1995

1995

THE
SISTINE
CHAPEL

THE SISTINE CHAPEL

A GLORIOUS RESTORATION

Edited by
PIERLUIGI DE VECCHI

CARLO PIETRANGELI, MICHAEL HIRST, GIANLUIGI COLALUCCI, FABRIZIO MANCINELLI,
JOHN SHEARMAN, MATTHIAS WINNER, EDWARD MAEDER,
PIERLUIGI DE VECCHI, NAZZARENO GABRIELLI, AND PIERNICOLA PAGLIARA

The essays in this volume were presented at a conference,
"Michelangelo: The Sistine Chapel," held at the Vatican 26–31 March 1990
and will appear in the forthcoming Proceedings,
edited by Kathleen Weil-Garris Brandt.

HARRY N. ABRAMS, INC., PUBLISHERS

THE SISTINE CHAPEL
A coproduction with NTV,
Nippon Television Network Corporation,
Tokyo

Photographs by Takashi Okamura
Design and editorial coordination:
Massimo Giacometti
General Editor: Pierluigi De Vecchi
Editor, English-language edition:
Diana Murphy

Texts by G. Colalucci, F. Mancinelli,
M. Winner, P. De Vecchi, F. Mancinelli/
G. Colalucci/N. Gabrielli, and P. Pagliara
translated by A. Lawrence Jenkens
with the assistance of Gabriele Poole.

Captions by Maria Piatto.
Captions and Lucanus, Aretino, and Tramezino
quotations translated by Karin Ford.

Biblical quotations taken from the Holy Bible, King
James Version, New York, Oxford University Press.
Vasari quotations on pp. 37, 45, 105, 136, 144,
148, 152, 154, 185, 186, and 204 taken from
Giorgio Vasari, *Lives of the Artists*, trans. George
Bull, vol. 1, Penguin Books, London, 1987.
Condivi quotations on pp. 66–67, 101, 108, 168,
173, and 175 taken from *The Life of Michelangelo*,
collected by Ascanio Condivi, D.B. Updike, 1904.
Ariosto quotation taken from *Orlando Furioso*, trans.
Barbara Reynolds, Hazell Watson & Viney Ltd.,
Aylesbury, Bucks/Penguin Books, 1975.

Unless otherwise noted, Italian texts quoted in
English were translated by A. Lawrence Jenkens.

Preceding pages: The *Azor-Sadoch* lunette, detail of
the figure on the right, which has been identified as
a portrait of Michelangelo
Right: *The Drunkenness of Noah*, detail of the shoulder
of Noah's son Ham

Library of Congress Cataloging-in-Publication Data
Cappella Sistina. English.
    The Sistine Chapel: a glorious
    restoration/Michael Hirst…[et al].
      p.   cm.
    Includes bibliographical references and index.
    ISBN 0-8109-3840-5
    1. Michelangelo Buonarroti, 1475-1564—Criticism
and interpretation. 2. Mural painting and decoration,
Italian—Conservation and restoration—Vatican City. 3.
Mural painting and decoration, Renaissance—
Conservation and restoration—Vatican City. 4. Sistine
Chapel (Vatican Palace, Vatican City)   I. Hirst,
Michael. II. Title.
ND623.B9C2913 1994
759.5—dc20   93-39787
                                        CIP

Copyright © 1992 Nippon Television Network
Corporation, Tokyo
English-language edition
copyright © 1994 Harry N. Abrams, Inc., New York
Published in 1994 by Harry N. Abrams,
Incorporated, New York
A Times Mirror Company

Printed in Italy

CONTENTS

Introduction

❧

An Account of the Restoration

I gratefully accept this opportunity to say a few words about the restoration of the Sistine Chapel on the occasion of the publication of the second volume on the restored frescoes, an enterprise supported by Nippon Television Network Corporation. It seems appropriate to review here the stages of that wonderful adventure, whose goal has been the redemption of Michelangelo's greatest achievement in the art of painting, the frescoes in the Sistine Chapel.

The cleaning of the frescoes was begun in 1965 on the initiative of Deoclecio Redig de Campos, who became general director of the Vatican Museums in 1971. It was to include only the fifteenth-century paintings depicting scenes of the lives of Christ and Moses. The restoration of the two sixteenth-century frescoes on the entrance wall, which are the final ones in that series, had been postponed at that time; their restoration would involve problems that were considerably different from those connected with the cleaning of the other panels in the series. This phase of the operation was completed in 1974.

In the spring of 1980, work in the Chapel was resumed and began with the frescoes on the entrance wall, which had become so dark with grime as to be almost indecipherable. The plan was then to move up the walls to the next register of paintings, the fifteenth-century series of portraits of the Popes, created by the same artists who had executed the scenes from the lives of Christ and Moses.

Once the scaffold had been erected in front of the entrance wall, the restorers were close enough to touch one of Michelangelo's lunettes, on which are represented the Ancestors of Christ. They took the opportunity to clean a minute sample of the lunette representing Mathan and Eleazar. The success attained encouraged them to proceed with the work until the lunette had been completely cleaned. The result was truly astonishing. The original colors of Michelangelo's painting, perfectly preserved under a thick layer of dust and glue, had reappeared.

We then stopped to consider what was to be done, since we were faced with the opportunity to perform a task involving enormous responsibility. Not only could the result be extraordinarily important, but also it was a step that appeared to be necessary and urgent. We had, in fact, noticed that in several places Michelangelo's painting was pulling off from the wall. This was happening as a result of changing atmospheric conditions, which were causing contractions in the layers of glue that had been applied to the frescoes in previous centuries. The glue, used to make the frescoes more visible, had grown dark with grime. Performing restoration work seemed therefore not only desirable in order to revive the original colors, but also a timely operation that should not be postponed if we wanted to ensure the preservation of the frescoes.

Except in isolated cases, it was not necessary to reinforce the plaster on which the frescoes had been painted, since this had been done during the preceding decades. While this work had been performed, no attempt had been made to tackle the cleaning of the paintings themselves because, with the tools available at the time, this would have presented insurmountable difficulties.

From the beginning the scientific aspects of the work were directed by Fabrizio Mancinelli and performed by Gianluigi Colalucci, chief restorer, together with Maurizio Rossi, Pier Giorgio Bonetti, and Bruno Baratti, master restorers. The laboratory analyses were performed by the Office of Scientific Research of the Vatican Museums, under the direction of Nazzareno Gabrielli. Professor Pasquale Rotondi, former director of the Central Italian Institute for Restoration, was consultant for restoration at the General Administration and, in that capacity, provided the necessary technical advice as he regularly followed the progress of the work. Upon his death in 1991, his work was continued by Professor Giorgio Torraca, the present consultant for restoration.

On 10 February 1981 a press conference was held; it was attended not only by journalists but also by many art historians and art critics, all of whom warmly encouraged us to continue with the work. At that time a schedule for the work to be done was drafted. It consisted of the following stages:

1980–84: Michelangelo's lunettes and the series of portraits of the Popes (a total of over six hundred square yards or meters of frescoes);

1985–88: Michelangelo's frescoes on the Ceiling (750 square yards);

1989–92: Michelangelo's Last Judgment (two hundred square yards).

In 1982 an agreement was signed with Nippon Television Network Corporation for the reproduction rights to the restored frescoes, reserving exclusive use of the photographs for a period of three years after the completion of each stage. Pursuant to the stipulations of the contract, the network was to film the entire course of the restoration free of charge.

The first stage of work was performed between 16 June 1980 and 13 October 1984; during that time the fourteen lunettes by Michelangelo (approximately 250 square yards) and the twenty-eight papal portraits were cleaned.

On 11 December 1984, on the occasion of the conclusion of the first stage of work, a second press conference was held, where the first criticisms of the restoration work were voiced by a small group of critics and artists. The same people continued to make these criticisms throughout the restoration. They did not, however, affect the timely completion of the work. We proceeded according to plan, secure in the knowledge that the results we had been obtaining were good and that they were inspiring the admiration of the greatest experts on Michelangelo's paintings as well as established critics throughout the world.

On 18–25 October 1985 a conference was held in order to examine the first results of the restoration. It was organized by the Wethersfield Institute, New York, in collaboration with the Vatican Museums and New York University's Institute of Fine Arts. The conference, held partly in Wethersfield and partly in New York City, at the Metropolitan Museum of Art and the Frick Collection, was attended by the most prominent Michelangelo scholars, who had come from all over Europe and the United States, and by the individuals in charge of the restoration. It was a huge success; fourteen hundred people, mainly art historians and critics, were present at the Metropolitan Museum alone.

On 7 November 1984 stage two, the restoration of Michelangelo's Ceiling frescoes, began.

For this stage of the work, a special aluminum scaffold, or bridge on wheels, was built under the direction of the General Administration of Technical Services for the Vatican Territories. The structure of the bridge was based on that of Michelangelo's bridge, and its supports were placed in the same holes in the walls used for Michelangelo's bridge. The bridge covered a section of the Ceiling only six yards long, so it was possible to follow the progress of the cleaning from below and observe the results obtained.

On 4 and 25 February 1986 a third press conference was held to present the results of the first phase of the Ceiling restoration.

In November 1986 the Italian National Research Council organized a conference on the restoration, during which Fabrizio Mancinelli and Gianluigi Colalucci gave presentations on the work in progress. In 1987 another report was given, at the Symposium on the Conservation of Wall Paintings, held in London and organized by the Courtauld Institute of Art and the Getty Conservation Institute. Conferences on this subject, directed by similar organizations and on the invitation of universities, museums, academies, and cultural institutions, have been held in almost every part of the world.

In December 1986 the first volume of the series that includes the present book was published by NTV in several languages. It contains essays by André Chastel, Pierluigi De Vecchi, Michael Hirst, John O'Malley, John Shearman, and, of course, Mancinelli and Colalucci. In April 1987 the Samuel H. Kress Foundation of New York, in collaboration with the International Foundation for Art Research, sent six master restorers to the Vatican to examine the work in progress: John Brealey, David Bull, Dianne Dwyer, Mario Modestini, Andrea Rothe, and Leonetto Tintori. They were accompanied by Marilyn Perry, president of the Kress Foundation, and Kathleen Weil-Garris Brandt of New York University, our consultant on Renaissance art. The opinion on the work performed to date submitted by these distinguished specialists was entirely favorable.

Also in 1987, at the request of the Administrative Office of the Vatican State, an international examining committee was installed to monitor the progress of the work. Members of the committee were: Norbert S. Baer, New York; Umberto Baldini, Florence; Carlo Bertelli, Lausanne and Milan; Kathleen Weil-Garris Brandt; André Chastel, Paris (until his death in 1991); Alfio Del Serra, Pistoia; Pierluigi De Vecchi, Milan; Christoph Luitpold Frommel, Rome; Michael Hirst, London; Paul Schwartzbaum, New York; Giovanni Urbani, Rome; and Matthias Winner, Berlin and Rome.

Concurrent with the restoration itself, numerous other related projects were organized and carried out. They are worth mentioning so the public may understand the complexity of this type of undertaking.

An examination of the records was conducted by Edith Cicerchia and Anna Maria De Strobel to collect all the available information about previous restoration work done on the frescoes.

To document the work in progress, fifteen thousand black and white photographs, ektachromes, and color slides were made. From the beginning NTV also documented the restoration on film. Every time a new stage of the cleaning process was begun, a Japanese television crew arrived from Tokyo and remained as long as necessary to film the work. Approximately forty-five thousand yards of 16mm film contained on eighty-three reels has been shot.

On 23 January 1987 an Apollo DN 3000 work station was installed on the scaffold, thanks to a financial contribution by Baron H. Thyssen Bornemisza. The data being collected by the computer relate to a variety of measurements and the state of conservation of the frescoes, as well as to the techniques used to produce them; in addition, information is being assembled on the various aspects of the restoration work. With the help of a second generous donation from the baron, we were able to take advantage of the opportunity afforded to make a photogrammetric relief of the Ceiling, which had never been done.

It should be mentioned that the bridge has at all times been accessible to qualified individuals from among the general public—critics, artists, well-known personalities. With their presence and their comments, most of them have encouraged us to continue the restoration work. Some have also written about their visits to the scaffolding. It is interesting to note that, in contradiction to what might have been expected, the critics who disapproved have rarely and only rather hastily visited the bridge. Since the time of its construction, approximately six thousand people have viewed the work.

The microclimate of the Chapel has been the subject of careful studies, begun in 1983 and published in 1986 by D. Camuffo and A. Bernardi. As a result of these studies, some precautionary measures have been taken to ensure that the results obtained by the restoration work will last. (It should be pointed out that no fixatives were applied to the frescoes after the cleaning.) A new lighting system equipped with cool, filtered lights has been installed; the system was contributed by the Osram Company. We are also in the process of installing a system that will filter and partially condition the air, thus eliminating changes in temperature and humidity.

The system has been installed by the General Administration of Technical Services for the Vatican Territories, with financing and technology provided by Delchi-Carrier. A monitoring system will check the functioning of the equipment, which will soon become operative.

Over the last few years several more events have taken place as the restoration work progressed. On 24 March 1990 an exhibition entitled Michelangelo and the Sistine Chapel: The Techniques, the Restoration, and the Myth and organized in collaboration with the Apostolic Library of the Vatican opened in the Charlemagne Wing of the colonnade in St. Peter's Square. In addition to a large amount of information about the restoration, the presentation included a series of original drawings by Michelangelo and his circle as well as engravings of works by Michelangelo. Also shown was the famous painting by Marcello Venusti from the Picture Gallery of Capodimonte, from which we may imagine how Michelangelo's Last Judgment looked with its original colors (which are now reappearing) and before the wraps were painted in by Daniele da Volterra. The exhibition traveled to the Cini Foundation, Venice, and to Montreal. Coinciding with the opening of the exhibition, 26–31 March, an international conference entitled "Michelangelo: The Sistine Chapel" was held at the Vatican. There, the most respected specialists in the field participated in a debate on numerous problems and issues raised by the restoration in progress. The full proceedings of the conference will be featured in a forthcoming publication supported by NTV.

The entire task of restoring the Ceiling was completed on 31 December 1989, having taken one year longer than projected. The surface that had to be restored was enormous and required a total of thirty thousand hours of work. Once it was completed, the bridge was dismantled and a scaffold erected that covers the Last Judgment wall from floor to ceiling. As noted above, the surface to be restored measures approximately two hundred square yards. The restoration was begun in early 1990 and, at the time of this writing, is expected to be completed by early 1994. The results so far are truly encouraging. Michelangelo's painting is reappearing from beneath layers of extraneous materials and its state of preservation is excellent. It is as if a window in a dark room is being opened to reveal a bright panorama. The marvelous adventure of the rediscovery of Michelangelo the painter is now reaching its much-anticipated conclusion.

Carlo Pietrangeli
General Director
Papal Museums, Monuments, and Galleries

Observations on Drawings for the Sistine Ceiling

Michael Hirst

An initial point that may be made about the drawings for the Sistine Ceiling is how few survive; the number appears all the smaller when we recall the square yards or meters of the decoration and its figurative complexity. If we exclude the eight leaves of the Oxford sketchbook and if we accept that rectos and versos of sheets may count as different drawings, the reckoning yields a total of scarcely more than fifty drawings. Even if we add the Oxford *taccuino* with its double-sided pages, we arrive at no more than sixty-six. It is instructive to compare this situation with the one relating to the Cascina project of a few years earlier. Here, there survive some twenty-five drawings for the physically much smaller undertaking of the Bathers section of the *Battle of Cascina,* a total approaching half the number we now have for the entire Ceiling. This very striking discrepancy could be the effect of chance. An alternative explanation could be found in the fact that the Sistine drawings remained in Rome, where they had been made; I have found no case of a sheet employed for the Ceiling which bears traces (such as drawings on the verso) suggesting that Michelangelo took it back to Florence with him in 1516. Michelangelo's own destruction of his drawings in Rome in the last weeks of his life in 1564 is a familiar fact. But that the destruction of Roman drawings began much earlier is proved by Leonardo Sellaio's letter of February 1518 reporting that he has had many drawings destroyed—he uses the word *chartoni*—at the absent master's insistence: "And they say all those drawings have been burned, but I don't think all. I tried to prevent it, but your wish was executed."[1]

So much for statistics. Two other general points may be made before we consider a few examples. One concerns scale. Probably none of the sheets for the Ceiling has escaped being subsequently cut down—usually on all four sides. Some of the most celebrated studies have suffered most, such as the two reproduced here, side by side on the same scale. That on the left is a sheet now in Florence, Uffizi 18720 F (Tolnay Corpus 141); the recto is a study for an *ignudo,* or nude. It is one of the most complete sheets to have survived, measuring nearly 16½ x 10⅜ in. (420 x 264 mm). Alongside is the celebrated British Museum study for the figure of Adam (Wilde 11 recto, Tolnay Corpus 134 recto); its area is now less than half that of the other. Both are life studies, and the evidence suggests that Michelangelo used uniform large sheets for this class of drawing for the Ceiling.[2]

My second point is that not a single drawing for the Ceiling was squared by the artist to facilitate enlargement to the cartoon; we do not find even blind squaring with a stylus. Such emancipation from methods used by artists of an earlier generation, like Signorelli, when making studies for murals may not be isolated; a comparison with Raphael's practice would be interesting. The whole question of squaring of drawings in this period warrants further study.[3]

Despite the fact that relatively few drawings for the Ceiling survive, those that we do have exemplify an amazing diversity of character. Their range extends from the British Museum early draft for the vault scheme in pen and ink to studies of physical extremities, including a study for the violently retracted left foot of Haman in one of the last areas of the program to be painted, the corner spandrel above and to the left of the altar wall.[4] This study, certainly made from life, was drawn at a moment when pressure from the pope on the artist to complete the program was intense; its existence shows that even at such a moment, Michelangelo was not prepared to take shortcuts when an exceptionally prominent figure was in question. Certain areas of the Ceiling do show him working at exceptional speed. For confirmation of this we need look no further than the last scene, *God Separating Light from Darkness,* painted in a single *giornata,* or

day's work (including a major improvised *pentimento,* or correction). But it is important that we distinguish between rapidity of execution and an abandonment of preparatory procedures; in this sense, the way the artist designed and painted the lunettes is very far from being paradigmatic.

Our most serious lacuna is the absence of compositional drawings, above all those for the Genesis scenes. Only one true compositional drawing for a narrative survives, the extremely rapid black-chalk sketch (Haarlem A 18 verso, Tolnay Corpus 51 verso) for the *Judith* spandrel. Although the artist drew part of an arc over the scene, the connection with the spandrel is, I believe, correct. The drawing shows how he planned the scene as a kind of mural triptych. Such a solution almost certainly came to him from his familiarity with very similar solutions in Domenico

Bastiano da Sangallo, copy of Michelangelo's lost cartoon for the Battle of Cascina. *Grisaille. Holkham Hall, Norfolk, England.*

9

Ghirlandaio's frescoes in the Tornabuoni Chapel, painted in the period of his own youthful apprenticeship. We may, for example, compare the similar device in the older artist's fresco of the *Visitation*. In a much subtler way, Michelangelo returns to it in the *Haman* spandrel, the one which, across the diagonal axis of the Chapel, faces the *Judith*. The idea we find indicated in the drawing, of the headless victim shown in extreme foreshortening on the stairs, was perhaps too big a challenge at this early stage. Or perhaps it seemed too indecorous. Did the initial drawings for the Genesis scenes approximate to this fleeting sketch? We now know that even at this early stage, when the artist was feeling his way as a fresco painter, he decided to dispense with a cartoon for the ancillary detail of the soldier in the *Judith* scene. He thus adopted an economy of effort for a marginal feature at this relatively early phase of his work; but I believe he had probably already

Opposite: Michelangelo, study for the ignudo above the Prophet Isaiah. Silverpoint, 16 ½ x 10⅜ in. (419 x 264 mm). Corpus 141 recto; Galleria degli Uffizi, Florence.

envisaged adopting such economy for the more marginal areas of the never-executed *Battle of Cascina* mural.

For only one of the Genesis scenes do we have evidence of his early thinking, on an Oxford sketchbook leaf for the last Creation narrative to be painted.[5] It contains three studies for this fresco's unique figure, one of them a remarkably complete draft with the framing lines drawn in. But the artist seems to have adopted this kind of small-scale *pensiero* mostly for single-figure inventions. And we are left with a question mark as to how the most famous Creation scenes in the history of art were themselves created. Since the specific topic of Michelangelo's compositions is beyond the parameters of this discussion, a word or two may be added here about one of

Michelangelo, study for the figure of Adam in the Creation of Adam. Red chalk over charcoal, 7½ x 10⅛ in. (190 x 257 mm). Corpus 134 recto; British Museum, London.

11

them, that which represents the *Temptation* and the *Expulsion*.

Confronted here for the first time in the Creation scenes with the problems so many Quattrocento artists had had to face and to which Leonardo gave thought—the problem of designing two episodes in a single field—Michelangelo solved the problem with a wonderful resourcefulness by

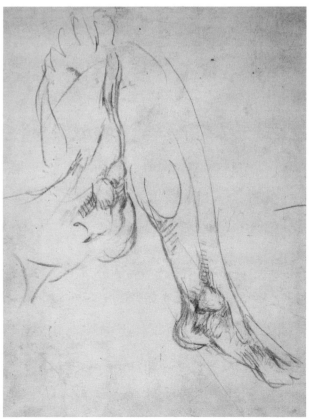

using the essential attribute of one of them, the tree, to create two episodes. But the steps by which he arrived at this solution are forever lost to us.

For the most part, the surviving drawings document his concern with single figures; the British Museum *Adam* is perhaps the most familiar. Yet in terms of numbers, the studies for *ignudi* are the most numerous we have. Does this reflect no more than accident? Perhaps this is so. Nevertheless, the chance afforded by the restoration to analyze how the *ignudi* were painted has served to underline their great importance for the painter. While in the earlier bays the *ignudi* were painted after the narratives, in those starting with the *Creation of Eve* their execution preceded that of the narratives. Perhaps this change was actuated by their substantially greater scale in the second part of the program, which in turn was facilitated by the drastic reduction in the number of figures in the narratives themselves.

Did the artist choose to preserve life studies while discarding so many others? That he took pains to study the fall of drapery is proved by a drawing such as the British Museum example, drapery that I suspect he placed over a wooden model.[6] The pen style very obviously recalls that of Ghirlandaio. But this is the only really significant drapery study for the vault we have. Did the particular task at this relatively early stage in the work lead him back to a technique there is no evidence he used in later

Judith and Holofernes *spandrel.*

Above: God Separating Light from Darkness, *detail.*

Below: Michelangelo, pen and wash studies, 5½ x 5⅝ in. (140 x 142 mm). Corpus 168 recto; Ashmolean Museum, Oxford. The sheet shows three versions of God Separating Light from Darkness, *one at bottom center, another on the left, and a third, better developed one at top right.*

Ceiling studies? No certain answer is possible. It is, however, a fact that elaborate nude studies in pen and ink, of the kind carried out for the Cascina project, do not survive for the Ceiling.

The studies for *ignudi* are themselves remarkably various.[7] For preliminary life-studies, Michelangelo seems to have favored black chalk, but almost all were made over a stylus under drawing. Then, for the more definitive life-drawings, he seems to have chosen red chalk, with a stylus used only very sparingly for the underdrawing.[8] By chance we have such

Domenico Ghirlandaio, the Visitation. *Tornabuoni Chapel, S. Maria Novella, Florence.*

studies for each of the *ignudi* above the *Persian Sibyl*. The Vienna example is stylistically the more retrospective of the two, very close in its lapidary detail to the British Museum's study for Adam, and indeed the two figures are adjacent on the Ceiling. For the Haarlem figure we have, as well, a brief head-study which is drawn on a sheet that Michelangelo had just used for the *Creation of Adam*. We find the same situation with the drawing for the whole figure, for on its verso there are studies for the putti who accompany God the Father in the Creation scene, and below them tiny chalk invention studies for the *ignudi* with their base blocks included (they measure just over 1⁹⁄₁₆ in. [4 cm], comparable to the scale of the figures in the Oxford sketchbook). The two Haarlem sheets confirm, in other words,

The Temptation *and the* Expulsion.

15

16

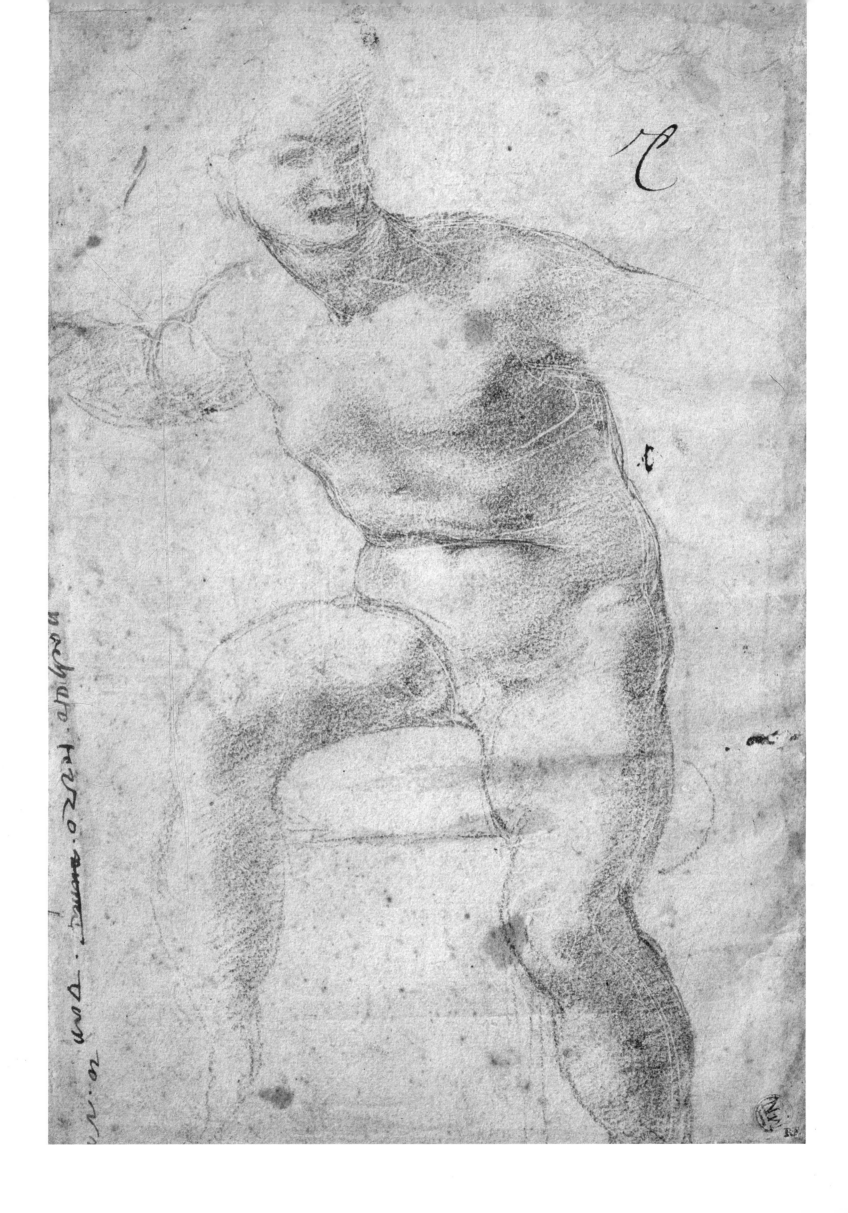

18

Michelangelo, study for an ignudo. Red chalk with touches of ceruse, 10¹¹/₁₆ x 7½ in. (271 x 190 mm). Corpus 144 verso; Albertina Museum, Vienna.

how the artist would pick up a sheet he had only just put down to use for an immediately subsequent task. With characteristic frugality, he did not throw away sheets of which he had used only one side. In formal terms it is the less lapidary style of the Haarlem *ignudo* study that points toward that of the latest life-studies such as those for Haman.[9]

Now in poor condition, the British Museum drawing for Haman was made with great technical refinement, in marked contrast to the brusque execution of the painted figure. The Haarlem studies for Haman raise interesting issues. Normally, in studies such as these, the artist would draw a form in its entirety even when part of it was to be obscured in the painting. Here he broke with the practice, leaving out the left side of the head, perhaps because he was already planning the greatly exaggerated scale of the outflung left arm and left hand so evident in the fresco, the most radically willful distortion of the decoration and one which, still not present on the Haarlem sheet, was evidently made at the cartoon stage.[10]

All these drawings were preparatory to making one-to-one cartoons. But before glancing briefly at the topic of cartoons, it is worth recalling that he did make drawings for parts of the decoration where he used no cartoons at all. The most extensive areas are the lunettes, where cleaning has revealed no trace of *spolvero* (pouncing) or *incisione* (incision). Most of

Opposite: Michelangelo, study for the trunk, legs, and right foot of Haman. Dark red chalk, 16 x 8⅛ in. (406 x 207 mm). Corpus 163 recto: British Museum, London.
Left: Michelangelo, studies for the Punishment of Haman. *Charcoal and red chalk, 9¹¹⁄₁₆ x 8⅛ in. (252 x 205 mm). Corpus 164 recto; Teyler Museum, Haarlem.*
Right: The Punishment of Haman *spandrel, detail.*

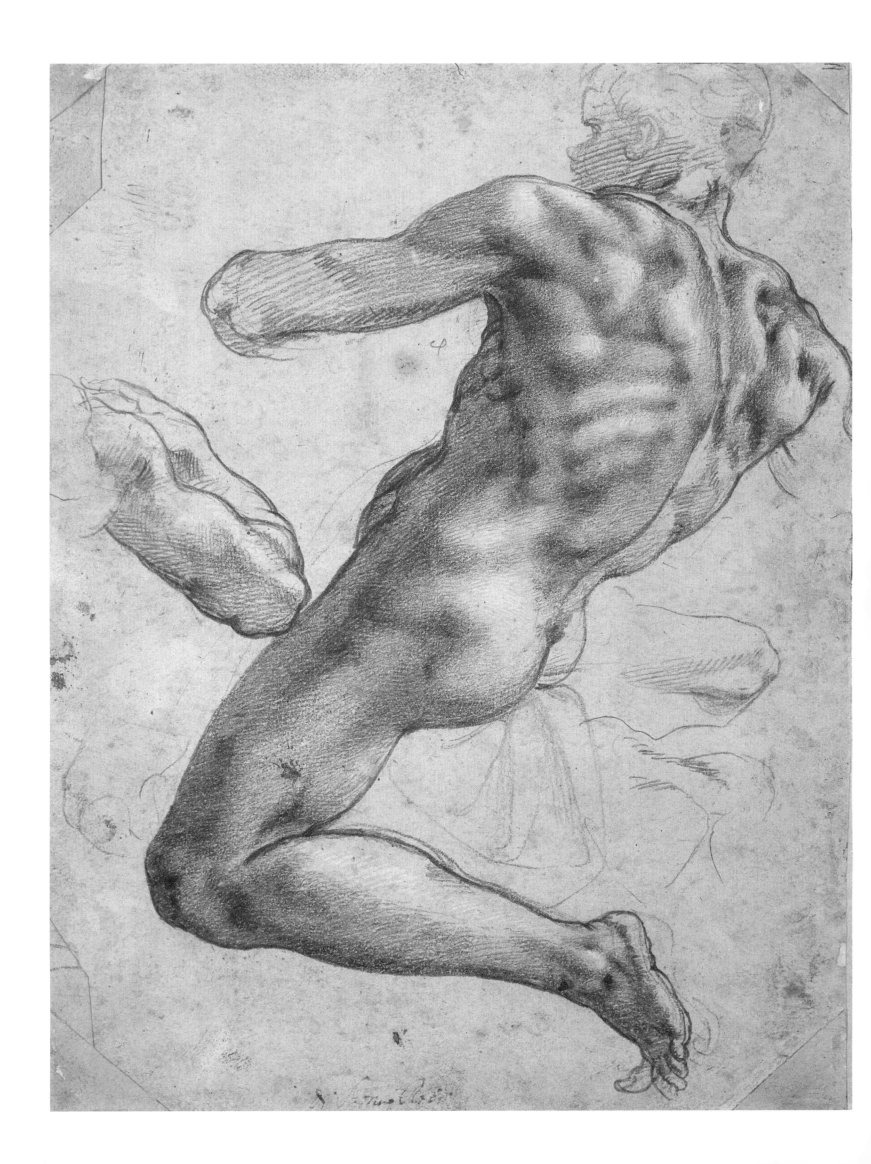

the motifs on the pages of the Oxford notebook leaves are concerned with
the lunettes. But two or three somewhat more substantial drawings for
them have survived. The most notable are two studies for the mother holding a child on the left of the *Ezechias* lunette, drawn on the verso of the
Turin sheet with the study for the head of the Cumaean Sibyl.[11] One is
bound to ask whether Michelangelo made more elaborate studies for the
lunettes than those few that now remain. Did he go so far as to make life
studies for these evocative and very large figures? A relatively small drawing in the Casa Buonarroti shows him making a nude study for a clothed
figure in one of the last lunettes.[12] We are again confronted with the issue I
raised earlier. It seems difficult to believe that a head with the realism of
that of Jacob was painted without a rapid drawing, such as that in the Uffizi
for the head of Zechariah.

Only one significant cartoon Michelangelo made for his own work now
survives. Carmen Bambach and I have independently concluded that the
Naples fragment for a part of the *Crucifixion of St. Peter* in the Pauline
Chapel in St. Peter's, Rome, is a section of a master cartoon, which was
too large to be applied to the plaster and was extensively pricked to allow

Above: Jacob-Joseph *lunette, detail of Jacob's head.*

Right: Michelangelo, study for the head of Zechariah. *Charcoal, 17⅛ x 10¹⁵⁄₁₆ in. (435 x 277 mm). Corpus 153 recto; Galleria degli Uffizi, Florence.*

smaller auxiliary cartoons to be made from it. She further observed that a piece of just such an auxiliary cartoon was used to patch a damaged part of the Naples cartoon.[13] This probably happened when the artist decided to give it away as a present, an act to which we must surely owe the survival of the Naples piece. I have suggested recently that the Cascina Bathers cartoon probably had the same function, a highly worked drawing perhaps seven yards long, which we know was glued together as one piece and from which more manageable cartoons could be made.[14] It does not seem unreasonable to conjecture that Michelangelo set out to make a large scene like the *Deluge* following the same procedure, a supposition the more likely when we recall his more difficult working conditions on the scaffolding beneath the vault. Militating also against the theory that he cut up his Sistine master cartoons and applied them directly to the *intonaco,* or upper layer of plaster, is Vasari's dependable statement that he gave the cartoon of the *Drunkenness of Noah* to Bindo Altoviti; a process of making secondary cartoons would have helped preserve it intact. However, because of considerations of scale, his procedure for the Genesis scenes may have been different from that for single figures like *ignudi.*

The amount of information we now possess about the Ceiling is so great that it will take years to digest. The evidence of how the painter carried out the *Persian Sibyl,* for example, shows his employment of pouncing for head, book, and hands, and *incisione diretta* (direct incision) for the drapery. This approach recalls very clearly that of Ghirlandaio and his team in the large chapel of S. Maria Novella. It may be that exact explanations of why the artist chose different ways of transferring his designs in different parts

Michelangelo, study of a male nude for the female figure in the Naason lunette. Black lapis, 5¹⁵⁄₁₆ x 4¹³⁄₁₆ in. (150 x 122 mm). Corpus 160 recto; Casa Buonarroti, Florence.

of the decoration will elude us.

How different these were is effectively shown by the different ways the artist used to transfer his designs in the final stages of painting. Despite the pressure on Michelangelo to complete the work (we should remember that his patron died just four months after the unveiling), it is only the figure of Haman, transferred by *incisione indiretta* (indirect incision, or incision through the cartoon), that exhibits the same kind of hasty execution as the figure of God in the neighboring Genesis scene. The lines etched into the plaster, while many, are very rapid and articulate the modeling in a very summary way. The painting of the foreshortened head is almost perfunctory. Nevertheless, for a number of details of other figures in the same spandrel, we find the artist using pouncing. It is, in other words, an area of the work that exemplifies a striking variety in a single scene. On the other hand, the figure of Jonah is transferred entirely by pouncing, unlike the majority of preceding Prophets and Sibyls. And so, likewise, is the whole of the *Brazen Serpent* spandrel, the most complex figure composition of the program.

The Technique of the Sistine Ceiling Frescoes

Gianluigi Colalucci

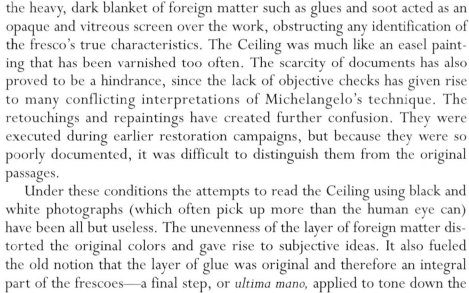

The technique Michelangelo used to fresco the Sistine Ceiling has long been the subject of passionate debate. Although past restorations offered an opportunity to study these paintings at close range, the heavy, dark blanket of foreign matter such as glues and soot acted as an opaque and vitreous screen over the work, obstructing any identification of the fresco's true characteristics. The Ceiling was much like an easel painting that has been varnished too often. The scarcity of documents has also proved to be a hindrance, since the lack of objective checks has given rise to many conflicting interpretations of Michelangelo's technique. The retouchings and repaintings have created further confusion. They were executed during earlier restoration campaigns, but because they were so poorly documented, it was difficult to distinguish them from the original passages.

Under these conditions the attempts to read the Ceiling using black and white photographs (which often pick up more than the human eye can) have been all but useless. The unevenness of the layer of foreign matter distorted the original colors and gave rise to subjective ideas. It also fueled the old notion that the layer of glue was original and therefore an integral part of the frescoes—a final step, or *ultima mano,* applied to tone down the colors. Biagio Biagetti, the painter who directed the 1936 intervention to consolidate part of the Ceiling's upper layer of plaster, or *intonaco,* intuited the truth when he wrote, "if and when I am able to address this issue, it will not be difficult to demonstrate that we see the colors of the Sistine ceiling as if through smoked glass...."

The recent cleaning, accompanied by extensive and thorough scientific research, has allowed us to confirm, finally, that Michelangelo painted in *buon fresco,* or true fresco, putting to rest the insubstantial notion that Michelangelo used tempera on a fresco base with other idiosyncratic additions. This notion coincided with the romantic vision of genius as solitary, tormented, and immune to all traditions including that of technique. Michelangelo was, on the contrary, very much immersed in the spirit of his own time. His work was characterized by the profound knowledge and rigorous technique, born of the highest standards of craftsmanship, that was typical of fresco painters in the Renaissance. Giotto had already set the highest standard for fresco painting, and he was followed by Domenico Ghirlandaio, Luca Signorelli, and the other great Florentine masters and their workshops. Michelangelo brought this technique to the height of perfection.

He achieved this result by paying particular attention to both choosing

God Separating Light from Darkness, *detail during the cleaning.*

Opposite: View of the Sistine Chapel after the restoration of the Ceiling.

and applying the plaster he would paint on, by rigorously controlling his brushstrokes, and by an equally careful choice of pigments. Michelangelo painted only with colors that were suitable for fresco and almost completely avoided those which, by their nature, had to be applied to dry plaster, that is, *a secco,* and were, therefore, less resistant to the vicissitudes of time and the external forces that worked on them.

Michelangelo's palette is restrained, with a few rare exceptions, to the oxide and silicate pigments. Nonetheless he preserves a fifteenth-century color scheme on the first half of the vault. On the second half of the Ceiling there is a marked shift to colder, sometimes livid, tones and to more sober juxtapositions of color. It is here that we find real innovations. The blue of the Persian Sibyl's sleeve, for example, consists of large grains of blue smalt applied, indeed, almost rubbed on, to the smooth, gray

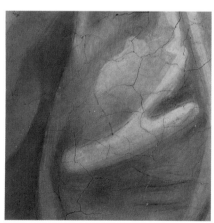

intonaco of black pozzolana with a hard brush. We also find new color combinations—in the *Libyan Sibyl,* for example—or unusual pigments such as the red-violet *morellone* used for the tunic worn by God the Father in the Creation scenes. The *ductus,* or form, and substance of Michelangelo's brushwork have an expressiveness which can be compared to the different surface textures of marble sculpture—polished, rough, or unfinished.

By manipulating the color fields and the corporeal differences of the pigments and by varying the width of his brushstrokes and the weave of his multicolored tapestry, Michelangelo succeeded in giving individual as well as groups of figures a remarkable three-dimensional quality. The youths behind the Prophets and Sibyls are almost always painted with a wide brush and liquid colors, often with little attention to specific details. The Prophets and Sibyls, on the other hand, are always well defined in every detail and easily admired, even from a distance of twenty yards or meters. The elements that project from the Ceiling's surface are not only painted with brighter colors but also with denser, thicker brushstrokes to give them a crystalline definition similar to the effect obtained today with a well-focused camera lens. Michelangelo's figures are built up by successive planes of color, each of which has its own individual focus. The first layer is usually, although not always, the most precise, and the successive levels become more and more blurred.

There are other optical juxtapositions that were not apparent until the recent cleaning. If we assume that the Sistine Ceiling was conceived as a large room spanned by ten arches but left open to the sky (the narrow bands of sky visible at each end of the vault suggest and confirm this idea), we note that all the figures placed inside the hall—the Prophets, Sibyls, and *ignudi,* or nudes—are painted with dense, fine brushstrokes that give the figures a sort of polished surface. The figures of the central scenes, on the other hand, hover in a space outside the vault and give the impression of a rougher surface. They are painted with more obvious, interwoven brushstrokes that recall marble blocks worked with a claw chisel. This slight difference in the figures creates an illusionary distance between those located inside the space of the Chapel and those placed beyond it. This subtle device is not obvious in the early sections of the Ceiling. It seems, rather, that the idea evolved as Michelangelo progressed. In fact, this differentiation is practically absent in the early sections of the Ceiling (with the exception of the lunettes), but is found in the *Expulsion* and in the first group of lunettes. It appears consistently on the second half of the vault.

The technique used to paint the lunettes is in some ways different from

Above: The Prophet Isaiah, *detail of the young assistants behind the Prophet.*
Below: The Creation of Adam, *detail of Adam.*

that used on the Ceiling. The lunettes were executed without cartoons and are characterized by a freedom of gesture and rapidity of brushstrokes that is seen only rarely on the Ceiling. There the difficulty of working on a curved surface that could never be seen from the proper angle required the constant use of preparatory cartoons. A rapidity of execution comparable to the lunettes is found only in the last three scenes of the Ceiling—*God Separating Light from Darkness,* the *Creation of the Sun, Moon, and Plants,* and *God Separating the Earth from the Waters*—where the cartoons were transferred by indirect incision.

The modulations of color and the technique of execution are also tied, in part, to their decorative function, which followed precise and codified rules that pertained especially to frescoes on high ceilings. We must keep this in mind as we try to understand the juxtapositions of color and the large color fields, the unpainted *intonaco* left bare for its chromatic effect, and the very luminous backgrounds painted with flat, liquid colors.

Michelangelo's workshop employed traditional techniques, yet the accuracy with which each detail was executed and especially the stylistic uniformity, which left little initiative to the various assistants, set it apart from contemporary shops and hinder the identification of individual hands. We can recognize various hands in the frescoes painted by the great workshops of the time (those of Ghirlandaio, Raphael, Perino del Vaga, and others) because each assistant was allowed to work according to his own custom and technical ability within the limits imposed by the master's design. Work was divided piecemeal—to the point that even small sections of a composition might be executed by several different artists. In the Stufetta of Cardinal Bibbiena, for example, two different artists painted the

Far left. Jacob-Joseph *lunette, detail of the figure on the left.*
Left: The Libyan Sibyl, *detail.*
Above: Michelangelo, Medici Madonna, *detail. Medici Chapel, S. Lorenzo, Florence.*

Stufetta of Cardinal Bibbiena, detail of the grotesques painted by two different artists on the two sides of a lunette.

grotesques in a single lunette that was only two yards wide, and each completely ignored the other.

Buon fresco begins with the choice of a good plaster. Although he had a better understanding of lime and sand mortars, Michelangelo chose in Rome to use a problematic mixture of lime and pozzolana (a volcanic material very common in Roman construction work). It is difficult to say whether this decision was based on technical considerations or if it was made for contingent reasons. In any case, the mixture of lime and pozzolana, although not always used for frescoes even in Rome (and almost never in ancient Roman frescoes), produced excellent results, judging as much by the quality of the painting as by its carbonization and its compactness, which made the plaster, if worked correctly, resistant to heavy infiltrations of water.

According to Vasari, however, Michelangelo had some trouble at the beginning of his work in the Sistine Chapel:

When he had completed about one-third of the painting, the prevalence of the north wind during the winter months had caused a sort of mould to appear on the pictures; and this happened from the fact that in Rome, the plaster, made of travertine and puzzolana, does not dry rapidly, and while in a soft state is somewhat dark and very fluent, not to say watery; when the wall is covered with this mixture, therefore, it throws out an efflorescence arising from the humid saltiness which bursts forth; but this is in time evaporated and corrected by the air. Michelangelo was, indeed, in despair at the sight of these spots, and refused to continue the work, declaring to the Pope that he could not succeed therein, but His Holiness sent Giuliano da Sangallo to look at it, and he, telling the artist whence these spots arose, encouraged him to proceed, by teaching him how they might be removed.[1]

We believe we have found traces of these problems in some areas of the *Drunkenness of Noah,* especially in the figure of the sleeping Noah.

The vault, an enormous mass of porous tufa blocks and pozzolana mortar (a concrete or Roman vault), retained the moisture produced by the abundant use of water necessary for the proper adhesion of the fresh plaster. The prolonged dampness of the *intonaco* favored good carbonization of the hydrated lime but could also lead to the inconveniences Vasari described. Nonetheless, even if Michelangelo had problems at the beginning and even if he perhaps had to remove work already completed, he soon mastered the technique. His frescoes carbonized perfectly—slowly and over an extended period of time—which made the *intonaco* very compact and durable.

As we have already noted, Michelangelo's *intonaco* is mixed from lime and black pozzolana, usually in the proportion of one to two (a "fat" mortar), and its average thickness is %6 in. (1.5 cm). The preparatory layer of plaster, or *arriccio,* which is also made of lime and pozzolana—although the latter is coarser—is never more than ¾ in. (2 cm) thick. This layer was applied very unevenly across the Ceiling since its main purpose was to fill the small gaps left after the previous *intonaco* had been scraped off and because it smoothed the readily apparent irregularity of the vault created by the casually joined tufa blocks, which are some 30 in. (80 cm) thick. In fresco painting (so-called because pigments are applied to fresh, or wet, plaster) the earth colors, diluted only by water, are fixed by the transparent and tenacious calcium carbonate that forms as the *intonaco* dries. The time the artist has at his disposal can vary with the seasons and the quality of the wall or the plaster. On average, however, the drying period is about six hours, although only the middle two allow for the best carbonization. During the first two hours the lime in the *intonaco* is still too strong and can damage the pigments. In the last two hours the drying plaster no longer carbonizes well enough to fix the colors; furthermore, some pigments applied at this stage can change markedly in tone once they are dry. For

Detail of the trompe l'œil architecture of the Ceiling, where a difference in the level of the plaster can be seen between the various giornate.

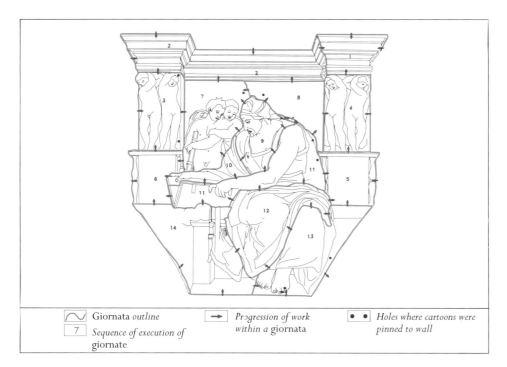

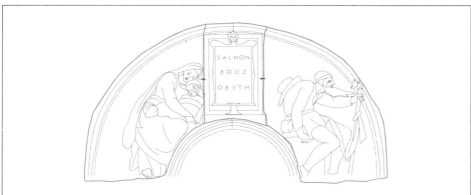

Giornata *outline*

7 Sequence of execution of giornate

→ *Progression of work within a giornata*

•   • *Holes where cartoons were pinned to wall*

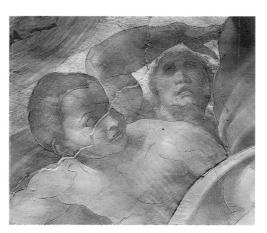

Above left: Diagram of the giornate *for the* Cumaean Sibyl.
Below left: Diagram of the giornate *for the* Salmon-Booz-Obeth *lunette.*

Top: The Deluge, *detail. It is possible to distinguish the black dots indicating that the des.gr. was transferred by pouncing.*
Above: The Creation of the Sun, Moon, and Plants, *detail. In this image, which was photographed in raking light, the indirect incising is clearly visible.*

The Prophet Isaiah, *detail of the throne with incision marks.*

this reason an artist can paint only a portion of *intonaco* at a time—each of these sections is called a *giornata,* or day's work.

Michelangelo's *giornate* are of various sizes, depending on how the composition could be divided and on the type of plaster used. The greater or lesser compactness of an *intonaco* influences the time it takes for the plaster to dry. Thus in the lunettes the rough and less-compact surface allowed days' work of unusually large size, about 5½ square yards. The *giornate* on the rest of the Ceiling tend to be smaller because the *intonaco* is more compact and polished and therefore stayed damp for a shorter period of time. This is true, for example, of the *ignudi* and the flesh areas of the Prophets and Sibyls. In many instances the surfaces of one day's work is not level with the next; around the fictive architecture there is sometimes as much as 3⁄16 in. (.5 cm) between them. In some cases the background around a figure or a part of the architecture is kept lower so as not to run over the areas already painted. In other cases Michelangelo manipulated the levels to create real shadows that accentuate and make palpable the junction between architectural elements and the open space beyond the vault.

Tasks within the workshop were assigned according to traditional practices. Nothing happened by accident. We find, for example, that similar figures were almost always divided into the same number of days' work, as in the large, central rectangle formed by the upper cornice of the thrones of the Prophets and Sibyls. This geometric construction supports and frames the entire composition of the Ceiling and separates the central scenes from the lateral figures. By studying the order of the *giornate* it is almost always possible to reconstruct the sequence an artist followed in executing his work. This is not possible on the Sistine Ceiling, however, because the central cornice and the fictive arches spanning the vault do not allow the progression of work to be traced across the various zones. By creating caesuras in the painting, the frames around the spandrels also impede any attempt to map the progression of *giornate*, which number 520 in total. A study of the days' work on the Sistine Ceiling is limited, therefore, to the individual areas enclosed by the fictive architecture or by frames.

The number of *giornate* used to paint the Prophets and Sibyls, including the thrones but not the cornice above them, varies between ten for the *Erythraean Sibyl* and *Zechariah* and eighteen for the *Libyan Sibyl*. The first two days' work always include the two pairs of monochromatic putti on the throne, followed by the background field behind the shoulders of the Prophets and Sibyls.

Above, left to right: The Deluge, *detail of the group of figures on the right;* Judith and Holofernes *spandrel, detail of the sleeping warrior; detail of the bronze nude to the right above the* Creation of Adam.

As work proceeded, the *giornate* of the four large, central panels of the Ceiling increased in size and their number was reduced. The *Deluge* was painted in twenty-four days' work, but the *Creation of the Sun, Moon, and Plants* was executed in seven. The smaller narrative scenes follow the same pattern; there are fourteen *giornate* in the *Drunkenness of Noah*, but *God Separating Light from Darkness* was painted in one. The lunettes are divided into three days' work, the first of which comprises the plaque inscribed with the names of Christ's ancestors. It is not always possible to find the seams between *giornate* in some of the lunettes executed during Michelangelo's second campaign on the Ceiling, which might allow us to conjecture even larger days' work. Yet even if we cannot exclude this possibility, we think it more likely that the mason applied fresh *intonaco* next to the still-damp plaster of the previous day's work, working it in such a way as to fuse the two areas.

Typically, frescoes were executed on the basis of full-scale drawings which the artist traced onto large sheets of paper and then cut into sections, following the lines of the composition and commensurate with what could be painted in a single *giornata*. Frescoes in and around Venice, even in the sixteenth century, remained an exception to this general rule; they were at least in part executed according to the more ancient technique of registers, or *pontate*—a method by which the *intonaco* was divided by vertical and horizontal lines corresponding to the various levels of the scaffolding.

Once they were divided into sections, the preparatory drawings could be transferred to the wet plaster in two ways, by pouncing (*spolvero*) or by indirect incision (*incisione indiretta*). In pouncing, a detailed and shaded drawing was placed over a second sheet, destined to be destroyed in the

Azor-Sadoc lunette, detail of the male figure's sleeve, finished with colors unsuited to fresco.

transfer process by the damp plaster on which it was laid. The first sheet was then pricked along the outlines of the composition and hit with a small bag of charcoal dust, leaving an outline of black dots on the *intonaco,* which served as a guide for the painter. In indirect incision, the drawing was usually made on *cartone,* a paper of consistent thickness. It was laid directly on the wet plaster and its contours incised with a metal or ivory stylus, producing an outline of the composition on the soft *intonaco.*

The pouncing technique did not damage the flat surface of the plaster and allowed complex and highly detailed drawings to be transferred to the wall. These cartoons were meticulously executed by the artist and required lengthy preparation. Indirect incision, on the other hand, allowed the artist to make quick sketches that were transferred as broad and summary outlines, which permitted a greater degree of freedom in executing the fresco. An outline incised too deeply, however, ruined the surface of the *intonaco.*

Michelangelo used both methods to transfer his drawings, although pouncing is found more often than incision. The lines of the architectural framework were traced directly onto the wet plaster with a stylus, without a cartoon. Nor is there evidence that he used either a snapped string or a roller, although large nails that anchored cords used as references lines are still in place in some parts of the Ceiling. The pouncing marks outlining the figures were often lightly traced with black paint, while within the figures one sometimes finds thin incisions directly on the plaster. These lines identify the areas to be shaded as well as outlining drapery and musculature, and they replace the *spolvero,* which was erased once the incisions had been made. All the lunette figures, as well as some on the Ceiling itself, were painted without cartoons, or at least without the direct transfer of a preparatory drawing to the *intonaco.*

With only a few exceptions, Michelangelo used pouncing for all the figures of Prophets and Sibyls and direct incision for their draperies and thrones. The compositions of the four large corner scenes were transferred largely by pouncing with some direct incising, although Michelangelo used indirect incision for the prone and decapitated figure of Holofernes and, in the *Punishment of Haman,* for the group of figures on the left, including the king, queen, and Haman himself. The preparatory drawings for the eight smaller spandrels between the Sibyls and Prophets were transferred by pouncing on the first half of the Ceiling and by indirect incision on the second.

One finds almost the exact same procedure for the monochromatic putti on the thrones of the Prophets and Sibyls: those on the thrones of Isaiah, the Delphic Sibyl, Zechariah, Joel, the Erythraean Sibyl, and Ezechiel were transferred by means of *spolvero,* while those on the thrones of the Cumaean Sibyl, Daniel, the Libyan Sibyl, Jonah, Jeremiah, and the Persian Sibyl were indirectly incised. One finds the use of *spolvero* and some direct incision in the central scenes, from the *Deluge* to the *Creation of Eve,* but only one instance of indirect incision—the angel expelling Adam and Eve from the Garden of Eden. In the *Creation of Adam,* the group of figures surrounding God the Father shows both pouncing marks and direct incisions, while Adam himself is incised from a cartoon. In the subsequent scenes up to *God Separating Light from Darkness,* the compositions were transferred by indirect incision.

The *ignudi* were all outlined by *spolvero,* but the bronze nudes show no trace of any method of transferring from cartoons, with the exception of the figure to the right of Jonah and above the *Brazen Serpent* spandrel. In this figure we do find some traces of indirect incision along the right arm; it is clearly the work of an assistant of modest ability. The shell and acorn motifs that decorate the frames around the lunettes were also transferred by indirect incision. In the lunettes themselves, as we noted above, there are no indications that cartoons were used. All across the Ceiling one notices figures or draperies painted freehand, including the little figure of

Top: Bronze medallion above the Prophet Isaiah.
Above: The Deluge, *detail of the group of figures on the right.*

33

Ignudo *to the left above the* Prophet Joel.

Noah planting the vine in the *Drunkenness of Noah,* or the sleeping soldier in the *Judith and Holofernes* spandrel. Michelangelo's use of different techniques to transfer cartoons does not follow the criteria of fifteenth-century workshops. He seems to have made his choices for different reasons, and since we can offer no objective conclusions, our study remains in the realm of conjecture. Because we can identify Michelangelo's hand, which is unmistakable by the brush handling, in those areas where no cartoons were used as well as in those prepared by pouncing or indirect incision, we must necessarily conclude that the choice of one method or the other was not made strictly on the basis of artistic need but also for reasons tied to workshop practice. The choice seems to be related as well to a greater sense of confidence, and perhaps to Michelangelo's evolution as a painter. The perceptible change in the artist's palette on the second half of the Ceiling is evidence of his technical development. On the second half of the vault we also find that cartoons were for the most part transferred by incising.

Michelangelo's use of fresco was so precise that he avoided, with only a very few exceptions of a limited and imperceptible scale, those intermediate techniques—*affresco aiutato*—which are frequently found even in murals that are commonly defined as *buon fresco.* I am referring here to a technique that, even though executed according to the rules of true fresco, allows the painting to be finished with a color to which a small amount of binder—animal milk or, more rarely, vegetable latex—has been added or which has been diluted with lime water or lime milk. In the first case the cohesion of the brushstrokes applied at the end of a day's work (generally the thick highlights or the most intense browns) is assured even without good carbonization of the hydrated lime in the plaster, while in the second the process of carbonization is facilitated.

These are the expedients taught by experience born of a thorough knowledge of the craft. Such techniques are almost never codified, but they neither alter nor modify the basic method. In the case of the Sistine Ceiling, however, one can always speak of *buon fresco* because the chemical process of carbonization supersedes the action of the binders. The opposite situation would by definition exclude the label of *buon fresco* and in some cases even of fresco, as in mural paintings, where only the summary, preparatory phase is fresco and the majority of the work is finished with pigments in animal-glue binders, often with a little oil added.

Given that not all pigments are able to withstand the strong alkalinity of lime, painters who wanted to use colors unsuitable to fresco had to rely on the *a secco* method, that is, applying the colors to dry plaster and binding them with glue. There is very little *secco* work in the frescoes on the Sistine Ceiling. It is found in the gilding and black shadows of the medallions and in the colonnettes of the thrones. There are some small, *secco* finishing touches executed in colors not adaptable to fresco: the green sleeve of the figure on the right of the *Zorobabel-Abiud-Eliachim* lunette; the cloak on the knees of the figure on the left of the *Eleazar-Mathan* lunette; the shaded part of the Delphic Sibyl's headdress; Ezechiel's blue drapery; and Zechariah's collar. In the *Deluge* the group of figures on the right were prepared mostly in *buon fresco* but finished in *secco.* This, however, is an anomaly attributable to the problems encountered as work began and to the assistants of whom Vasari wrote.

There are, moreover, corrections, or *pentimenti,* which Michelangelo almost always made to either reduce or enlarge the dimensions of various parts of a figure (arms, legs, flanks, drapery) by a few millimeters or even nearly an inch. One of the larger *pentimenti* is found on the nude youth to the left of the group above *Joel.* This figure's left arm was completely erased. Corrections occur most frequently in the Prophets and Sibyls (there is a considerable number, for example, on the *Zechariah*). On the first half of the Ceiling, the *pentimenti* were made in one of three ways: in fresco, in half-fresco, and on the dry plaster. When done in fresco, the area to be corrected was cut away and then repainted on new, wet *intonaco,* even for very small sections (*Zechariah,* the *Drunkenness of Noah*). To make a correction in half-fresco, the plaster was scraped away before it had set. An upper layer of *intonaco* was then reapplied, using slow-drying plaster applied with a brush and then painted with pigments diluted in water (*Zechariah,* the *Drunkenness of Noah, Joel,* the *Deluge,* the *Erythraean Sibyl*). If the correction was to be *a secco,* it was painted with colors in an animal-glue binder. The last method was used when corrections were made late in the process, mostly on the second half of the Ceiling. There is only one lime intervention, on Zechariah's wooden footstool. There are no *pentimenti* in the lunettes, with the exception of the figure on the left side of the *Achim-Eliud* lunette. This is not, however, a correction in the true sense, but rather a complete reworking in fresco since all that remains of the initial painting is a small part of the upper background and the head.

During the cleaning of Michelangelo's frescoes, the restoration was criticized by those who were convinced, wrongly, that autograph areas of *secco* work were numerous and would be lost, and that the artist himself had applied the layer of glue. As we have seen, the study carried out over the nine years of the restoration answered these questions definitively. Apart from the evidence of objective data like the fragment of original fresco buried since 1570 in a crack across the chest of one of the *ignudi,* we can also say that the application of a layer of glue as a method of varnishing would have been very unusual for a true-fresco painter. It would also have been a grave error since the materials in a fresco consolidate and are enhanced with time while an organic material like glue deteriorates and changes much more rapidly. Artists applied a layer of very liquid glue over plaster or frescoed *intonaco* only when painting *secco* murals or works sketched out in fresco and then finished on the dry plaster. On the other hand, glue was frequently used by restorers of old as a way to revivify colors or to prepare pictures in cases when the restoration entailed a complete repainting of the image.

All *secco* finishing touches on the Sistine Ceiling were identified before the cleaning and were obviously protected and conserved, yet one should note that the high degree of finish and the thoroughness of the fresco work exclude the possibility that Michelangelo planned an *ultima mano.* But even if some embellishments in a fifteenth-century style had been planned, and the manner of the last part of the vault makes this unlikely, they were certainly never carried out, as the unfinished areas at the bases of the lunettes demonstrate.

In the light of what we know today, Vasari's comments now seem very clear: "Pope Julius…whose temper was hasty and impatient, would insist on having the pictures opened to public view, without waiting until the last touches had been given thereto…." He continues later, "Michelangelo had much desired to retouch portions of the work *a secco,* as had been done by the older masters who had painted the stories on the walls; he would also gladly have added a little ultramarine to some of the draperies, and gilded other parts, to the end that the whole might have a richer and more striking effect. The Pope, too, hearing that these things were still wanting, and finding that all who beheld the Chapel praised it highly, would now fain have had the additions made, but as Michelangelo thought reconstructing the scaffold too long an affair, the pictures remained as they were…."[2]

The Prophet Joel, *detail.*

A fragment of original fresco had been buried since 1570 in this crack across the chest of an ignudo.

JUDITH AND HOLOFERNES

The spandrels above the entrance wall tell
the story of how the Hebrew people were
miraculously saved by two unusual heroes.
The hero in the first episode is a widow,
Judith; in the second it is a young man,
David. According to the symbolic
interpretation of the paintings in the Sistine
Chapel, these two scenes represent the triumph
of the Church and of Christ over evil.
Holofernes, commander in chief of the Assyrians,
had been assigned to make war on the western
countries that had not obeyed the orders of King
Nebuchadnezzar. He would have exterminated
the Israelites as well had it not been for the
beautiful Judith, who deceived him with
feigned submissiveness and then
killed him after letting him get drunk.

JUDITH 13.8—10

And she smote twice upon his neck with all her might, and she took away
his head from him,
And tumbled his body down from the bed,
and pulled down the canopy from the pillars; and anon after she went
forth, and gave Holofernes his head to her maid;
And she put it in her bag of meat: so they twain went together
according to their custom unto prayer.

THE CEILING OF THE SISTINE CHAPEL

"The ceiling has proved a veritable beacon to our art, of inestimable benefit to all painters, restoring light to a world that for centuries had been plunged into darkness....In the nudes, Michelangelo displayed complete mastery: they are truly astonishing in their perfect foreshortenings, their wonderfully rotund contours, their grace, slenderness, and proportion." (Vasari)

The effortlessness and perfection of these frescoes have been praised universally, from the time they were unveiled in the summer of 1511 until today. But Michelangelo experienced the process of creating a work of art as a battle that involved, on the one hand, the struggle with the block of marble to free the form imprisoned in it and, on the other, the agony of trying to attain the ideal figure the mind had conceived by means of lines that the hand had to draw.

The Ceiling is divided into three sections. The first contains the lunettes and the triangular severies in which the Ancestors of Christ are depicted, beginning with Abraham and ending with Joseph, as they are listed in the first chapter of the Gospel according to Matthew. They are the people of the Old Testament and are represented in poses that symbolize the condition of mankind before the Redemption. At the four corners, the Ceiling is connected to the walls by means of spandrels on which are painted episodes in which the chosen people were miraculously saved from destruction. These scenes foreshadow the salvation promised to all humanity through Christ. The second and third sections comprise the Ceiling itself. An external band running around the perimeter features the thrones on which are seated the seven Prophets and the five Sibyls who announced the coming of Christ in their writings. The progressive manifestation of the Revelation culminates on the highest part of the Ceiling, the central rectangle. It is divided crosswise into nine spaces by a fictive architectural framework whose supporting elements rest on the plinths of the Prophets' and Sibyls' thrones. In the panels formed by this framework, scenes of the Book of Genesis are represented in chronological order. The first, at the altar, is God Separating Light from Darkness, *and the last, at the entrance door, is the* Drunkenness of Noah. *As we enter the Chapel and observe the scenes in reverse order, we can interpret them symbolically as the story of the Redemption, from the Incarnation to the Last Judgment. Five of the nine panels are smaller because, at their short sides, corresponding in location to the thrones, Michelangelo painted the figures of the* ignudi, *or nudes. They hold ribbons tied around swags of oak leaves and acorns, which allude to the house of Della Rovere, of which Pope Julius II, who commissioned Michelangelo to decorate the Ceiling, was a member. The* ignudi *also support ten bronze medallions with representations of scenes from the Old Testament. It took Michelangelo several years to execute the frescoes, due mainly to a lack of funds that led to a long interruption in 1510, when momentous political developments kept the pope far from Rome. Michelangelo began painting at the entrance and proceeded toward the altar. The first half of the Ceiling was revealed in August 1511, and in the fall of the following year the cycle was complete.*

…placing the head on a shallow basket resting on the head
of her servingwoman.
This old woman is so tall that she has to stoop to allow her mistress
to balance it properly;…and to cover it up, she turns her face
towards the trunk….This disturbance causes her terror and alarm,
which are clearly seen in her expression.

VASARI, "Life of Michelangelo Buonarroti"

Overleaf: Detail with Judith and her maid.
Gatefold: The Sistine Ceiling restored.

DAVID AND GOLIATH

It is difficult to devise a composition to cover a concave, triangular surface. In this case Michelangelo used the vertical axis of his composition to arrange the scene, and he increased the vertical effect by painting the field tent in the background, which helps deemphasize the lateral spaces.
During the war between the Philistines and the Israelites, the giant Goliath challenged the Israeli army to find a man who would fight him in a duel. The army to which the winner of the duel belonged would be considered victorious, and the people of the vanquished would become slaves. Young David was the only one courageous enough to accept the challenge, and although unarmed, he won.

I SAMUEL 17.50—51

So David prevailed over the Philistine with a sling and with a stone,
and smote the Philistine, and slew him;
but there was no sword in the hand of David.
Therefore David ran, and stood upon the Philistine, and took his sword…
and cut off his head therewith.

Preceding page: Detail of David striking Goliath.

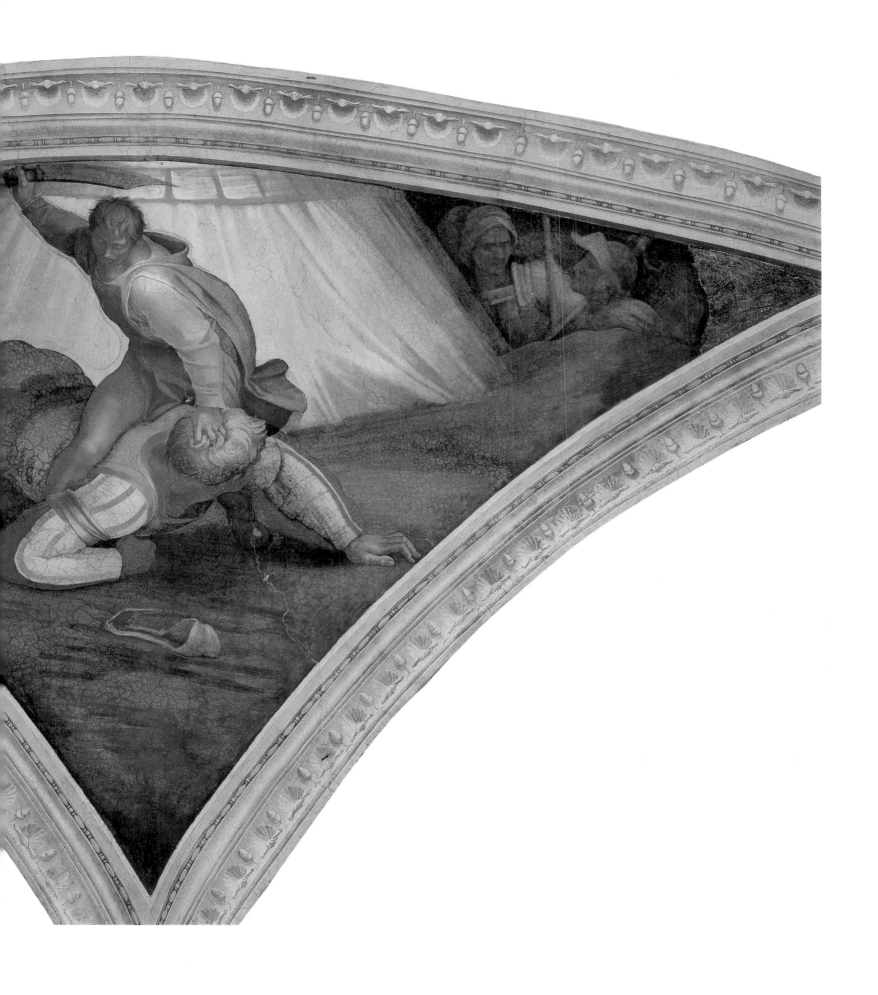

…exerting all his boyish strength,
there is David cutting off the head of Goliath, while some soldiers
in the background look on in amazement.

VASARI, "Life of Michelangelo Buonarroti"

The Problem of Michelangelo's Assistants

Fabrizio Mancinelli

The question of whether Michelangelo employed assistants to help him fresco the Sistine vault and if so to what extent has always been problematic. The documents offer two possible and contradictory answers. Scholars, who have often puzzled over this issue, usually described a limited intervention by assistants, although without clarifying the fundamental questions of how or when they were used or about the actual extent of their work on the Ceiling. Vasari's biography of Michelangelo is the oldest source we have that mentions the assistants, and it says explicitly that the artist delayed beginning the work of painting "until certain of the Florentine painters who were his friends should arrive in Rome, partly to decrease his labor by assisting in the execution of the work, but also in part to show him the process of fresco-painting, wherein some of them were well experienced. Among these artists were Granacci, Giuliano Bugiardini, Jacopo di Sandro, and the elder Indaco, with Agnolo di Donnino and Aristotile da Sangallo." Concerning the actual work done by his assistants, Vasari explains that:

the work was begun, and Michelagnolo caused them to paint a portion by way of specimen, but what they had done was far from approaching his expectations or fulfilling his purpose, and one morning he determined to destroy the whole of it. He then shut himself up in the chapel, and not only would he never again permit the building to be opened to them, but he likewise refused to see any one of them at his house. Finally therefore, and when the jest appeared to them to be carried too far, they returned, ashamed and mortified, to Florence. Michelangelo then made arrangements for performing the whole work himself, sparing no care nor labor, in the hope of bringing the same to a satisfactory termination....[1]

This version of events, reported in the 1568 edition of Vasari's *Lives*, corresponds with only a few minor variations in language to that in the 1550 edition. Vasari obviously thought that this part of his text needed no revision, the publication of Condivi's biography clearly at Michelangelo's request and Vasari's own research and modifications after the artist's death notwithstanding.[2] He must have found it sufficiently accurate and true.

We find no hint of the use of assistants in Condivi's biography of the artist. Unlike Vasari, he maintains that Michelangelo "finished this entire work in twenty months, without any help whatever, not even someone to grind his colors for him."[3] The tone of Condivi's biography, however, was shaped both by a desire to dispute Vasari's work and by an obvious wish to mythicize the persona of Michelangelo. From this point of view, Vasari's statement that Michelangelo decided to seek the help of *garzoni*, or assistants, and especially that he wanted them to "show him the process of fresco-painting," could not but have provoked Condivi's counterassertion that there were absolutely no assistants on the scaffolding, "not even someone to grind his colors for him." His position on this issue is similar to the one he takes at the beginning of his biography, when he sharply denies Vasari's assertion that Michelangelo was an apprentice in Ghirlandaio's workshop.[4]

Michelangelo's own *Ricordi* and correspondence provide definite evidence that assistants came to Rome. In a *ricordo*, or record, P. Barocchi dates to April 1508, that is, just before the contract for the Sistine Ceiling was signed, Michelangelo fixed the salary of each of his five assistants at twenty gold ducats: "for assistants to help with the painting whom he called from Florence, that is, five helpers, twenty gold ducats from the [Apostolic] chamber apiece."[5] Francesco Granacci identifies these five *garzoni* in a letter he sent to Michelangelo, in July according to Charles Wilson,[6] in August according to Karl Frey and Ernst Steinmann,[7] or in April, as Barocchi more convincingly dates it.[8] Granacci mentions

"Giuliano e Iachopo," that is, Giuliano Bugiardini and Jacopo di Sandro, who could not come to Rome before Easter—23 April—because of previously agreed upon obligations. He also mentions "Agnolo di Donnino" and "Bastiano," that is, Bastiano da Sangallo, who was also called Aristotile.[9] These artists, including Granacci, are the same as those Vasari lists in his *Lives,* although he also mentions a sixth assistant, Indaco the Elder.

We know from Michelangelo's letters that there were serious problems with Jacopo di Sandro from the beginning of October 1508; he left Rome at the end of the following January.[10] Therefore, unless we assume that Vasari's list is inaccurate, the most likely hypothesis is that Jacopo di Sandro (active 1500–1554) was replaced after he left by Indaco the Elder, Jacopo di Lazzaro di Pietro Torni (1472–1526), who also apprenticed in Domenico Ghirlandaio's shop and had, therefore, a technical background similar to Michelangelo's.[11] It is also possible that Jacopo di Lazzaro was in Rome at this time, where he may have worked with Pintoricchio in the Borgia Apartments, and where, according to Vasari, "he remained... for a long while and worked very little [because] he never worked except when he was obligated."[12] Vasari remarks specifically on Jacopo's friendship with Michelangelo, including, to explain the closeness between the two artists,

Top: Michelangelo (?), detail of the putti on the false relief to the right of Zechariah's throne.
Above: Michelangelo's workshop, detail of the putti on the false relief to the left of Zechariah's throne.
Left: Michelangelo's workshop, detail of the putti on the false relief to the right of the Delphic Sibyl's throne.

the fact that since Indaco was "a witty, pleasant and good-humored person," Michelangelo sought him out, every so often, when he wanted "to divert himself from his ceaseless exertions of mind and body, [for] no-one suited him better than Jacopo."[13]

Friendship and a common tie through Ghirlandaio's shop proved, in most cases, to be the basis upon which Michelangelo chose his assistants. This is certainly true for his two principal *garzoni,* Granacci and Bugiardini. Granacci (1460–c.1543) was the childhood friend who first interested Michelangelo in painting and introduced him into Ghirlandaio's work-shop.[14] Bugiardini[15] was a friend from Ghirlandaio's workshop; "there was besides a certain natural goodness and a kind of simplicity in the manners and mode of life of Giuliano who was wholly devoid of all malice and envy, and the qualities infinitely pleased Michelangelo."[16]

Agnolo di Donnino and Bastiano da Sangallo were chosen for different reasons. The former, Agnolo di Domenico di Donnino Mazzieri (1466–1513), came from Cosimo Rosselli's shop and was, according to Vasari, a close friend of that artist's.[17] Granacci chose him because of his technical skill, "because he is better than others in fresco painting."[18] Bastiano (1481–1551), known familiarly as Aristotile, trained first in Pietro Perugino's shop but was really formed by his study of Michelangelo's cartoon for the *Battle of Cascina,* after which he later painted an oil copy, now at Holkham Hall in Norfolk, England.[19] Furthermore, "as were others of his family," he was interested in "architectural things." In particular, he worked on perspective under Donato Bramante's guidance, evidently on-site at St. Peter's, where he had been brought by his brother Giovan Francesco, who had "a large establishment, consisting of Tufa and Puzzolana works" in Rome.[20] The team of *garzoni* mentioned thus far was made up of an organic group of fresco specialists, all with relatively similar skills, with the exception of Granacci and Bugiardini, who were undoubtedly the most gifted of the lot.

The homogeneity of this group was reinforced by the fact that all its members, with the exception of Bastiano, who was six years younger than Michelangelo, were either the same age or slightly older than the master. They were also for the most part bound by ties of friendship—Vasari called them Michelangelo's "painter friends"—and above all by the fact that they all, with the exception again of Bastiano and of Agnolo di Donnino, came from the same workshop. That the majority of this team emerged from Ghirlandaio's shop was obviously a consequence of Michelangelo's own apprenticeship there; he wanted collaborators who were schooled in the same workshop practices and who understood the technique and subtleties of fresco painting. Typical in this regard was the use of lapis lazuli and blue smalt in fresco rather than *a secco* (*buon fresco,* or true fresco, is executed on wet plaster; fresco *a secco* on dry plaster).

Assuming that Indaco replaced Jacopo di Sandro, the group of *garzoni* who assisted the master during the initial phase of work on the Ceiling seems to have had only five members, as Michelangelo himself says in his *ricordo* of April 1508. In a letter to Michelangelo dated 28 September 1510, however, Giovanni Michi, writing from Rome to Florence, mentions "Gismondo and Bernardino" and specifies that they were "drietro a ritrarre."[21] They have been identified as Giovanni Trignoli and Bernardo Zacchetti,[22] two practically unknown artists from Reggio Emilia whom Michelangelo perhaps knew in Bologna. He stayed in touch with them even after the Sistine project, particularly with Zacchetti, who lived with him in 1517.[23] It is not clear when these two began to work with Michelangelo or exactly in what capacity. Michi's use of the term *ritrarre,* to draw, suggests something of a graphic nature, perhaps connected to the drafting of cartoons since it was impossible that some work not continue on the scaffolding in the master's absence.

It is clear, then, as William Wallace has observed, that Michelangelo's workshop consisted of more than Vasari's five *garzoni della pictura* and included both permanent and temporary assistants.[24] We can be certain, however, that Giuliano da Sangallo was never a member of the workshop; his role on the project was something completely different. Among those who were not painters, Piero di Jacopo Rosselli (1474?–1531) should be mentioned first. He was the master mason employed by Michelangelo to prepare the surface of the vault for frescoing, that is, "to scrape the ceiling, plaster it and to do whatever else was necessary," and to construct, or at least to assist in building, the scaffolding.[25] Rosselli was paid for the last time on 27 July 1508; this date must mark the completion of the preliminary phase of the project. It is not known if Piero stayed on afterwards, but Michelangelo must have used the services of at least one expert mason since the *intonaco,* or upper layer of plaster, is very skillfully laid, especially on the first half of the Ceiling.

During this same period we find Piero Basso (1441–1525) in Michelangelo's shop.[26] He had the same general duties that Giovanni Michi would later assume. As was also perhaps the case with Rosselli, Basso left Rome at the end of July for health reasons. On 29 July Michelangelo wrote to his brother, Buonarroto, "I am letting you know that Piero Basso has left here Tuesday morning—that is, the 25th—sick, and whether I wanted him to or not."[27] In his missive Michelangelo asked Buonarroto to give Michi a letter on his behalf, in which he asks him to come to Rome as quickly as possible, "because I cannot remain alone and also because I can find no-one to trust." Michi had already written on 22 July to offer his services,[28] and confirmed that he was available on 5 August. He most likely arrived in Rome around the middle of that month.[29] The documents, which cover only the period from 1508 to 1510, reveal little about Michi; they do not even say whether he was a painter, a sculptor, or something else.[30] Michelangelo treated him as a general factotum, assigning him minor tasks and leaving him to manage his household.

The task of overseeing financial matters for Michelangelo, at least at the beginning of the Sistine project, fell to Granacci. It was he who in April gave Michelangelo the names of possible assistants; he gave him Fra Jacopo di Francesco's name the following May when the master wrote to this friar asking him to send "a certain amount of pretty blues... since I have certain things to paint here."[31] In May or June Granacci was also made responsible for supervising Piero Rosselli's work, and it was he who paid the mason, with the exception of the first payment, which came directly from Michelangelo.[32] In July Granacci was in Florence,[33] and we find him there again in August and at the beginning of September, when Michelangelo charged him with buying pigments, or rather, given the quantity, samples of pigments, for painting the Sistine Ceiling.[34] At the end of September or perhaps the beginning of October, the colors purchased and the preliminaries at least partially finished, the operation was moved to the scaffolding in order to begin work. According to Charles de Tolnay, who based his opinion on stylistic analysis, Granacci took no part in this phase.[35] If Michelangelo indeed used assistants as he began to paint—and Jacopo di Sandro was still in Rome in January—then it is difficult to imagine that he did so without the help of Granacci, given his role in the months previous, who was the best of them. Such a supposition is even more problematic in a case like the Sistine Ceiling, where stylistic analysis cannot furnish conclusive evidence for the identification of individual hands.

With the exception of Granacci, the dates the *garzoni* arrived in Rome are not clear. We know from Michelangelo's often-cited letter of April 1508 that Granacci and Bastiano were immediately available but that Jacopo di Sandro and Bugiardini had first to finish work already under way elsewhere. On 24 May Granacci had certainly been in Rome for some time, since he made the first payment to Rosselli on Michelangelo's behalf on that date. It is possible, although there is no documentary evidence to support it, that Bastiano was also in Rome with Granacci. Indeed Bastiano possessed several qualities that would have made him extremely useful to Michelangelo during the early stages of the decoration of the Sistine Ceiling. These included a better knowledge of the building materials used in Rome—lime, tufa, and pozzolana—which he had learned working with his brother, Giovan Francesco, and an equally profound understanding of the problems of perspective—which he would later use for stage sets and festival machines—acquired, at least in part, from Bramante. Finally, given that he came from a family of architects, and given his training and his experience in Bramante's shop at St. Peter's, Bastiano brought a familiarity with the problems of structural engineering, which would have been useful in designing the scaffolding.

Michelangelo had set aside twenty ducats a month for each *garzone*.[36] Yet it would have been difficult for him to keep all five of them working full-time at the same time, since the planning of the decoration most likely began only after the contract was signed and because the master would hardly have delegated any of the drawings, be they studies or preparations of cartoons, to others.[37] If we also consider that Granacci was dismissed temporarily in June, it seems very unlikely that the other assistants were called to Rome before September or October, when, as we have already noted, the operation moved to the scaffolding in the Sistine Chapel. In this context it is particularly significant that the first disagreements with Jacopo di Sandro occurred on 7 October.

According to Vasari the *garzoni* worked on the scaffolding for only a short time. Dissatisfied with their services, Michelangelo is said to have locked himself on the scaffold and refused to admit his assistants. In the end shame compelled them to return to Florence. As has been observed many times, such a traumatic conclusion to the story of the assistants would necessarily have prejudiced future contacts between Michelangelo and the *garzoni*.[38] Yet documentary sources, including Vasari's description in his *Lives* of continuing relationships between the master and his assistants, contradict his account of this episode. Bugiardini, for example, painted a portrait of Michelangelo for Ottaviano de'Medici in 1522, and Michelangelo turned to Granacci at the beginning of April 1512, while work was still under way in the Sistine Chapel, for news of Alonso Berruguete—something he would not have done if their relationship were anything but friendly.[39]

Vasari also reports an incident in his biography of Indaco that is curiously similar, except for its end, to that which puts an end to the story of the Sistine assistants.[40] Vasari recounts that one day Michelangelo, who was tired of Indaco's constant chatter, sent him to buy figs. After he had left on this errand, Michelangelo locked the door and refused to let him back in when he returned. Indaco was obviously offended, and "for many months he did not want to speak to Michelangelo. Finally, however, he was reconciled and was a better friend than ever."[41]

This happy ending, perfectly plausible in a simple relationship like that with Indaco, is difficult to imagine in a group situation which involved more than strictly private interests. The episode, which we might call the story of the closed door and which repeats itself many times in Michelangelo's biography—not only in the artist's relationships with the *garzoni* and Indaco but also with Julius II—both documents an aspect of Michelangelo's character and provides, in the case of his assistants, a literary-theatrical expedient to end a story about which Vasari was not very well informed.[42] The myth of Michelangelo as a superhuman and solitary genius remained almost unaltered for more than three centuries, and only with Wilson's study of 1876 did scholars begin to reexamine the possibility that he may have used assistants when painting the Sistine Ceiling.[43] The most reliable analyses were done first by Steinmann and then by Biagetti and de Tolnay.[44] More recently Wallace has dealt with this subject in his careful reconstruction of Michelangelo's workshop and his analysis of the available documents.[45]

Both Steinmann and Biagetti formulated their hypotheses on the basis of the two restoration campaigns undertaken in the Sistine Chapel in the first half of this century: the first in 1904 and the second in the 1920s and thirties. Steinmann, and de Tolnay later, ventured a series of tentative attributions; Biagetti more prudently limited himself to pointing out areas where the intervention of assistants could be identified with relative certainty. The recent cleaning allows us to confirm the accuracy of Biagetti's survey and to clarify the extent and quality of the workshop interventions.

The hands of assistants can be detected both in the exclusively decorative parts of the cornices and in the more complex fictive reliefs on the thrones, the *tondi,* and the narrative scenes. Yet wherever the *garzoni* painted, they worked under the strict guidance of the master, who often exercised ruthless control and painted passages of less important decorative detail himself to demonstrate how it was to be done. The series of extremely accurate cartoons that Michelangelo drew were his essential tool in controlling his shop.[46] These allowed the assistants no room for any personal initiative and forced them to follow the master's compositions with great care. It is not surprising, then, that there were even cartoons for the architectural frames around the narrative scenes, although only at the beginning, and for the decorative moldings, with their acorns and shells, around the spandrels. The cartoon for the capitals of the Delphic Sibyl's throne—the first to be executed—called for a more complicated decorative scheme that was modified only after painting had begun.[47] This change documents a direct intervention by Michelangelo, who evidently closely supervised the execution even of these seemingly less important details.

Ghirlandaio's use of his workshop in the Tornabuoni Chapel in S. Maria Novella in Florence proves rather different from Michelangelo's, despite numerous similarities, and the organization of Perugino's shop in the Stanza dell'Incendio in the Vatican is totally the opposite. In the Tornabuoni Chapel, where Michelangelo himself may have worked as a young boy, the most important areas of the frescoes, those nearest the viewer, were executed in part by Ghirlandaio and in part by his assistants, who worked from the master's detailed cartoons.[48] The upper and less easily legible zones were entrusted entirely to the workshop, which painted them based on summarily executed cartoons transferred to the wall by indirect incision. The master's direct intervention in the painting was thus dictated by the importance of the subject and its visibility. This left his pupils a great degree of freedom in the less important areas, where the presence of different hands is clearly detectable, especially when observed at close range.

Perugino's working method on the ceiling of the Stanza dell'Incendio, executed at the same time Michelangelo was working in the Sistine Chapel, was the opposite of Ghirlandaio's. Here the master's hand is hardly present, except in the preparation of the cartoons—although their repetitive details suggests at least some workshop intervention even here—and in the finishing touches.[49] Several assistants worked on the ceiling, but because Perugino painted *a secco,* he had more time to work and could study the whole, retouch it, and make it more homogeneous, even much further along in the execution of the ceiling. Here, too, however, close inspection permits us to identify individual hands rather easily.

The intervention of assistants is much less evident in Michelangelo's workshop, due both to the extremely detailed cartoons used and to the master's rigorous control. These artists also subordinated their own style to Michelangelo's, as testified to by the lack of changes or interruptions in the sequence of *giornate,* or days' work. It is very difficult, therefore, to identify individual hands, and any such attribution is usually debatable. The presence of workshop assistants is nonetheless clearly detectable in tech

Below: Detail of the decorative band around the spandrels and severies. It is possible to make out the indirect incision and, to the right, the traces of pouncing that indicate a preparatory cartoon was used.
Bottom: Detail of one of the capitals on the Delphic Sibyl's throne. When viewed against the light, one can see the ornamental tracing that had initially been planned.

51

niques that vary from Michelangelo's and especially in the perceptible diminution of creative tension, indicated by a weakness of execution, the handling of the brush, and the use of heavy outlines as guides—something the recent cleaning has shown that Michelangelo himself would be very unlikely to do.

The *Deluge* is a particularly significant example. The recent restoration has confirmed that this is without doubt the first scene Michelangelo painted on the Ceiling and that he painted it in two stages, using a different technique for each.[50] The first was executed partially *a secco;* in the second this technique was abandoned for *buon fresco.* Michelangelo apparently demolished the first version almost entirely—for reasons that are unclear—leaving only the small island crowded with people fleeing the rising waters. It was incorporated into the definitive version, of which it constitutes the first six days' work.[51]

Such technical uncertainties are typical of the initial stages of the painting of the Ceiling, and they include numerous *pentimenti,* or corrections, and partial repaintings that can be detected on the left side of the composition. The breaks in the continuity of the drafting that characterizes the different sections of the scene are wholly different. They are easy to see when one compares the figures in the foreground on the left with those under the tent on the right. The former, especially the family group with the donkey, although vigorously modeled, are somewhat simplified in the articulation of the planes. The latter are executed with much more diluted and transparent colors and with such careful attention that it borders on pedantry. The technique used to paint the old man carrying his son's corpse is completely different. The planes are treated with greater analytical vigor, pigments are more or less diluted according to the desired expressive quality, and the often hatched brushstrokes tend to define the areas in the foreground by a precise rendering of detail and to simplify and blur those behind.

These technical differences cannot easily be attributed to a single painter, even one still searching for his artistic identity, as Vasari believed Michelangelo was when he started to paint the Sistine Ceiling.[52] This is evident when one compares the *Deluge* with the more or less contemporary and certainly autograph figures of the Prophets, Sibyls, and *ignudi,* or nude youths, which surround the scene. We must remember, too, that the man carrying his dead son, also without a doubt by Michelangelo himself, was executed with the same technique as the much later Creation scenes. Furthermore, it was painted on one of the very first *giornate* in this scene and not, as is the case with the family and its donkey, on one of the last. If, as it seems, Michelangelo did indeed paint this figure, then neither the figure on the left of the composition nor those under the tent are by his hand. The scene was executed by assistants, perhaps by Granacci and Bugiardini, given that they were the most talented and that the qualitative level of the scene is very high. The work of assistants, probably the same who painted part of the *Deluge,* can also be found in the adjacent scenes—in the figures of Noah's sons in the scene of his drunkenness and in the *Sacrifice of Noah,* especially in the figure of the patriarch's wife. It appears that despite what Vasari thought, the entire workshop was active on the scaffolding for some

time. Furthermore, Michelangelo seems not to have destroyed their work but on the contrary profited from their help for as long as possible—most likely, as we will see, until the end of 1509.

Michelangelo's assistants were clearly active on the first third of the vault, most obviously in the *tondi* and on the fictive reliefs of the thrones, where the master employed his less-able helpers.[53] Perhaps Michelangelo himself worked only on Zechariah's throne, painting the fictive relief on the right while assigning that on the left to a less-skilled assistant. The *tondi* are more complicated both because they were painted *a secco* and because they were damaged by earlier restorations and appear to have been largely repainted.[54] And yet, since previous restorers always tried to reconstruct the passages lost in the cleaning as accurately as possible, a general evaluation of the *tondi* is still possible. It is fairly obvious that the medallions above the *Delphic Sibyl* and *Joel* were painted by two different artists, and a third seems to have painted the remaining roundels up to the *Creation of Eve.* The intervention of assistants on the figures of the Prophets and Sibyls can be excluded because of both the quality and the size of the figures. The same is true of the Ancestors of Christ, who were painted without preparatory cartoons.

The four *ignudi* of the first bay are uncharacteristic. They are very different from those in later bays for the simple reason that they are the result

Top: Michelangelo, detail of the old man and his dead son in the Deluge.
Above: Diagram of the giornate *for the* Deluge. *The zone in gray shows what remains from Michelangelo's first version of this scene.*

Opposite left, top to bottom:
Michelangelo's workshop, the Deluge, *detail of top left corner showing the woman with child next to the donkey;*
Michelangelo's workshop, the Deluge, *detail of the young man leaning against a small cask, in the group under the tent;*
Michelangelo, the Deluge, *detail of the legs of the old man and his dead son;*
Michelangelo, the Creation of Adam, *detail of God the Father.*

Opposite right: Michelangelo and his workshop, the Deluge, *detail of the group on the island painted during the first six* giornate.

Above: Michelangelo's workshop, the Sacrifice of Noah, *detail of Noah's wife.*
Right: Michelangelo's workshop, the Drunkenness of Noah, *detail of Noah's sons.*

of experimentation. Although much admired in the past for their originali-ty, the two *ignudi* above the *Delphic Sibyl* are rather weakly executed, par-ticularly when compared to the two opposite them. Their qualitative level is high enough, however, that to attribute them to a workshop hand is risky. The situation changes radically in the last two panels of the first cam-paign on the Ceiling, the *Temptation* and the *Expulsion* and the *Creation of Eve*. Here the compositions are reduced to only a few figures and their size increases notably—the later figures are more than two yards or meters tall.[55] The rhythm of work also changes; there are thirteen and twelve *gior-nate* in the *Drunkenness* and *Sacrifice of Noah*, respectively, but only four in the *Creation of Eve*. The days' work are so large that only Michelangelo could handle them—Eve in the *Expulsion* and God the Father in the *Creation of Eve* were painted on single *giornate* and are each about two yards tall. The qualitative level also remains exceptionally high throughout the *Creation of Eve*, without the uneven quality one finds in the three earlier panels. Nor does it seem coincidental that Michelangelo changed the order in which he painted the various components of the bay, including the *ignudi*. The *Drunkenness* and *Sacrifice of Noah* were both painted before the *ignudi* around them, but this sequence was reversed in the bay with the *Creation of Eve*, with the narrative panel painted after the nude figures.

It is likely, therefore, that it is at this point and not earlier that Michelangelo drastically limited the participation of his workshop in the execution of the Ceiling, giving them only the less-important areas to paint.[56] The more qualified of the *garzoni* returned to Florence and were perhaps replaced by less-gifted assistants. Yet because they were less

skilled, they may also have been better suited to the new working conditions. This may well have been the case for Giovanni Trignoli and Bernardino Zacchetti.

It is very difficult to establish with any certainty when this change occurred. In the passage cited above, however, Condivi gives us a clue to the chronology, which Vasari omitted in his 1568 edition of the *Lives,* perhaps because it made little sense with regard to the Ceiling as a whole. Yet if Condivi's statement is related to the departure of the assistants, it is, on the contrary, very illuminating. Condivi says that Michelangelo "finished the entire work in twenty months." Taking a quick look at the chronology of the Sistine project, we know from Michelangelo's correspondence with his father and Buonarroto that he finished the first half of the Ceiling in August 1510 and that in September he had to interrupt his work because of the pope's departure from Rome.[57] The scaffolding in the Chapel was dismantled for the Feast of the Assumption in August 1511, and the work was shown to Julius II, who paid Michelangelo four hundred ducats on 1 October.[58] Michael Hirst believes it possible that work on the Ceiling resumed around this time and that in the meanwhile the scaffolding had been reassembled in the second part of the Chapel.[59] Exactly a year later, at the beginning of October 1512, the artist could finally write to his father, "I have finished the chapel which I was painting, and the Pope is very well pleased."[60]

If one takes into account the interruption caused by Julius's leaving and then subtracts the twenty months cited by Condivi, one comes to around November or December 1509, which must correspond to the time when

Michelangelo's assistants left. There are obviously no certainties, but there are clues. On 17 November 1509 Michelangelo sent his brother a letter that seems to indicate a change in the rhythm of work and, above all, a different kind of solitude: "I am here very hard pressed for time and very exhausted, with no friends of any sort, nor do I want them."[61]

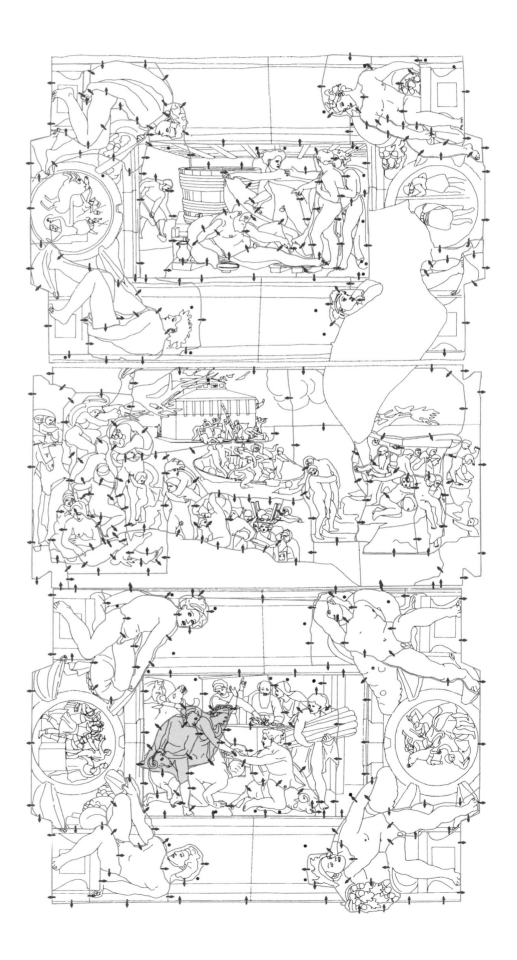

Diagram of the giornate *for the* Drunkenness of Noah, *the* Deluge, *and the* Sacrifice of Noah.

Diagram of the giornate *for the* Temptation *and the* Expulsion, *the* Creation of Eve, *and the* Creation of Adam.

Overleaf: The ignudi *to the left of the* Drunkenness of Noah *panel.*

GENESIS 9.20—23

And Noah began to be an husbandman, and he planted a vineyard:
And he drank of the wine, and was drunken;
and he was uncovered within his tent.

The scenes telling the story of Noah, which were the first to be painted, are the first ones the visitor sees on entering the Chapel. Chronologically, however, they are the last stories of the cycle that makes up the Book of Genesis. The sequence of the illustrations in this volume follows this reverse order since it is also valid for a typological interpretation of the scenes that are placed in the center of the Ceiling. Paintings often conveyed doctrinal messages, and the better-educated sixteenth-century spectators were able to interpret the symbolism of these images.

The panels with the patriarch's stories were the first ones Michelangelo undertook and he probably began with the great, central scene of the Deluge. The scenes consist of three complex compositions with a narrative style that is epic and solemn. As there are more figures in these scenes than in those painted subsequently, the dimensions of the figures are less monumental. Parts of these figures have been identified as having been done by Michelangelo's assistants. The initial trial-and-error stage, which shows his indecisiveness on how to proceed with the work, is apparent in the way the figures were executed.

Above: The Drunkenness of Noah, detail.

And Ham, the father of Canaan, saw the nakedness of his father,
and told his two brethren without.
And Shem and Japheth took a garment, and laid it upon both their shoulders,
and went backward,
and covered the nakedness of their father.

The Drunkenness of Noah.

The Drunkenness of Noah, *detail of the sleeping Noah. The grapevine is a plant with symbolic meaning in the Old Testament, where it represents Israel, as well as in the New, where Christ states, "I am the true vine..." (Gospel according to St. John 15.1). Hence, the drunken Noah is the symbol of man reverting to his sins once the Deluge has passed, but there is also an allusion to the Word that makes itself humble by accepting to come into this world as the "grapevine of Israel."*

Opposite: The Drunkenness of Noah, *detail with his sons. Noah's ridicule by his son Ham, in the foreground, was interpreted by St. Augustine as foreshadowing the mocking of Christ.*

The two ignudi *above the* Delphic Sibyl.
*The figure on the left has been lost almost
entirely as a result of the 1797 explosion of
the gunpowder magazine in Castel Sant'Angelo.
However, we know from a sixteenth-century
engraving that this figure was a mirror image
of its companion.
The medallion they support shows Joab, nephew
of David, as he kills Abner (2 Samuel 3.27).*

This pair of nudes, who are turned toward the
Delphic Sibyl, *is one of the first painted by
Michelangelo. Although the pair was greatly
admired in the sixteenth century, they do not
possess the level of excellence of the* ignudi *he
painted later. All these extremely beautiful
nudes, on which the artist lavished great
attention, should probably be considered
representations of angels; with regard to the
hierarchy of the Ceiling's images, they are
in fact the closest to the biblical scenes.*

Opposite: Detail of the ignudo *to the right of
the* Delphic Sibyl.

GENESIS 7.15–19

And they went in unto Noah into the ark, two and two of all flesh,
wherein is the breath of life.
And they that went in, went in male and female of all flesh,

The dynamic composition of this large painting,
with its diagonal axes, emphasizes the actions of
the fleeing people, while the ark is placed in the
background. In the upper right corner we see
that part of the plaster has come off. This

occurred in 1797, as a result of an explosion in
the nearby Castel Sant'Angelo. Directly above
the tent that shelters a small group of fleeing
people, Michelangelo had painted, "...the
wrath of God is turned against them in torrents,

as God had commanded him: and the Lord shut him in.
And the flood was forty days upon the earth; and the waters increased,
and bare up the ark, and it was lift up above the earth....
And the waters prevailed exceedingly upon the earth; and all the high hills,
that were under the whole heaven, were covered.

and lightning and thunderbolts." The fragment portraying the lightning, as recorded in Condivi's description, can be seen in a sixteenth-century copy of the painting located at the Louvre. The symbolic interpretation of this scene is very clear: the water of the deluge that wipes the sinners from the face of the earth is the symbol of baptism, which washes away original sin. The ark symbolizes the Church and tells us that man can save himself only through it.

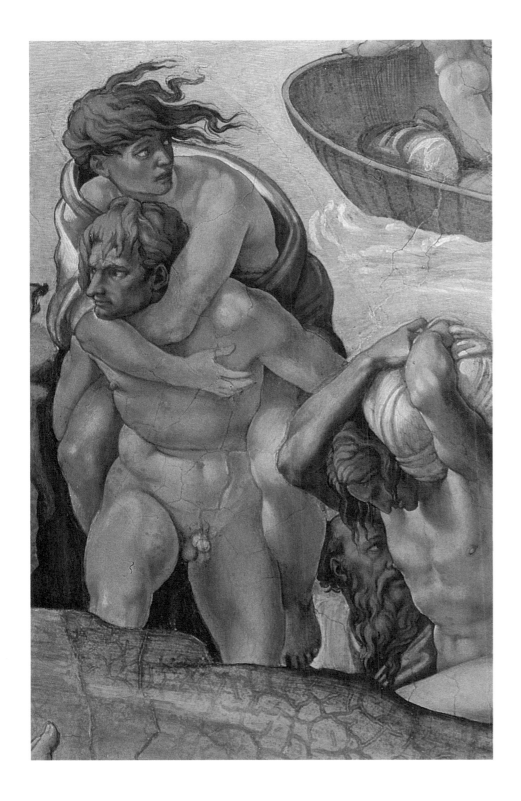

As compared to the biblical version of the story, Michelangelo emphasized the reactions and anguish of the people. Although they are sinners, they are not automatically evil. The ones who are seeking safety on higher ground are helping and trying to comfort each other, but they are impeded by their love of material things, as they laboriously drag along their possessions while climbing up the hill.

The Deluge, *details.*
"…*in the history of the Flood, where there are
depicted some dying men who are overwhelmed
by terror and dismay at what has happened and
in various ways are striving their utmost to find
safety…. Michelangelo also showed the pious
actions of many people who are helping one
another to climb to safety to the top of a rock.
Among them is a man who has clasped someone
who is half dead and is striving his utmost to
save him; and nothing better than this could be
seen in living nature." (Vasari, "Life of
Michelangelo Buonarroti")*

Overleaf: The two ignudi *above the* Erythraean Sibyl. *The two figures are placed in very similar positions and differ essentially in the way the chiaroscuro has been handled.*

71

THE SACRIFICE OF NOAH

GENESIS 8.20–21

And Noah builded an altar unto the Lord; and took of every clean beast,
and of every clean fowl, and offered burnt offerings on the altar.

According to chronological order, the scene representing Noah as he pays homage to the Lord for saving him from the waters should have been placed after that of the Deluge. Instead, the Sacrifice was placed before the Deluge so it could be read as the Sacrifice of Christ according to the symbolic program, which proceeds in reverse order across the Ceiling.

If, therefore, the three stories of Noah are read starting from the entrance and proceeding toward the altar, they symbolize the Incarnation, the Baptism, and the Sacrifice of the Word.

Above: The Sacrifice of Noah, *detail of the young man who receives the viscera of the sacrificial animal.*

And the Lord smelled a sweet savour; and the Lord said in his heart,
I will not again curse the ground any more for man's sake;
for the imagination of man's heart is evil from his youth;
neither will I again smite any more every thing living, as I have done.

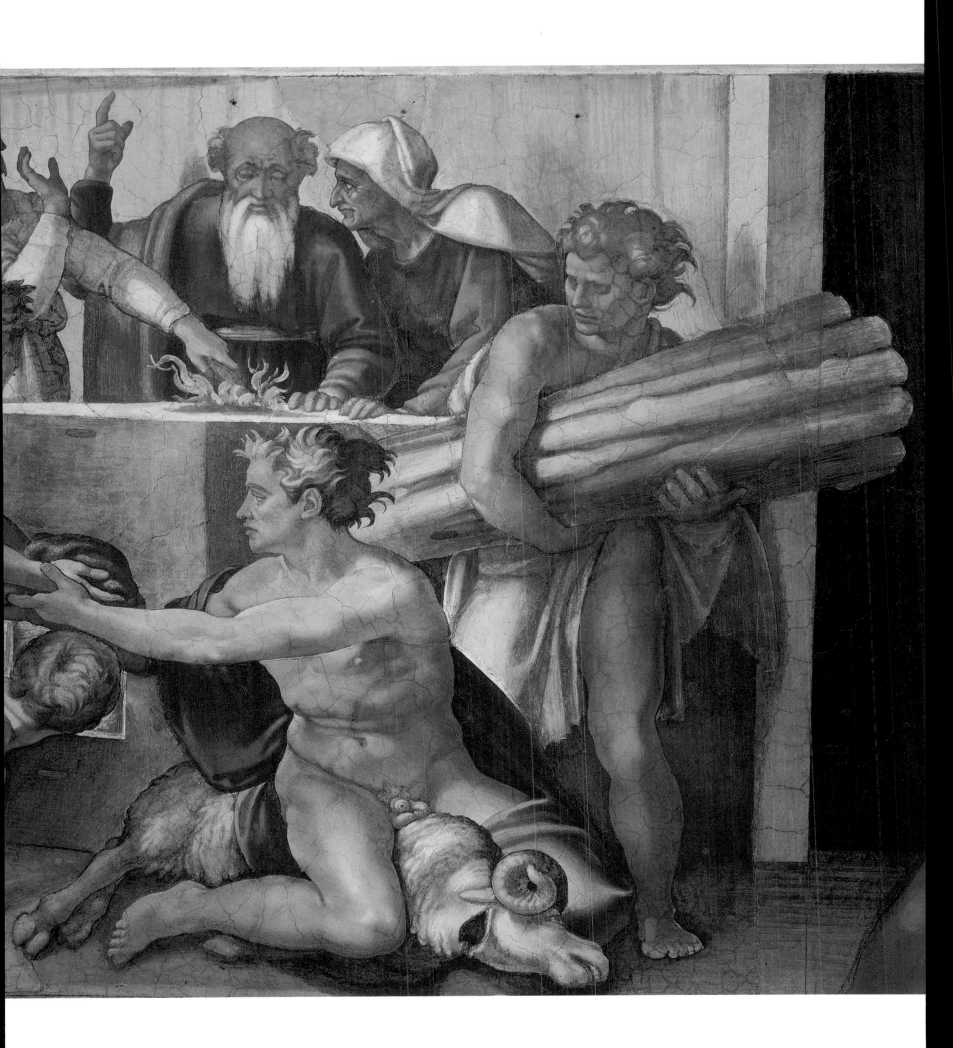

The Sacrifice of Noah, details. According
to the writings of Vasari and Condivi, the scene
represented the Sacrifice of Cain and Abel.
The two historians were perhaps deceived by the
panel's erroneous chronological placement
immediately after the Temptation and the
Expulsion and before the Deluge, instead
of following it.

The Sacrifice of Noah, *detail of the group performing the sacrifice.*
The upward movement of Noah's gesture is underlined by the arrangement of the three figures in a pyramidal composition. In particular, the gesture of the woman to the left, shielding herself from the heat and sparks, extends and reinforces the dynamic impact of the movement of wise old Noah's arm.

Overleaf: Nudes above the Prophet Isaiah, *details.*
"He made them of all ages, some slim and some full-bodied, with varied expressions and attitudes." (Vasari)

The Functions of Michelangelo's Color

John Shearman

That the study of color needs demystification, and that it needs liberation from deplorable clichés, are not as much commonplaces as they ought to be. Most of the clichés may be allowed to fade away in peace, but perhaps there is one that needs on this occasion to be dispatched summarily and without sympathy, for it has done us a notable disservice: that is the notion that there is something less essential about Florentine color than about Venetian, a notion that has taken an extreme form in the idea that Florentine painting is colored drawing. There is not one grain of truth in such distinctions and there never was, even when the Brancacci Chapel and the Sistine Ceiling were hard to read. For, to take a fundamental, formal issue, it was always clear that the presence of form is as much dependent on color in Masaccio as in Giovanni Bellini, as much in Michelangelo as in Giorgione. That is not to say it works in the same way.

It might go without saying that the following observations on Michelangelo's color are made in the Chapel, from the frescoes, and not from photographs or slides. And that should not be thought to be some unusual claim. But I have the impression that most of the initial reactions to the cleaning of the Ceiling were not so made. The strident critics of the conservation campaign seem to have formed their reactions to strident color from color photographs, particularly from details, and especially not from looking at the vault from the floor. The rhetoric of criticism has not yet, on either side, readjusted to the experience of reading the frescoes from the floor without artificial light. Only when that is done, it seems to me, can the functionality of Michelangelo's color be assessed and appreciated. When I look at the Ceiling from the floor I do not see brilliant color and strong contrasts—indeed, I see them less than I had expected to.[1] Rather, I see an extraordinary clarity of form, of expression, and of action, and a harmonious cast of color dominated by the stony flesh of the *ignudi*, or nudes.

Opposite: The Temptation *and the* Expulsion, *detail of the serpent.*

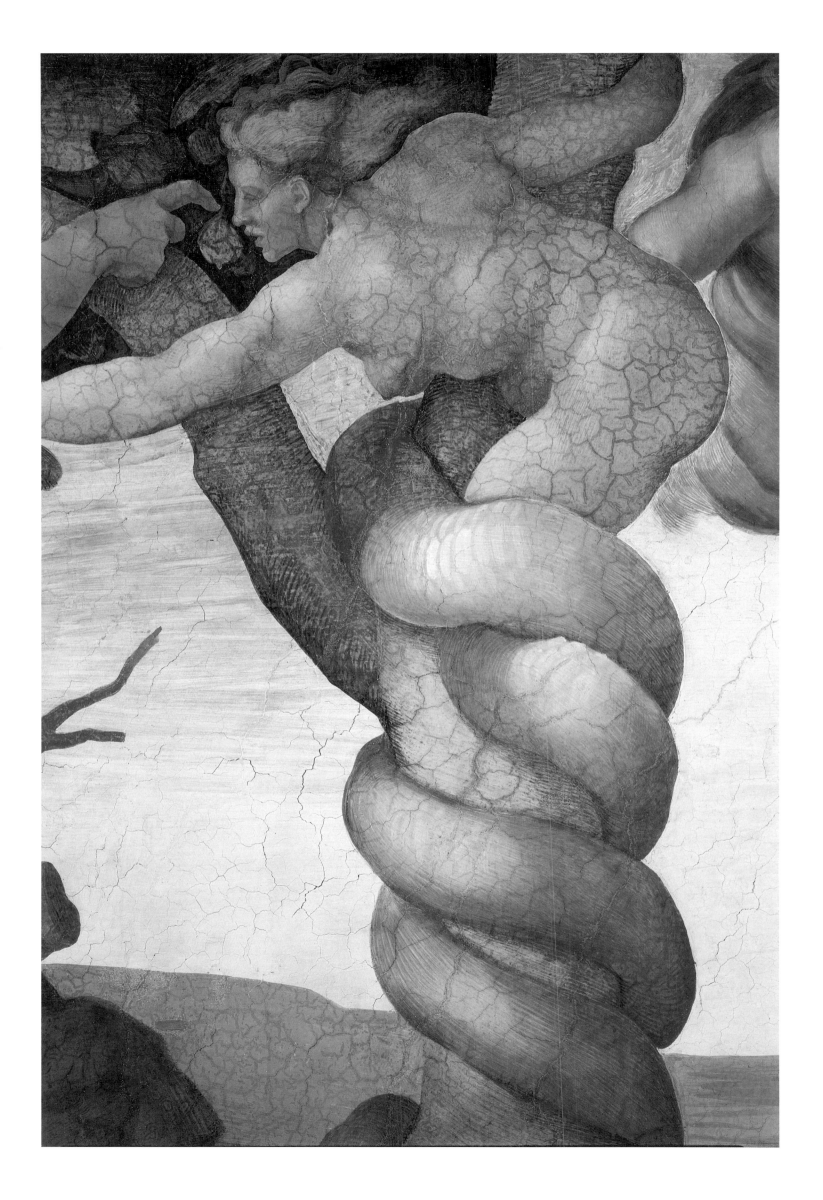

Now, if we are to privilege the reading from the floor in natural light over readings from the scaffold or from color reproductions, it follows that we need to be especially aware of and sensitive to changes both of surface and of ambience. By changes of surface what is meant is the mellowing and lightening effect over distance of the uneven, moderate but not negligible breakup of the hard crystalline fresco-skin, an effect like a mild form of interference or scatter. And by changes in ambience what is meant is above all the small but perhaps significant change in the nature of the light itself, which was never, in fact, entirely natural. The present stained-glass windows are pallid reconstructions based on the less colored of the painted windows of the entrance wall, themselves contradictory as evidence of the original windows. It is worth remembering that the originals were removed early in the nineteenth century with the express intention of making the frescoes more legible, frescoes which by that date, of course, were already very dirty.[2] Now that they are clean, we need all the more to allow a probable correction of the ambient light, for the light's subtle but specific effects may once more be operative and significant. It is probable that Michelangelo painted the Ceiling, and his public saw it, in a coloristically stronger and less stable light than we have now. The combined effect of changes in surface and ambience is probably to diminish the richness of the original color experience.

In attempting to deal with three principal functions of color in the Ceiling I shall leave such a correction implicitly operative. But before approaching the three chosen functions, I should mention two which are not to be treated in detail. It would be insensitive, I think, to the now-revealed color not to comment on its manifest function to give pleasure to the eye, pleasure like that of a bouquet. The biggest surprise, indeed, has been to find in Michelangelo a capacity and an evident intention to give pleasure in this sense like another Federico Barocci, and therein lies perhaps the most radical reassessment we now must make of Michelangelo the painter. Its understanding must take into account self-discovery in the very process of painting the vault. While it has always been clear, for example, that in many respects the color of the Ceiling would emerge from some future cleaning resembling the clarity of pure pigment we could see in the *Doni Tondo,* that picture was not painted by a Barocci-like artist who could touch the poetry of color. At that point in Michelangelo's career the polemics of painting, engendered by his rivalry with Leonardo, would not naturally have led him in that direction. And when Michelangelo began on the Ceiling, whether with the *Delphic Sibyl* or with *Zechariah,* he was still, one is forced to say, the less-imaginative painter for whom the value of color was structural and clarifying. By slow degrees, and accelerating after the break in the work, perhaps precisely as Florentine polemics receded, the poet in him was released. He poured coloristic beauty as if from a cornucopia into the *Libyan Sibyl* on the pendentive opposite his patron's throne, with plain intent to please, and scarcely less so into *Jeremiah* and *Jonah.*

It is much more difficult to find a clear solution to an apparently more objective issue, which is whether there is a structural function for color in the Ceiling, in the larger sense of compositional structural function. Did he, to be specific, intend to articulate the vast and awkwardly shaped field of the vault by the device of isochromatic alternation and exchange?[3] It was a system in use in Domenico Ghirlandaio's workshop, and one with a long, almost exhausted tradition in Tuscan art—almost exhausted because the absolutism of color on which it rested was itself practically dissolved by about 1500. In the earlier parts of the Ceiling, some hint of such an articulating approach to coloristic unity is not difficult to find. The articulation, however, seems to assume the developmental license of imperfect or approximate isochromatism, which to the skeptical may bring the whole question into disrepute unless they have thought about such cases as Duc-

Michelangelo, Doni Tondo, *after its restoration. Gallerie degli Uffizi, Florence.*

83

cio's *Rucellai Madonna.* Thus a yellow-and-green sequence which moves diagonally across the earliest pendentives on the Ceiling is subject to development and eventual dissolution:[4] starting axially on *Zechariah* the yellow/brown undergarment and apple-green robe exchange location in a canonical way, moving left to the *Delphic Sibyl,* for yellow/red-brown robe and pale-yellow/apple-green undergarment. The sequence may be seen to continue, without change of location, moving across to the *Erythraean Sibyl* (yellow/gray robe) and back to the *Cumaean Sibyl* (yellow/brown robe), and thereafter that trail is lost. And the pale-yellow/apple-green of Delphica's dress is nearly exactly repeated across in Erythraea's, reasserted as a simple green across again in *Cumaea,* and finally across once more as a pure apple-green in the Persian Sibyl's dress. Such analyses, of course, are unreadable, so it may be enough to sketch a complementary sequence that moves across the other diagonals: a red-to-pink series begins axially in the third strong accent of *Zechariah,* moves right to *Joel,* across to *Isaiah,* across again to *Ezechiel,* and across once more to dissolve into violet in *Daniel.* Violet and gray make another thread running through this sequence. It seems, however, that the links articulating these movements, reinforced though they may be by linear and plastic diagonal shifts, weaken progressively, their intention overtaken by a supervening system of color unity. This newer system depends less on contrasts and chromatic separatism that can be structured than upon a structural relation and commonality in the very fabric of each color. But by the same token it may be said that after a certain point my observations become imprecise and my argument does not work. For this reason the idea that Michelangelo began intending to organize by isochromatic structures (as stained-glass windows had for long been organized) had better be expressed unassertively. To the extent that it is convincing it will draw attention to a function of color inherited from a great tradition.

The form-creating function of color is the first of the three I want to describe in more detail. The expressively significant forms of the Ceiling tend to be executed in one of two systems of color modeling, both derived from the mosaic tradition and both exploited to great effect in Florentine Gothic painting. Neither can be construed straightforwardly as an effect of light. One, the simpler, is a saturation system: the change of tone that describes relief (and a direction of light, in this case) is contributed by increasing or decreasing the saturation of a single hue, that is, a single pigment or a consistent mixture of pigments. A tone gradient is coexistent with a saturation gradient. In practice it is much easier to find the uncomplicated, unqualified system of pure color-modeling in earlier artists, for example Ghirlandaio; nevertheless, there are many passages where the system is effectively operative in the Ceiling, especially in the earlier parts, where the technique approximates the dogmatic purity of the *Doni Tondo.* The saturation system is tonally but not coloristically descriptive of effects of light and form.

For the second system of color modeling, often called *cangiante,* I prefer the more descriptive term color change, mainly because the perfectly sufficient Italian word has been invested, evasively, with a mysticism we can do without. A study of its history and incidence will show that color change is almost never a representation of shot silk or indeed of any texture or material. It is simply a substitute, with certain advantages, for saturation change, and it is in the same way constructional. It exists in Late Antique mosaic and has a special flowering in Late Gothic painting. To clarify its working and to separate it from the rare cases of shot-colored fabric imitation, we need to start by considering the intrinsic properties of pigments.

Whether naturally or because we have been taught, we tend to arrange colors in a spectrum, that is, in a gradient of hue, from blue by way of green and yellow to red. But there is another taxonomy. If we fasten on the intrinsic tonal properties of pigments, then we can construct a gradient of

The Libyan Sibyl, *detail.*

tone, which will place the yellows at one end and will descend by way of vermilion (cinnabar), green, and rose-red (madder), to the blues at the other. Significant separation on this gradient may then be exploited by modeling in fully saturated hues, one for highlight and the other for shadow. The resulting change of tone describes relief, as before; but this time it is coexistent with and in fact caused by a change in hue. Some artists will apply only the intrinsic tone-scale. Most, like Michelangelo, will allow themselves occasionally to dilute a tonally stronger pigment, say blue, to make a highlight to an inherently paler shadow-color, say red. But in fact Michelangelo largely respects the intrinsic tonal gradient on the Ceiling, and I think one sees why: it allows a purer value of each color. It is helpful to consider the special case of yellow, which cannot be effectively modeled with yellow itself because the tonal variations between all yellow pigments are insignificant. This color always needs supplementation, either with another color, most often red, red-brown, or green, or (with horrible results) with a monochrome additive. The product of the color-change system is like that of saturation change: a tonal but not a coloristic description of lighting and form, and not a description of texture, substance, or light effect. But of course it also multiplies the colors and may produce clearer values of them.

To define the very limited descriptive intent or value of color change would require a broad historical survey of its incidence in mosaic and in painting. Here it may be enough to select from its copious use in Gothic painting the case of the Salimbeni brothers' frescoes in the Oratorio di San Giovanni in Urbino, where *cangianti* construct not only passages of fabric, but also architecture and rocks.[5] The case is not unusual and it must be taken seriously. There are no shot-silk rocks. By about 1500 color change is generally restricted to fabrics, perhaps because in anything else it is unrealistic in a declamatory way. And it is precisely by examining the convention historically and realistically that we may see it is almost never intended as descriptive of fabric texture.

Are there objective criteria we might apply to the recognition of effects of shot silk and the like, or the still-rarer effect of iridescence, as of fish scales, had the artist intended them? We ought perhaps to focus on the most sensational case on the Ceiling—at least the one most often reproduced—which is in a lunette on the east wall, Eleazar's undeniably exotic hose. The modeling sequence in this passage is white/apple-green/plum; and observing it carefully one sees that the sequence is precisely coincident with light and its privation—that is to say it produces not only form (wrinkles, or the rotundity of the thigh), but also cast shadow (as the shadow cast by the hand on the ankle). That is what would not happen if the hose were made of shot silk or a similar fabric.

To make this distinction clearer it may be helpful to see that there is a well-defined tradition in Renaissance painting (and prints) for the imitation of shot silk; the artists knew what they were doing, and they did it in appropriately restricted descriptive situations. One finds it frequently in a circle around Giovanni Bellini applied with mimetic decorum to the linings of robes; a dazzling Roman paradigm is the lining of the high priest's robe in Barocci's *Presentation of the Virgin* in the Chiesa Nuova. What these artists knew was that the complex optical phenomenon produced by highly particularized surfaces and weaves should be represented by a dissociation of color change from the fall of light, for in these cases the shift in hue is related instead to the shift in inclination of surface or thread. It follows that the shot effect may be securely identified only when the maverick independence of color shift from lighting is localized in a larger context where the tonal laws of light and shade are observed. Confirmation comes from an unexpected quarter. Because there is a tonal component of color change a shot effect may be perceived monochromatically and represented in a monochrome medium. Thus it is a mark of Albrecht Dürer's virtuosity in

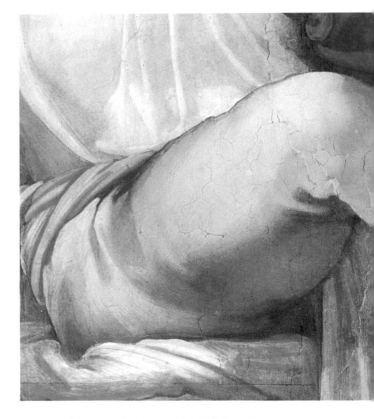

Eleazar-Mathan *lunette, detail of Eleazar's hose.*

his mature woodcuts that in very restricted passages (mimetically decorous) he will switch from a modeling system descriptive of a unified contextual light to a subversion of its laws for localized textural description: there is a beautiful case in the sleeves of the Virgin in the *Marriage of the Virgin* from the Marienleben (B. 82), and another, still more discrete, in the inner sleeve of Salome in the *Beheading of the Baptist* (B. 125).[6] The example testifies not only to the understanding of the optical phenomenon by the artists, but also to their expectation that the painted analogue will be properly interpreted. If, now, we apply this criterion—that a shot effect is identified by dissociation of color shift from lighting—there are almost no passages in the Ceiling, even among the apparently exotic ones like Eleazar's hose, that can be interpreted with such a descriptive intention. Those famous hose are not, it turns out, maverick in the ambient lighting system, but they conform and indeed enhance it; so that if we persist in saying that they are all the same made of shot silk or a similar fabric, we are saying that that is not what Michelangelo has painted, or that he did not know how to paint it, which strikes me as the reductio ad absurdum that closes this interpretative route. Over the whole painted vault there is, in the end, almost no case of the phenomenon to be seen; an exception, mimetically decorous, may be the squamous coils of the serpent in the *Temptation* and the *Expulsion*.[7]

It is agreeable, I think, to be rescued from unreality—to be rescued, for example, from the remarkable conclusion that Michelangelo (of all people) thought of Jonah, survivor of a rough journey by sea that ended in the whale, and of a night in the open under the gourd, wearing expensive silks for these activities. We get a better reading of his intentions, I think, by reattaching him to a vibrant and sophisticated tradition. For the real difference between his *cangianti* and those of his fifteenth-century predecessors lies not so much in the deployment or range of his color as in his fresco technique. Revisiting Pietro Perugino, for example, his *Nativity* fresco of 1503 in San Francesco at Montefalco, one finds passages very like those on the Ceiling: on St. Joseph's yellow/pinkish-violet robe over a pale-blue/red undergarment, and on an angel's yellow/red robe and pinkish-orange/green robe lining. There is also a rich repertory in the work of Ghirlandaio, Melozzo da Forlì, Benozzo Gozzoli, and so on. There are even good precedents in this tradition for the occasional triple-color sequences on the Ceiling, such as the white/dove-gray/green of Judith's robe in the northeast spandrel; they remind me of such subtle sequences as Benozzo's pink/blue-gray/purplish-gray robe in his *Birth of St. Francis*. This eminently imitable tradition is transformed in certain conspicuous cases on the Ceiling by sfumato transitions—Eleazar's hose are again a good example—which create an individualistic effect: it is a sfumato of color gradient polemically responding, once more, to Leonardo's recent achromatic example. In any case, to return to functionality, Michelangelo reasserts a tradition of using pure color for constructional purpose, and there is no fundamental difference between his intentions in a polychrome sequence, such as the white/yellow/green robe of Erythraea, and that of a single-color saturation change, as in the red of her dress. The advantage of color change may be, in his mind, both quantitative and qualitative: it produces a greater variety of hue and yields form with the clarity of purer, less compromised color. The value of pure color-modeling in the clarifying sense is well illustrated by an experiment in the *Azor-Sadoch* lunette, the first on the north side. To the left the yellow-ocher robe is modeled with monochrome reinforcement, yielding the most inarticulate passage in the lunette; it is clearly less effective as form than the same figure's pale-bluish-gray/rose-pink dress or, over on the right, a similar yellow robe modeled with pale-violet. The experiment, never repeated in the Ceiling, yielded a "dead" passage, especially dead when read from the floor.

This argument has already led us from the one function of Michelangelo's color to a second, from construction to clarification. But we might now distinguish between two senses in which his color clarifies. Color in painting—pure color, that is—always has the potential beneficial function of distinguishing form from form, of marking separate identities. Michelangelo particularly exploits this function of polychromy in the Ceiling, and this fact goes a long way to explaining the preferred choice of pure color modeling. Variations, separations, of pure color help enormously to clarify complex structural passages such as the figure of Libica—clarifying, that is to say, the structural action of separate components of her body and costume. This extraordinarily complex figure's legibility, and hence its animation, is far greater in color than in a black-and-white photograph. The same point may be made for much smaller units. Returning to the *Azor-Sadoch* lunette, one sees that the concentration of great formal complexity in the mother's headdress is concomitantly a concentration of much strong and diverse color-modeling, including emphatic color-change. The same may be said of the woman's head in the *Ezechias-Manasses-Amon* lunette, the third on the north side. The proof of functionality is that these details retain a phenomenal legibility and distinction of form from form over the great distance entailed in their reading from the floor. For the same purpose, I think—that is, for clear articulation and emphatically separate identity—one notices collections of strong color and vivid color-change in larger passages of great figural complexity, as in the *Brazen Serpent* spandrel. This scene would otherwise be quite hard to read from the floor.

But there is another aspect of the clarifying function of color and especially of color change: that it enhances legibility not only over distance but also in difficult places, in dark corners or areas of *contre-jour,* around windows. I think it is probable that in his practice Michelangelo drew upon a pragmatic workshop tradition, very reasonably as a pupil of Ghirlandaio. For I have a general impression that in the Tuscan tradition, vaults and *contre-jour* areas tend to be painted with stronger color and more color-change. One thinks back beyond Ghirlandaio and Benozzo Gozzoli to Spinello Aretino, whose Evangelists in the vault of the Sacristy at San Miniato al Monte are distinct in this way from the Stories of St. Benedict on the walls. Such a tradition is very probably exemplified in the Sistine Chapel itself, in a difference between the coloration of the Popes between the windows and that of the narrative cycle below; but this apparent difference may be confused by uneven cleaning. If such a pragmatic approach is real and general, it may be interpreted as a compensatory device, not unlike the sculptural rhetoric (selective emphasis for persuasive effect) of Giovanni Pisano, Donatello, and Michelangelo himself, when their figures were to be read over a great distance.

It would seem in any case that such an approach, traditional or not, was pragmatically followed by Michelangelo. The vivid clarity and sharp contrasts, so striking when the newly cleaned frescoes are studied from the scaffolding, work, when now seen from the floor, as compensation for distance and difficult viewing conditions. From the floor there remains, I find, no effect of sharpness, but rather of really exceptional legibility of plasticity, action, expression, and other detail. And while we avoid fallacies when we recognize them, such as the fallacy that effects are a sure guide to intentions, it seems reasonable to suggest motivation when it appears effective in resolving major problems in a task. There may be, in other words, a better explanation in functionality for the concentration of brilliant color-change in the lunettes closest to the windows and to the Popes, than in chronological sequence (whatever that may be). For it is true, I think, that the cleaning of the Ceiling would have been less surprising at first if it had been begun somewhere else but in the lunettes. And then again there may be another element of proof for this reading of Michelangelo's color in the lesson that Pontormo seems to have learned from it when he went to

Rome in about 1520. Shortly before the Roman journey, he had painted the (coloristically speaking) Leonardesque altarpiece in San Michele Visdomini, and in the event he could hardly have been less disappointed than we are today when we try, in the dark church, to discern what is represented or what is happening. The imitation of the coloration of the Sistine lunettes in Pontormo's Capponi Chapel (begun in 1525) has been very properly noticed. But more specifically there is a difference we can now understand between the *contre-jour* fresco, the *Annunciation,* and the better-lit altarpiece, a difference similar to that between lunettes and pendentives in the Sistina, which suggests the serious purpose underlying the imitation.

It is not customary, and it may not prove to be popular, to talk of a rhetoric of color. But if by such a term we mean a prioritizing manipulation of emphasis, we may pursue this thought somewhat further to clarify a third functional aspect of Michelangelo's color. I will try to describe here an increasingly sophisticated distinction, during the Ceiling's progress, between larger and smaller forms, in effect between mass and surface detail. For convenience rather than elegance I will use the terms macroform and microform.

In the *Doni Tondo* and in *Delphica,* forms of equivalent rotundity are constructed by saturation change or color change over approximately the same segment of the tonal gradient, irrespective of differences in their absolute scale. In the case of *Delphica* the cluster of small folds around her right hand may be compared in terms of modeling intensity with the larger passage constructing the left leg. The result, here and in the *Tondo,* is a quantity of unprioritized detail and a certain confusion of the larger form. The control of plastic detail in favor of the macroform seems thereafter to become a general concern, a general strategy, developed through a reduction of tonal emphasis in the microform. Looking at the pendentives of the north side of the Ceiling there is in this sense a marked difference between *Delphica* at the beginning and *Libica* at the end; for in the later case there is clearly a diminished tonal intensity (this means, always, color intensity) in the small surface-folds over the knee relative to the construction of the larger knee form itself, or in the small folds over the hip relative to the macroform of the torso. The distinction is systematic and operates over widely diverse colors. The same systematic discrimination is wonderfully consistent in the latest Sibyl on the south side, *Persica.* But this sophisticated control of color modeling clearly begins within the first half of the Ceiling, unequivocally in *Isaiah* already. It is analogous in effects of mass, prioritizing the larger form, to the growing unity in effects of color as color.

I think that anyone who looks closely at the Ceiling's color will be forced in the end to abandon the schematic simplification that is necessary as a first heuristic step. Michelangelo's restless experimentation produces much inconsistency. The last observation I want to make concerns one such experiment, or inconsistency, which appears to arise from the search for a coloristic resolution of the macroform/microform distinction. The extraordinary robe of Josaphat in the fourth lunette on the north side in fact pulls into focus most of what I have tried to say. On this single form or object, the robe, Michelangelo gives different responsibilities to different modes of color modeling: the construction of the microform is entrusted to saturation change (greenish ocher lightening toward white), and superimposed on this is a larger system enacted in color change (greenish-ocher/orange), which constructs the macroform, the envelope of the whole figure. The contingent nature of the experimental innovation is underlined by its repetition in *Daniel,* just to the left and above (we are here in the second half of the Ceiling, where I think the lunettes were painted pari passu with the vault proper). The eccentricity in this case lies in the passage over Daniel's right knee, where again saturation change (white/yellow-ocher) constructs the microform and color change (white/yellow-ocher/green) constructs the macroform. The independent

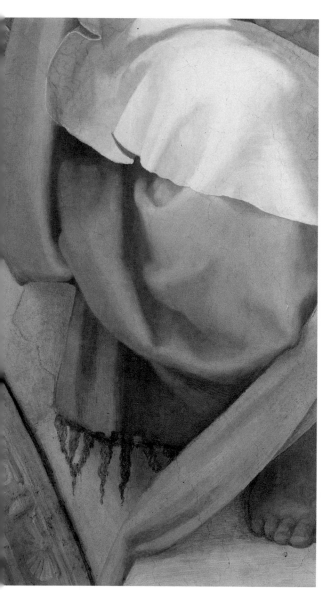

The Prophet Daniel, *detail of his right leg and knee.*

functions assigned to the two systems here superimposed, normally employed as alternatives, seem to show very clearly the pursuit of a prioritized larger form, perhaps one might say a rhetoric of color. They show also a mind at work on fundamental problems of color, and Michelangelo absolutely a painter. But I am not convinced that the experiment works. It was a passing moment, and he reverts to a more normative realization, in the last phase, of what was to be an extraordinarily creative discrimination—a discrimination in favor of the larger form, which is once more a clarifying response to the viewer's difficulties in the Chapel. To be read is understandably his first priority, and color is his instrument. When we needed strong artificial light to see anything at all from the floor, his very nature as an artist was traduced.

Asa-Josaphat-Joram *lunette, detail of the figure on the left.*

GENESIS 3.2–3

And the woman said unto the serpent,
We may eat of the fruit of the trees of the garden:
But of the fruit of the tree which is in the midst of the garden, God hath said,
Ye shall not eat of it, neither shall ye touch it, lest ye die.

This large panel is divided in two by the Tree of Life, which is a symbol of the cross. On the left is the Temptation, *showing Adam touching the forbidden tree and Eve, one of the most beautiful female figures Michelangelo ever painted, accepting the fruit from the serpent.*

Paradise is characterized by luxuriant foliage and a rocky landscape. On the right, in the Expulsion, *Adam and Eve have been banished by the angel and find themselves in an arid and desolate place, without the grace of the Lord.*

Overleaf: In the first scene, Michelangelo emphasized Eve's physical perfection before her knowledge of sin; in the second, in striking contrast, he portrayed an older woman who has succumbed to temptation. For Michelangelo, physical beauty was an external sign of spiritual perfection.

THE BRONZE MEDALLIONS

On the Ceiling there are ten bronze medallions, each held up by a pair of ignudi. *They differ slightly in diameter, which varies between 51 and 55 in. (130 and 140 cm). They represent scenes from the Old Testament, taken from the Books of Genesis, Samuel, Kings, and the Machabees. On the basis of their number and*

Thou hast killed Uriah the Hittite with the sword, and hast taken his wife to be thy wife, and hast slain him with the sword of the children of Ammon. Now therefore the sword shall never depart from thine house.

their shape, the medallions have been interpreted as allusions to the Ten Commandments or as eucharistic symbols. Painted partly in true fresco and partly in secco, they have been restored several times over the centuries and in some cases even repainted. There have been doubts about the authenticity of the medallions; for some of them at least the design has been attributed to Michelangelo, and many are thought to be the work of his assistants.

2 KINGS 10.16–17

And he said, Come with me, and see my zeal for the Lord.
So they made him ride in his chariot.
And when he came to Samaria, he slew all that remained unto Ahab in
Samaria, till he had destroyed him.

Opposite: Medallion held up by the nudes above
the Cumaean Sibyl. *Represented is David as he*
kneels before the prophet Nathan and asks
forgiveness for his sin.
Below: Medallion supported by the nudes above
the Prophet Ezechiel. *The composition, with*
its circular movements, is appropriate to the
shape of the medallion. The scene depicted is the
destruction of the tribe of Achab.

Overleaf: The two ignudi *above the* Prophet
Ezechiel.

But for Adam there was not found an help meet for him.
And the Lord God caused a deep sleep to fall upon Adam, and he slept:

*The Creation of Eve is generally considered
the first scene Michelangelo painted when he
resumed work on the Ceiling in 1511.
Progress on the frescoes had been interrupted
due to the pope's absence from Rome when he
became involved in the struggle against the
French.*

*"The brush of this wonderfully ingenious
craftsman arrestingly reveals the difference that
there is between sleep and wakefulness and how
the divine majesty can be portrayed in the firm
and tangible terms that humans understand."
(Vasari, "Life of Michelangelo Buonarroti")*

*The typological interpretation of this biblical
event must have been known to educated
people who came to the Sistine Chapel on a
regular basis during the time of Julius II. The
creation of Eve from Adam's rib probably
alluded to the birth of the Church from the
blood that had flowed out the side of the
crucified Christ.*

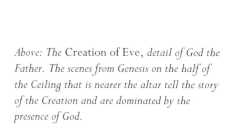

*Above: The Creation of Eve, detail of God the
Father. The scenes from Genesis on the half of
the Ceiling that is nearer the altar tell the story
of the Creation and are dominated by the
presence of God.*

and he took one of his ribs, and closed up the flesh instead thereof;
And the rib, which the Lord God had taken from man, made he a woman,
and brought her unto the man.

The Creation of Eve, *detail with the sleeping*
Adam.

The Creation of Eve, *detail with Eve.*
"...and as she comes forth bowed with a sweet
movement, with her hands joined and raised
towards God, it seems that she offers him
thanks, and that he blesses her." (Condivi)

Above and right: Nudes above the Cumaean Sibyl.

Let us make man in our image, after our likeness:
and let them have dominion over the fish of the sea, and over the fowl of the air,
and over the cattle, and over all the earth,
and over every creeping thing that creepeth upon the earth.
So God created man in his own image, in the image of God created he him.

...a figure whose beauty, pose, and contours are such that it seems to have been fashioned that very moment by the first and supreme creator rather than by the drawing and brush of a mortal man.

VASARI, "Life of Michelangelo Buonarroti"

Michelangelo's great compositional skill is exemplified in this painting. The focal point of the action, consisting of the two hands that are about to touch, has been moved slightly to the left of the center of the painting. In addition, the dynamic line forming the lower edge of the figure of God parallels the diagonal of the landscape behind Adam. Together, these elements create a convincing expression of movement, and the moment is charged with tension and expectation.

This page: The Creation of Adam, *detail. According to some, this beautiful female face represents Eve before she was created but as she already existed in the mind of God. With one hand she holds onto the arm of God that is placed around her shoulders, while from beneath the pink mantle that protects her and the angels she observes the birth of man.*

In the fourth [panel] is the creation of Man,
wherein God is seen with his arm and hand outstretched,
as if giving precepts to Adam, concerning what he needs must do,
and what not do;...

CONDIVI, *The Life of Michelangelo*

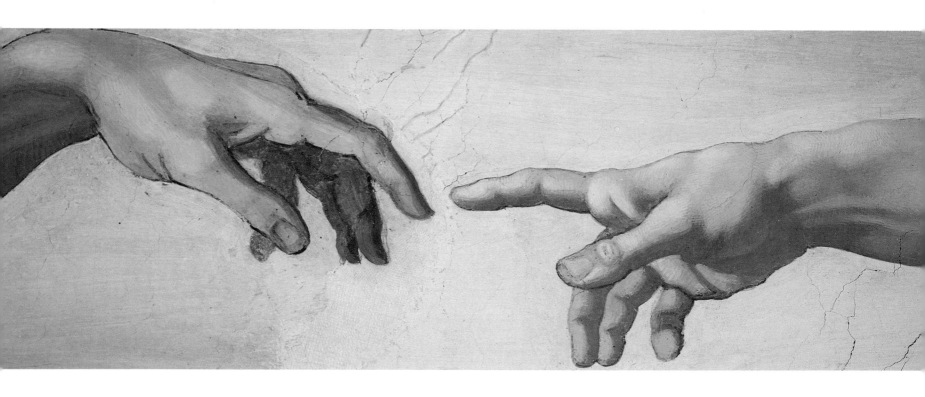

Opposite: The Creation of Adam, *detail of the* *face of God.*

Jonah's Body Language

Matthias Winner

As early as 1550 Giorgio Vasari, in his oft-cited praise of Michelangelo's *Jonah*, noted the fact that the figure leaning backward cancels the effect of the vault's curvature.[1] Thanks to the opposing movements, the Ceiling appears to be flat. Vasari does not, however, mention the trompe l'œil of the painted architecture, which has such a remarkable influence on the viewer's perception. Michelangelo originally intended to fill the natural convexity of the vault between the severies and over each of the windows with painted niches.[2] The effect of the niches, projected on corbels and situated between two severies and the intervening lunette, would have created the illusion that the wall around them receded. The trompe-l'œil would thus have been more effective than the final architectonic system we see today. This solution would also have taken into account the spectator's vantage point from the floor below. Another project, in which medallions were to be framed by oculi flanked by small, winged genii, would also have hinted illusionistically at the thickness of the wall.[3] Each niche, filled by a Prophet or a Sibyl, would have underscored the connection between those Michelangelo painted and the ones below, containing figures of the Popes, that were part of Sixtus IV's campaign to decorate the Chapel.

At this level of the painted Ceiling, however, Michelangelo seems to have been more interested in the wall as surface or background rather than for its perceived volume. Jonah and the other Prophets and Sibyls are all represented seated on stone thrones, each defined by two corner-pilasters. The volume of the rear walls of the thrones, like that of the fictive walls connecting them, cannot be precisely measured. The suggestion of spatial depth over the thrones is limited to the cornice, which breaks backward above the heads of the Prophets and Sibyls. The cornice runs uninterrupted around all four sides of the vaulted Ceiling, implying an attic story above the four walls of the Chapel. In terms of perspective, each throne is constructed independently and has a single vanishing point, located just above the knees of the seated figure. Thus the viewer sees the footrests of the thrones from above, while the *ignudi,* or nude youths, and their pedestals are seen slightly foreshortened from below. The human figures, then, are the principal tool used to suggest volume and relief. Their placement—in the lunettes, on the corbels, and at the center of the vault—determines their varying degrees of optical reality. The viewer who enters the Chapel from the Sala Regia perceives the figures of the Prophets and Sibyls as more real than those of the Genesis scenes, which appear as pictures within pictures. Anyone wishing to orient himself or herself will surely see Jonah, on

Opposite: Copy of the Prophet Jonah, *attributed to Giulio Clovio. Rugby School of Art, England.*

110

IONAS

the altar wall, as the most important mediating figure. He leans back on the throne; the corbel on which it sits was once located atop a pilaster that was part of the architecture of the Chapel but is now covered by the *Last Judgment*. His body reclines on a diagonal axis, in front of the fictive pilaster on the left side of the throne; it is almost as if Jonah is trying to take in the

Michelangelo, pen and wash sketches, 5⁷⁄₁₆ x 5⅝ in. (138 x 143 mm). Corpus 170 recto; Ashmolean Museum, Oxford. In the top left is a quick sketch of a seated nude whose position suggests it is a sketch for the Prophet Jonah.

entire central section of the Ceiling in a single glance. The pilasters of the throne do not support pedestals which could serve as bases for *ignudi*. In the foreshortening of his body, which emphasizes the irritated, hornlike gesture of his crossed hands rather than disguising it, one perceives the full extension into depth of the volume of this figure. The relatively smaller size of the whale and the two putti heads beside the Prophet only underline the effect of the gestural language toward the left. Jonah's naked legs seem to project from the wall, and his left arm crosses over his reclining torso, pointing behind him toward the dark background of the fictive wall next to his throne. Jonah's movement transforms the vertical axis of the seated figure into the horizontal, or at least diagonal, axis of a lying figure. The horizontality of the frescoed corbel above the short wall of the Chapel connects with the parallel axis of the Genesis scenes.

There are many *pentimenti,* or corrections, in the *Jonah,* although no more than we find in other figures on the Ceiling. Michelangelo used a car toon for this figure, and the traces of *spolvero,* or pouncing, are visible even to the naked eye, especially around the Prophet's head and torso. Jonah's relative nudity ties him thematically to the other *ignudi* on the Ceiling, although he was depicted in colossal dimensions. It seems possible that Michelangelo may originally have wanted to leave the right part of Jonah's

shoulder and his collarbone uncovered. The green drapery adheres so tightly to his body that his muscles and navel can be seen through the transparent material. *Pentimenti* are also found on Jonah's calves and feet; Michelangelo increased the size of the Prophet's legs with respect to the incisions lines and *spolvero* that mark the original outline of the figure as it was transferred to the Ceiling from the cartoon.

In the so-called Oxford sketchbook we find three poses for the figure of Jonah.[4] The standing figure on the right side of f.168 verso in Charles de Tolnay's Corpus, leaning to the left and pulling his left leg up to rest it on the seat of the throne, offers one alternative design. The seated figure to the left of this figure introduces the idea of movement into Jonah's torso, which here is drawn leaning too far back. As in the preceding sketch, however, the figure's left leg is still placed above his right. In any case this figure shown in *contrapposto* is sketched between the two pilasters of a throne and cannot, therefore, be associated with any of the *ignudi.*

Michelangelo, pen and wash sketches, 5 7/16 x 5 5/8 in. (138 x 143 mm). Corpus 170 verso; Ashmolean Museum, Oxford. In the bottom center is a sketch for the sleeping figure of the lost Phares-Esrom-Aram lunette, but in reversed position.

113

At the same time Michelangelo formulated poses for the various figures who were to be located relatively close to the *Jonah* but in distinct pictorial fields; an example is the red chalk sketch of the sleeping figure of Hezron (an Ancestor of Christ, he was painted in the lunette, later destroyed, below and to the right of Jonah). A sort of convex corbel must have acted

Michelangelo, one large charcoal sketch and eight pen and wash sketches, 5½ x 5⅝ in. (140 x 142 mm). Corpus 168 verso; Ashmolean Museum, Oxford. At top right are two sketches for the figure of Jonah; in the center, a study for the sleeping figure of the Phares-Esrom-Aram *lunette, which was subsequently destroyed.*

as the pictorial model for the sketches of Jonah; the sleeping ancestor was intended, instead, for the vertical wall of the lunette, pierced in the middle by a two-light window. The figure's pose, leaning to the right, was suited to the arch of the window. We find the same sleeping figure again on another sheet in the sketchbook, but here turned around and resting on his left side.[5] This figure belongs to an earlier stage in the planning of the painting, given that the executed fresco follows exactly the pose of the figure leaning to the right as he sleeps. On the recto of the same sheet we find another idea for Jonah, or perhaps for an Ancestor of Christ, with the head represented in three different positions.[6]

In his analysis of the Oxford sketchbook, Michael Hirst suggests that all these drawings were executed after the interruption in the work on the first part of the Ceiling in September 1510, or even after September 1511, when Michelangelo unveiled the first part of his fresco.[7] It has often been observed that each figure on the vault was conceived in relation to the others. The artist had planned this connection between the body language of individual figures of different proportions and belonging to different realities in the overall image from the very beginning of his work on the Ceiling. The poses of the *ignudi* over the thrones of the Prophets and Sibyls demonstrate this point; each nude has to be seen in relation to the youth

Nude to the right above the Prophet Jeremiah.

with whom he is paired, in relation to the larger, seated figure beneath him, and to the second pair of *ignudi* on the other side of the same bay. Yet the Genesis scenes on the first half of the vault constitute a unity of action in themselves. The *Deluge,* with its numerous nude bodies, can be read as a finished whole. The four *ignudi* on the illusionistic arches of the Ceiling turn their backs to the narrative scene and do not interfere with it. The next bay, with the smaller panel representing the *Drunkenness of Noah,* emphasizes the unity of action of the two pairs of nudes. All four hold the medallion ribbons carefully and gently touch the garlands of oak leaves. None of them extends beyond the painted bands of the illusionistic architecture, nor do they interrupt the pictorial field where Noah's drunkenness is depicted.

It seems significant that Vasari tells us there was a cartoon for the *Drunkenness of Noah,* which Michelangelo gave to the young Bindo Altoviti.[8] All the other cartoons for the Ceiling have either been lost or were intention ally destroyed by the artist himself, evidently because they did not contain single, complete scenes. The marked shadows the heads of the *ignudi* cast on the light bands behind them create, in this first phase of work, a second pictorial reality containing the nude youths and the stone framework. Yet in the following bay Michelangelo lightens the shadows behind the nudes, and he gradually eliminates them altogether as he works toward the altar wall. The artist wanted body language to speak alone, independently of the fictive architecture around his figures. It has been noted that the movements of the *ignudi,* constructed in a tightly woven sequence, become more agitated with each bay until the figures actually penetrate the Genesis scenes themselves. Their body language serves to increase the expressiveness of the scenes of the days of Creation. It almost seems as if there is a psychic connection between God's creative acts and the four living beings seated at the corners of the frames. The *ignudi* always turn their backs to the larger bays, and the dialogue is always between the two figures seated above the throne of one of the Prophets or Sibyls.

The bays painted after the break in 1510–11, beginning with the *Creation of Eve,* demonstrate just how much Michelangelo intensified the movement of the *ignudi.* Starting with *God Separating the Earth from the Waters,* the gestures of the *ignudi* invade the adjacent scenes. The nude next to Adam, being touched by the finger of God, has his hand so close to that of the Progenitor that we can imagine both bodies as belonging to the same pictorial reality. They are, furthermore, of similar size, although their bodies correspond to two different levels of representational reality. The movement of the *ignudo*'s extended legs is similar to that of the supine figure of Adam. The nude on the right, above the Persian Sibyl's throne, is represented from behind, both because of the formal dialogue with the corresponding *ignudo* on the left and because he responds to the agitated figure of God in the Genesis scene above him. In the last bay of the Ceiling, *God Separating Light from Darkness,* Michelangelo represented Him from below and with His arms extended upward in an oblique position with respect to Jonah's. The floating body of the Divinity relates to Jonah's body language, and the Prophet's ecstatic gaze seems to search for the elusive figure of God the Father, located in a different pictorial unit and pictorial reality. The nude who looks down at Jonah in a helical *contrapposto* mediates between the two figures. A vertical axis connects Jeremiah, on the throne below, to the two *ignudi* above him and to the figure of God, who stretches across the whole pictorial field at the center of the bay. The Libyan Sibyl on the opposite wall corresponds to this axis. The movement with which she turns to place her book on the upper part of the throne above and behind her is clearly related to God the Father's extended arms in the scene above, on the same vertical axis. In the representation of the first act of creation we see the Divinity in action along the horizontal axis of the scene. The vertical axis of the last bay of Prophets and Sibyls and the horizontal axis of the first Genesis scene coincide.

Michelangelo did not resolve the conflict inherent in the position of Zechariah's throne, located over the short entrance wall of the Chapel and at right angles to the thrones of the Prophets and Sibyls on the long walls. Above the pilasters flanking his seat, where on the long walls one finds the pedestals of the *ignudi,* the artist painted a strip of sky. We find the same strip of sky above Jonah; here, however, the nude youths intrude upon it. The *ignudo* near Jonah's head, for example, kneels on his plinth in such a way that his foot protrudes into this area of sky. The lower part of his leg repeats, on a lesser scale, the motif and direction of Jonah's gigantic, dangling leg, and his foot seems to want to rest on the broken cornice above the Prophet's head. In this way the axes created by the placement of the thrones at right angles are connected by the *contrapposto* movement of the figures.

In the last bay, nearest the altar wall, the contrast between the single

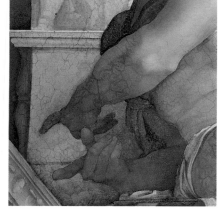

Detail of the expressive gesture of the Prophet Jonah's hands.

scenes framed by the fictive architecture and the voluminous figures seated in front of the architectonic trompe l'œil disappears. The three-dimensional reality of the entire Ceiling is more evident in Jonah's body language than it is in the trompe l'œil architecture around it. Beginning with Jonah's body it is necessary to find a logical, figurative connection between the fig-

ures on this part of the vault, thus reducing the architectural system of the Ceiling to a rhythmic, ornamental frame for the active figures. Michelangelo did not alter his system of pictorial frames from one half of the Ceiling to the other, although he made small changes in the proportions of the frescoes. The rhythmic alignment of individual scenes and their architectural frames evolved until a dramatic unity of the entire Ceiling was achieved. Jonah's backward movement seems not only to cancel the natural convexity of the vault, as Vasari observed, but the figure, by way of its movement, also dominates all the pictorial units seen from the entrance of the Chapel.

View of the last three bays near the altar wall.   *117*

Ascanio Condivi repeated Vasari's praise, stating that Michelangelo's ability "in his handling of lines in foreshortenings and in perspectives," created this effect.[9] Michelangelo accentuated the *contrapposto* of the figures in the corner scenes that flank the *Jonah.* Haman crucified, on the left, seems to grasp at something outside of the picture; the effect is emphasized by the figure in front of him, represented from behind. The tangle of people being bitten by snakes in the *Brazen Serpent* spandrel, to the right of *Jonah,* can be separated into pairs acting in two different pictorial spaces. In this image one figure seen from the back is joined to the legs of another figure

Copy of the lost Abraham-Isaac-Jacob-Judah *lunette, among the Ottley engravings, nineteenth century.*

stretched out beneath it in extreme foreshortening, almost creating a monster consisting of a back with legs turned forward. With just the *contrapposto* torsion of torso and limbs, Michelangelo suggests the possibility of moving around the figure, even though the viewer is constrained to a single point of view.

Michelangelo willfully contrasted Jonah's extreme frontality with a variety of other representations of bodies in the picture fields around him. It is possible, however, that a similar, artificial contrast between a variety of figures was also originally found in the pendentive where the Prophet is painted. One generally assumes that there was once a Della Rovere coat of arms fixed to the wall beneath the figure of Jonah, similar to the one below Zechariah on the entrance wall of the Chapel. Pier Matteo d'Amelia, in his project to decorate the vault with a field of stars, had already planned to put the coat of arms of Sixtus IV in the pendentives above both short walls of the Chapel.[10] If indeed the Della Rovere arms were placed on the altar wall, as they were at the other end of the Chapel, toward the Sala Regia, Michelangelo would have removed them, at the latest when he was preparing the wall for the *Last Judgment.* The bracket at the feet of Jonah must postdate 1534. In 1550 Vasari did not mention the coat of arms, which must have been there. In 1568, however, he recounts that "Pope Paul [III] desired to have his own Arms [of the Farnese] placed beneath the statue of the Prophet [Jonah], where those of Julius II had previously been. But when the master, not wishing to do wrong to Julius or Clement, declined to execute them there, saying that it would not be well to do so, His Holiness yielded at once...."[11] Vasari obtained his information from Condivi, who had written his biography of Michelangelo after interviewing the artist himself. There, on the contrary, we read that Paul III wanted him "to carry out what he had already begun in Clement's time; and he had him paint the altar wall of the Sistine Chapel, which he had already prepared with rough plaster and closed off with boards from the floor to the vault. Because it had been Pope Clement's idea and begun in his time, Michelangelo did not put Paul's coat of arms in this work, although the pope had besought him to."[12] Condivi affirms, therefore, only that Michelangelo did not want to affix the Farnese arms to the *Last Judgment*. Vasari alone and at a later date claims that Julius's arms were found there first, but it is impossible to prove this.

The only graphic evidence we have concerning the two lunettes that flanked the *Jonah* are the so-called Ottley engravings of the nineteenth cen-

Copy of the lost Phares-Esrom-Aram *lunette, located to the right on the altar wall.*

tury.[13] We do not know what sixteenth-century model was used for these prints, but they show the Della Rovere arms under the Jonah, as they are on the entrance wall under the *Zechariah*. Arnold Nesselrath has recently discovered a sixteenth-century copy of the entire *Jonah* bay in England, in which a putto is shown holding up a tablet inscribed with the name of the Prophet in place of the coat of arms.[14] The connection with the male and female putti under the other Prophets and Sibyls is obvious. Yet the putto under Jonah in the copy is different in that he is represented from behind. He crosses his legs and holds up the inscribed tablet with both hands. That he is represented standing and from behind acts as a foil to the seated figure of Jonah with his huge legs, shown frontally and in extreme foreshortening. The putto then might be understood as a pictorial joke. Yet if one understood it as such, it would be difficult to attribute its invention to a copyist. This version of the whole pendentive might, therefore, be either a lost original idea of Michelangelo's or evidence about the very last part of the Ceiling to be painted. Such an optical joke gave way to the seriousness of the *Last Judgment*, planned under Clement VII and executed under Paul III. The preparations to paint the altar wall had already erased both the putto and the Ancestors in the surrounding lunettes. Condivi tells us that in the Last Judgment Michelangelo expressed, "all that the art of painting can do with the human figure, leaving out no attitude or gesture whatever."[15] Michelangelo's artistic purpose in his representation of the human body on the Sistine Ceiling, painted some twenty years earlier, could not be better expressed.

Rejoice greatly, O daughter of Zion; shout, O daughter of Jerusalem:
behold, thy King cometh unto thee: he is just, and having salvation;
lowly, and riding upon an ass,
and upon a colt the foal of an ass.

*The figures that have the largest dimensions
of all those on the Ceiling have been placed in
the band that surrounds the narrative panels.
They are the Sibyls, who were pagan diviners, and
the Prophets, the seers of the Old Testament,
who concurred in prophesying the advent and
the message of the Savior. As a group
they demonstrate the universality of the
Redemption—the belief that there is one God
for all, whether Gentiles or Hebrews. They are
shown with their writings, holding their own
book or reading on a scroll the divine message
each brought. With them are small figures,
perhaps the angels or spirits that, in many of
these Prophets' books, act as intermediaries
between God and man. Their presence confirms
that the Genesis scenes painted on the Ceiling
must be viewed as symbols and prefigurations of
Christ's work, from the Incarnation until the
end of time.
As in the other panels, the figures became
gradually bigger as the work progressed. Their
movements became more fluid but also more
complex, and the execution of the figures
attained a supreme ease and sureness.*

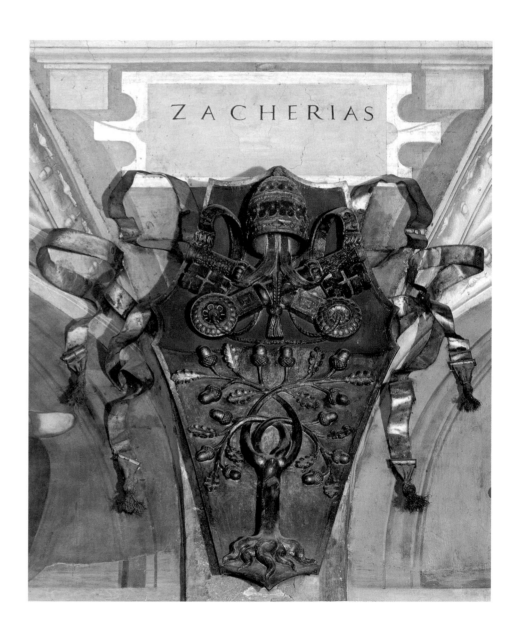

ZECHARIAH

*He prophesied Christ's entrance into Jerusalem
and this may be the reason his image was placed
above the entrance to the Chapel.*

*Above: The plaque bearing the name of the
Prophet, located above the coat of arms of Julius
II della Rovere, the pope who commissioned the
work on the Ceiling.
Right and overleaf:* Zechariah, *full view and
detail.
Vasari described Zechariah, "who holds a book
in which he is seeking something that he cannot
find."*

THE DELPHIC SIBYL

First she encircles the hair covering her forehead with a band,
then, on the hair that hangs loose around her shoulders,
she places a shiny white mitre,
around which she has wound Delphic laurel.

She still shifts
her fierce eyes all around, and her pupils that roam
every which way; at times she looks frightened,
then grim and threatening, and the look on her face
changes all the time.

MARCUS ANNAEUS LUCANUS, *The Civil War, or Pharsalia*

The tunic, belted under her breasts and fastened on the side with a round brooch, reminds us of her Greek origins. In the Oracula Sybyllina, she was attributed with prophesying the coming of a savior, "who shall be betrayed into the hands of the infidels and crowned with a crown of thorns." Hence it does not seem a coincidence that her image was placed high on the wall to the right of the entrance, below the Drunkenness of Noah. *In fact, the episode of Noah ridiculed by his son is a prefiguration of Christ's mocking by the soldiers, about which the Delphic Sibyl also spoke in her oracle.*

Right: The putto who supports the plaque below the Delphica.
Opposite: The Delphic Sibyl.
Overleaf: Details of the putti behind the Delphic Sibyl and of her face, which is that of a very young girl. The style is still very close to that of Michelangelo's early paintings.

Behold, I will send you corn, and wine, and oil,
and ye shall be satisfied therewith: and I will no more make you
a reproach among the heathen.

The Prophet Joel *is located to the left of the* Drunkenness of Noah *and opposite the* Delphic Sibyl. *It seems that his link to the Drunkenness scene can be ascertained by the presence of the symbolic grapevine. In his book, Joel proclaims to Israel the destruction of their vineyards and grape harvests. It will be a divine punishment followed, however, by a promise of abundance, which is a sign of God's mercy.*

Right and opposite: The putto who supports the plaque with the prophet's name, and Joel. *Overleaf: Detail of the Prophet reading and his "assistants" discussing.*

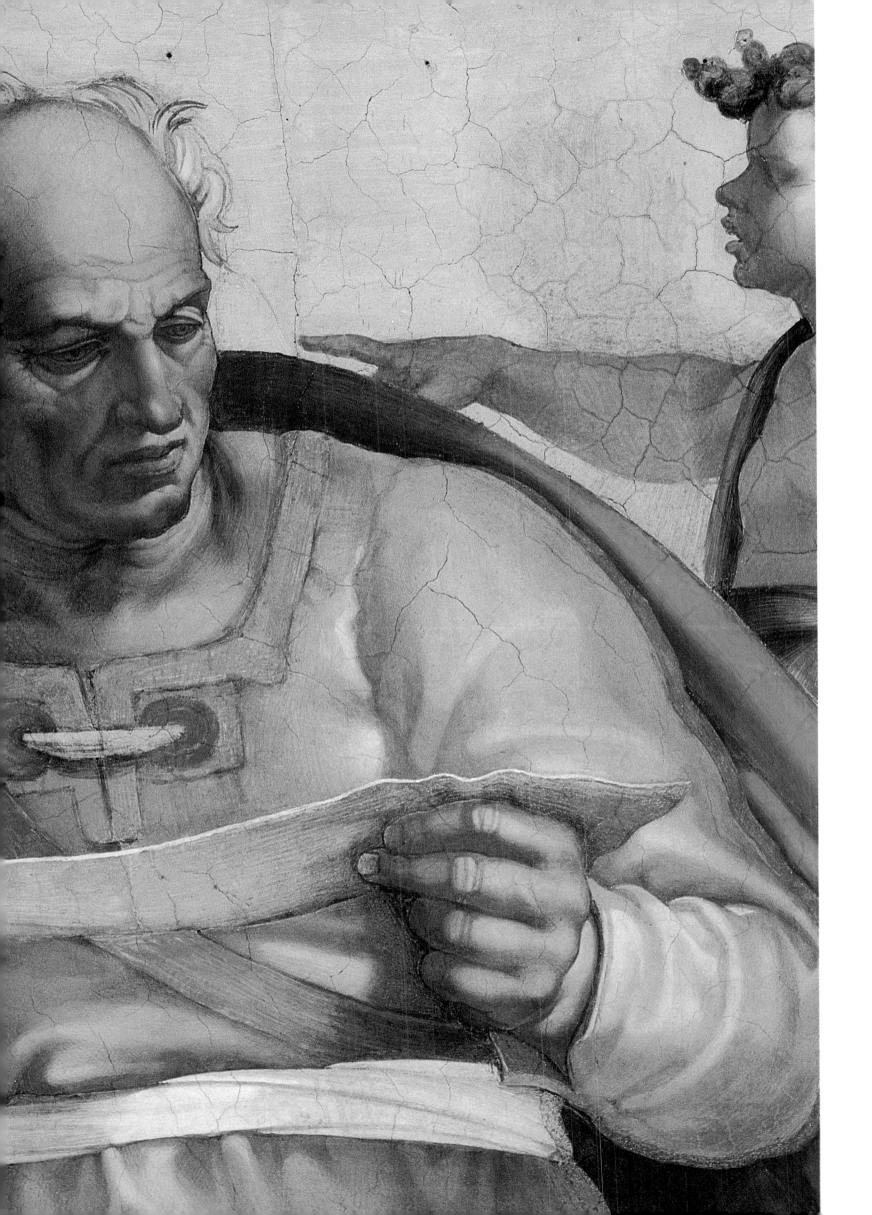

But he was wounded for our transgressions,
he was bruised for our iniquities:
the chastisement of our peace was upon him;
and with his stripes we are healed.

*The fundamental message of the Prophet Isaiah
is contained in the Songs of the Servant, lyrical
passages that introduce a servant of Yahweh
who preaches the true faith, expiates the sins of
the people with his death, and is glorified by
God. For Christians this is clearly a
prefiguration of Christ's mission. There is an
obvious relationship between the words of Isaiah
and the nearby scene of the Sacrifice of Noah,
which symbolizes the sacrifice of the Word.*

*Right: Putto with the plaque, standing at
Isaiah's feet.*
Opposite: The Prophet Isaiah.

He is lost in thought,
and with his legs crossed
he keeps one hand inside
the pages of his book,
to mark his place,
while he rests the other elbow
by the book and presses
that hand to his cheek;
he is called by one
of the putti behind him,
but stays motionless,
turning only his head.

VASARI, "Life of
Michelangelo Buonarroti"

The Prophet Isaiah and one of his "assistants"
in discussion. The putti that appear with the
seers are divine messengers. Michelangelo
conceived them as integral parts of his
portrayals of the Prophets. They accentuate the
movement, tension, or equilibrium by which he
intended to convey to each image its own
character.

…holding a book at some distance and about to turn one of the pages,
sitting deep in contemplation, with one leg over the other,
while she ponders what she must write;
and then a little boy behind her blows on a burning brand to light her lamp.

VASARI, "Life of Michelangelo Buonarroti"

Although all the figures of the Prophets and Sibyls are placed very high and on a curved surface, Michelangelo painted them as if the viewer stood before them. We even see the footrests of their thrones from above.

Right: Putto serving as plaque-bearer.
Opposite: The Erythraean Sibyl.

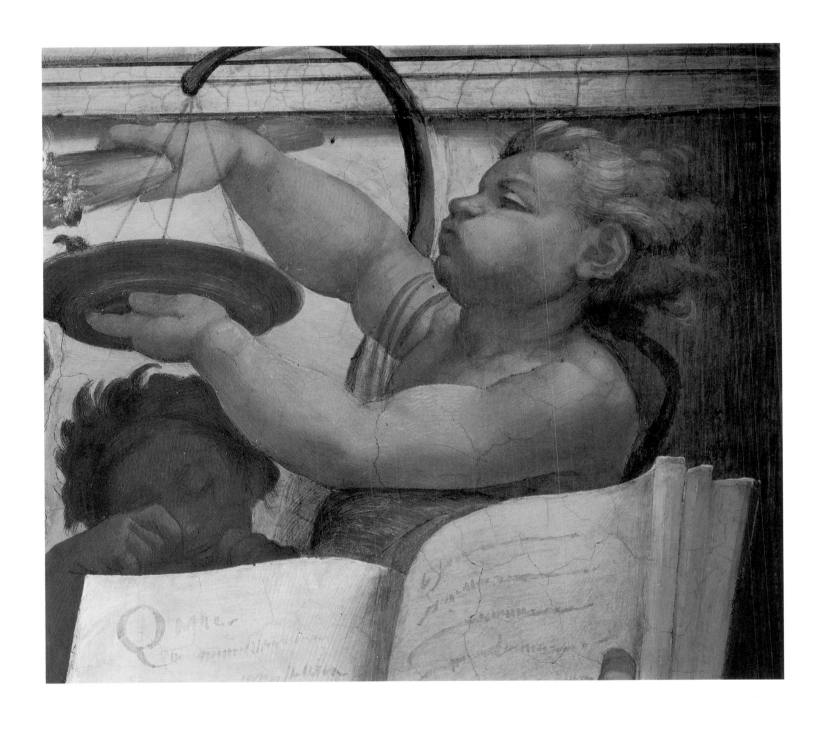

Opposite and above: The Erythraean Sibyl, *details of her and two attending spirits. Next to the putto who "lights her lamp," a metaphor of divine illumination, hides another who seems to be half asleep. This is probably an allusion to the trance that overcomes seers at the moment of inspiration.*

139

THE CUMAEAN SIBYL

In truth, Alcina was, without a quibble,
Wrinkled and frail; her hair was sparse and white,
And from her toothless mouth there ran a dribble....
Older than Hecuba or Cumae's Sibyl,
She had outlived all other women quite.

LUDOVICO ARIOSTO, *Orlando Furioso,* Part 1, Canto 7, Stanza 93

*In the fourth of his Eclogues, Vergil prophesied
the advent of a new age of gold, and his verses
were interpreted by the Christians as a
prediction of the coming of Christ.
The imposing figure holds a book open with her
large, sturdy hands. Her wrinkled face, a
convincing portrait of an old woman, contrasts
with her powerful shoulders. The simplicity of
her garment and the added detail of her bag,
which hangs from the marble throne, bespeak a
wise but frugal personality.*

*Right: Putto with plaque in the corbel below the
Sybil's throne.
Opposite: The Cumaean Sibyl.
Overleaf: Detail of the two "assisting genii" and
the face of the old Sibyl.*

EZECHIEL

Ezechiel was a priest and his prophecy concerned the temple of the Lord. A guiding spirit showed him, first, the temple contaminated by sin and abandoned by God, and then, the construction of the new temple to which the Lord would return and from which a fruitful and miraculous river would flow.

The symbolic connection with the scene of the Creation of Eve, painted above Ezechiel, *is clear. Mary is the new Eve, the image of the Church founded by the blood that had flowed from the Redeemer's side and, as such, the new temple from which sin had been erased.*

Right: Putto in the corbel below Ezechiel. The figures of the putti who stand in the corbels below each facing pair of Prophet and Sibyl are sometimes taken from the same cartoon, but reversed. This is the case with the putto of Ezechiel, who is the mirror image of that of the Cumaean Sibyl.

Opposite: The Prophet Ezechiel.

Detail of the Prophet Ezechiel as he converses with the genius standing behind him. The latter is perhaps a personification of the spirit who, in the Holy Scriptures, acts as guide for the Prophet when he visits the new temple and says to him: "Son of man, behold with thine eyes, and hear with thine ears, and set thine heart upon all that I shall shew thee; for to the intent that I might shew them unto thee art thou brought hither: declare all that thou seest to the house of Israel" (Ezechiel 40.4).

DANIEL

Then comes the figure of a young man, representing Daniel,
who is shown writing in a great book,
copying things from certain other writings with eager intensity.
As a support for the weight Michelangelo painted between Daniel's legs
a putto who is supporting the book while he writes.

VASARI, "Life of Michelangelo Buonarroti"

*The painting seems to capture Daniel at the
moment when he receives the prophecy
announcing the final judgment. At that time,
the Lord said to him, "But I will shew thee that
which is noted in the scripture of truth..."
(Daniel 10.21) and, at the end of the telling of
the Apocalypse, he concluded by saying,
"But thou, O Daniel, shut up the words, and
seal the book, even to the time of the end"
(Daniel 12.4).*
*The use of color to create and model the figures
achieved exceptionally successful results in
Daniel, who is more striking and beautiful than
the first seers Michelangelo frescoed.*

*Right: Putto as plaque-bearer at the feet of the
Prophet.*
Opposite: The Prophet Daniel.
*Overleaf: The Prophet Daniel, details of the
angel that holds the Prophet's book and of
Daniel's face.*

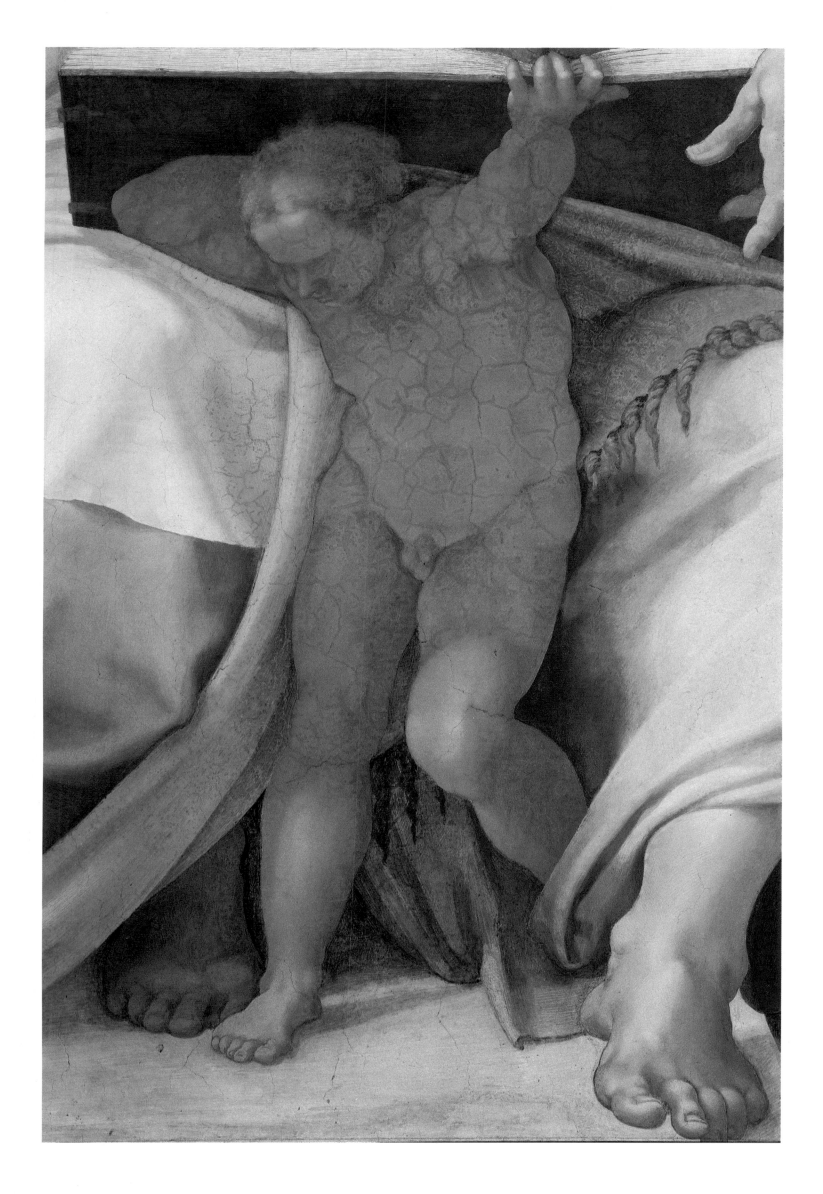

THE PERSIAN SIBYL

She is enveloped in draperies, to suggest that her blood had frozen
with the passing of time.
And since her sight has failed, Michelangelo has depicted her
holding the book she reads very close to her eyes.

VASARI, "Life of Michelangelo Buonarroti"

She has been placed opposite Daniel; *she is also
a prophetess of the end of time. To her was
attributed a prediction relating to the triumph
of the Virgin over the beast of the Apocalypse.*

Right: Putto bearing the plaque of the Persian
Sibyl.

Opposite: The Persian Sibyl.

THE LIBYAN SIBYL

The same holds true for the lovely figure of the Libyan sibyl who,
having written a great volume drawn from many books, is about to rise
to her feet in an attitude of womanly grace;
and at one and the same time she makes as if to rise and to close the book, something
most difficult, not to say impossible, for anyone
but the master to have depicted.

VASARI, "Life of Michelangelo Buonarroti"

*The pose of the Libyan Sibyl is one of the most
dynamic and complex inventions Michelangelo
created with the last figures of the Ceiling. The
twisting motion of the Sibyl, intensified by the
movement of her robes, expresses a "furor
divinus," or divine fury, that is present on other
scenes on the second half of the Ceiling as well.*

*Right: Putto supporting the plaque of the
Libyan Sibyl.*
154 *Opposite: The Libyan Sibyl.*

The small figures were executed with wide brushes, highly diluted colors, and little definition of detail, as is natural for a painting that will be viewed from a distance. However, the Sibyl's face is portrayed with greater accuracy, both in the design and in the way the pigments have been applied. The colors are bolder and they have been applied in fine but densely arrayed brushstrokes. Hence the painted surfaces produce a more polished, better defined image, as if it were closer to us.

The Sibyl never reveals the truth,
unless she is furious, demented and wretched;
and the divine plan
is discerned when her mind is affected, not when it is sound.

LEONARDO BRUNI ARETINO, *Ballad in Praise of Venus*

Right: The Libyan Sibyl, *detail of the young assistants.*

156

Opposite: The Libyan Sibyl, *detail.*

Cursed be the day wherein I was born:
let not the day wherein my mother bare me be blessed....
And let him hear the cry in the morning,
and the shouting at noontide;...
Wherefore came I forth out of the womb to see labour and sorrow?

He was called upon by God to be the prophet of tragedies and, with his sensitive disposition, he felt great sorrow for the agonies that the Omnipotent had decided to inflict upon the Hebrew race of sinners. Michelangelo presents Jeremiah as someone intent on his grief but resigned to the will of God. The tormented personality and physical appearance of the wise old man have often been compared to those of the artist.

Right: Putto as plaque-bearer.
Opposite: The Prophet Jeremiah.

Details of the Prophet Jeremiah
*that demonstrate Michelangelo's strong
psychological characterization of this personage.
Above and above right are the two genii
standing behind him, who are touched by his
sadness; at right, the Prophet's naturalistic
hand, held slack on his lap in resignation;
opposite, the face of the old Prophet.*

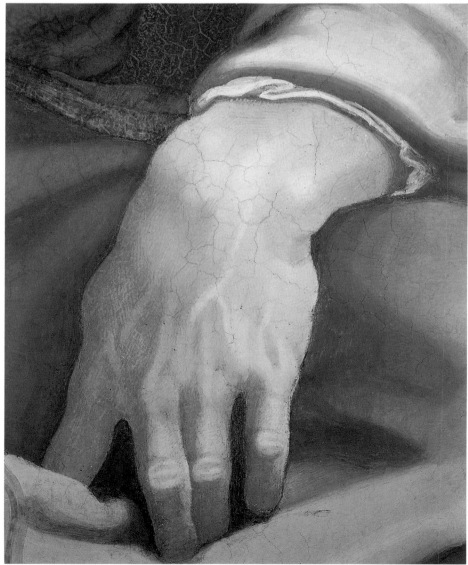

In his brief and singular book is told the story of how the sinners of the city of Nineveh were converted, precisely as a result of the preachings of the reluctant Prophet. The mercy God showed the people once they had repented outraged Jonah. It seems Michelangelo was portraying this moment in the story when he painted the impetuous gesture of the Prophet. Around Jonah are other attributes of the scene: the fish that swallowed Jonah, who remained inside his stomach for three days (an episode that foreshadows the three days spent by Christ in the tomb before his Resurrection), and the branch behind the Prophet's head, a reminder of the castor-oil plant that God caused to grow to protect him from the desert sun.

And God said to Jonah, Doest thou well to be angry for the gourd?…
Thou hast had pity on the gourd, for the which thou hast not laboured,
neither madest it grow; which came up in a night,
and perished in a night:
And should not I spare Nineveh, that great city, wherein are more than
sixscore thousand persons that cannot discern between their right hand
and their left hand; and also much cattle?

The theme of divine judgment, which is the subject of the Book of Jonah, is linked to the scene that has been placed above the Prophet and at which he seems to be looking. It is the scene of God Separating Light from Darkness, a clear symbol of the Last Judgment.

Above: Plaque with the name of the Prophet.
Opposite and overleaf: The Prophet Jonah, full view and details.

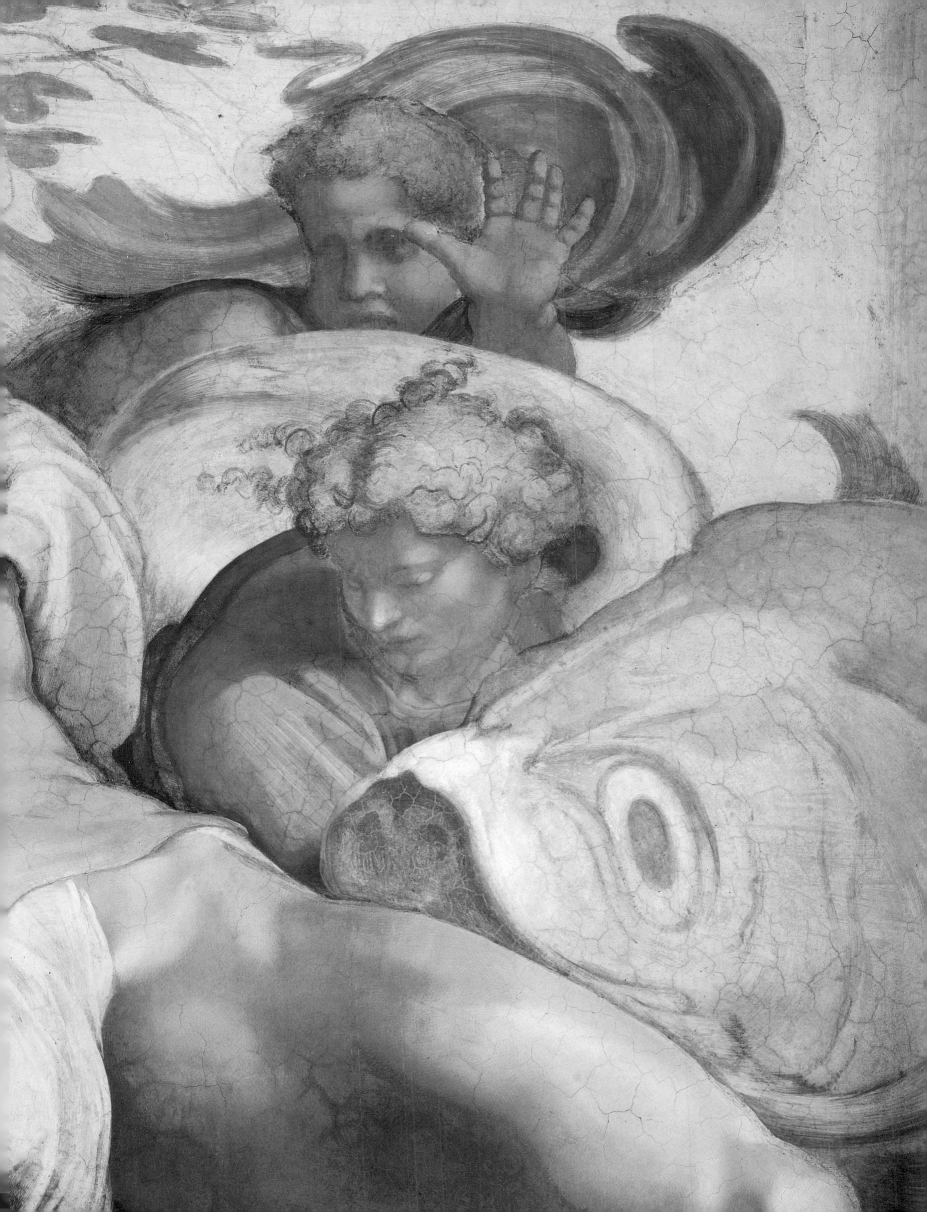

GOD SEPARATING THE EARTH FROM THE WATERS

In the third space, the Lord God appears in the air,
and in like manner with angels; and looking upon the waters,...

CONDIVI, *The Life of Michelangelo*

The Eternal Father is the only protagonist in the Creation scenes and throughout the scenes He becomes an increasingly strong presence. The whirling movement of the robes and "the extremely beautiful and artfully done foreshortenings" aid in conveying the impression of a mighty primordial force.

It has not been easy to identify the particular biblical event this painting illustrates. Experts have formulated differing views, seeing the scene as the Separation of the Earth from the Waters, the Creation of Marine Animals, or the Separation of the Sky from the Waters. The first seems to be the most credible.

Preceding pages: The two nudes above the Persian Sibyl. *The medallion they hold up is the only one without a narrative scene. The movements of the nudes become gradually more agitated toward the altar wall. The two here seem to be buffeted by a strong wind, especially the nude on the right, who is off balance in his backward-leaning pose.*

The ignudi Michelangelo painted at the beginning of his work on the Ceiling are in balance as a result of the symmetry between each pair. In the subsequent stages of the work, the artist preferred the dynamic equilibrium resulting from the contraposition of their movements. The dramatic power of the poses of these characters, which increasingly invade the pictorial fields of the Genesis scenes, seems to be an amplification of the gestures of God in the act of creating.

168

GENESIS 1.8–10

And the evening and the morning were the second day.
And God said, Let the waters under the heaven be gathered together
unto one place, and let the dry land appear: and it was so.
And God called the dry land Earth; and the gathering together
of the waters called he Seas.

*Overleaf: The two nudes above the Prophet
Daniel. Represented on the medallion is the
Death of Absalom (2 Samuel 18.9).*

And God said, Let there be lights in the firmament
of the heaven to divide the day from the night. . . .
And let them be for lights in the firmament of the heaven to give light

Two consecutive scenes have been painted in this
panel. The first, on the right, shows God
creating the sun and the moon. He seems to be
giving a peremptory command that takes even
the angels around him by surprise. Half of his
figure, which is "very terrifying," is exposed to
the light of the sun in front of him. The other
half is in darkness, where the moon can be seen.
To the left, God causes plants to grow on the
earth.

upon the earth: and it was so.
And God made two great lights; the greater light to rule the day,
and the lesser light to rule the night: he made the stars also.
And God set them in the firmament of the heaven to give light upon the earth,
and to rule over the day and over the night, and to divide the light from the darkness.

Overleaf: The Creation of the Sun, Moon, and Plants, *detail of God creating the plants. The figure is shown from the back, "down to the soles of its feet. It is indeed a most beautiful work, and one which shows what is possible to foreshortening" (Condivi).*

There are some little angels in his company, one of which, on the left side,
hides its face, as it nestles close to its Creator,
as if to shield itself from the baneful influence of the moon.

CONDIVI, *The Life of Michelangelo*

The Creation of the Sun, Moon, and
Plants, *detail of the angels in the sunlight. One
of them shades his eyes with his arm.*
Overleaf: The Creation of the Sun, Moon,
and Plants, *detail of God in the act of creating.*

GOD SEPARATING LIGHT FROM DARKNESS

Both Vasari and Condivi testify to the fact that Pope Julius II pressured Michelangelo to hasten the completion of the frescoes. The pope, who died four months after the unveiling of the Ceiling, was determined to see the undertaking brought to completion. The increased pace is clear from the technique Michelangelo used during this stage: the brushstrokes are broader, quicker, and more decisive. An example of his increased speed is God Separating Light from Darkness, *which was painted in just one* giornata. *The simplicity of the concept and the novel design are the mark of a genius.*
The last scene Michelangelo painted represents the first act of creation, but it also has an eschatological meaning. God Separating Light from Darkness *is a symbol of the division of good from evil, and the scene is therefore an allusion to the day of Judgment.*
"For his holiness was always asking him importunately when it would be ready.... [Michelangelo] retorted that the ceiling would be finished 'when it satisfies me as an artist.' And to this the Pope replied, 'And we want you to satisfy us and finish it soon.' Finally, the Pope threatened that if Michelangelo did not finish the ceiling quickly he would have him thrown down from the scaffolding." (Vasari)

Preceding pages: The ignudi *above the* Prophet Jeremiah.
Overleaf: The ignudi *above the* Libyan Sibyl.

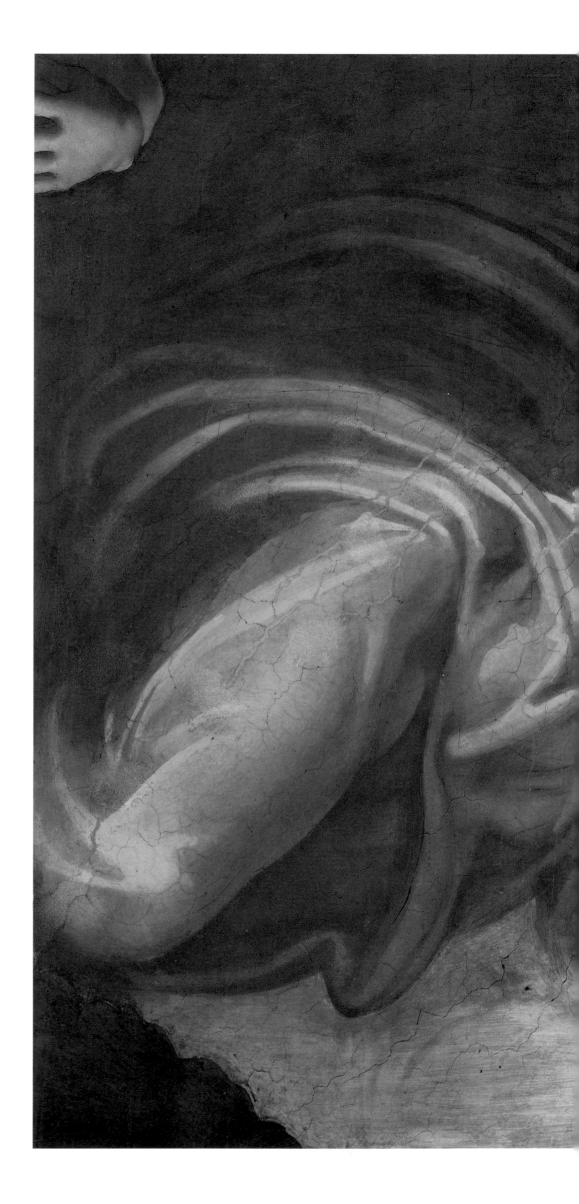

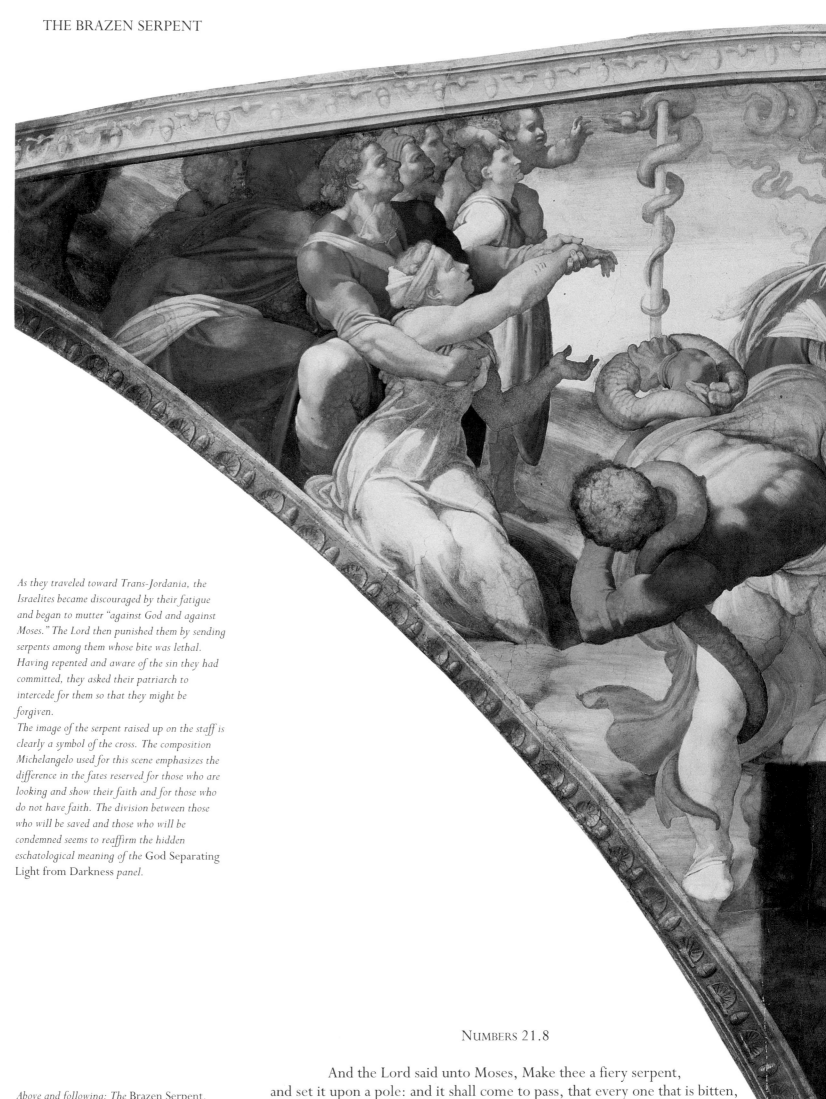

As they traveled toward Trans-Jordania, the
Israelites became discouraged by their fatigue
and began to mutter "against God and against
Moses." The Lord then punished them by sending
serpents among them whose bite was lethal.
Having repented and aware of the sin they had
committed, they asked their patriarch to
intercede for them so that they might be
forgiven.
The image of the serpent raised up on the staff is
clearly a symbol of the cross. The composition
Michelangelo used for this scene emphasizes the
difference in the fates reserved for those who are
looking and show their faith and for those who
do not have faith. The division between those
who will be saved and those who will be
condemned seems to reaffirm the hidden
eschatological meaning of the God Separating
Light from Darkness panel.

NUMBERS 21.8

And the Lord said unto Moses, Make thee a fiery serpent,
and set it upon a pole: and it shall come to pass, that every one that is bitten,
when he looketh upon it, shall live.

Above and following: The Brazen Serpent,
details.

Even more beautiful and inspired…is the story of the serpents of Moses,
over the left-hand side of the altar.
For here one sees the deadly havoc wrought by the rain of serpents
as they bite and sting,
and the brazen serpent itself that Moses placed upon a pole.

VASARI, "Life of Michelangelo Buonarroti"

185

The deadly poison is causing the death of countless men
and women in terror and convulsion, not to mention the rigid legs
and twisted arms of those who remain just as they were struck down,
unable to move, and then again the beautifully
executed heads shown shrieking and thrown back in despair....

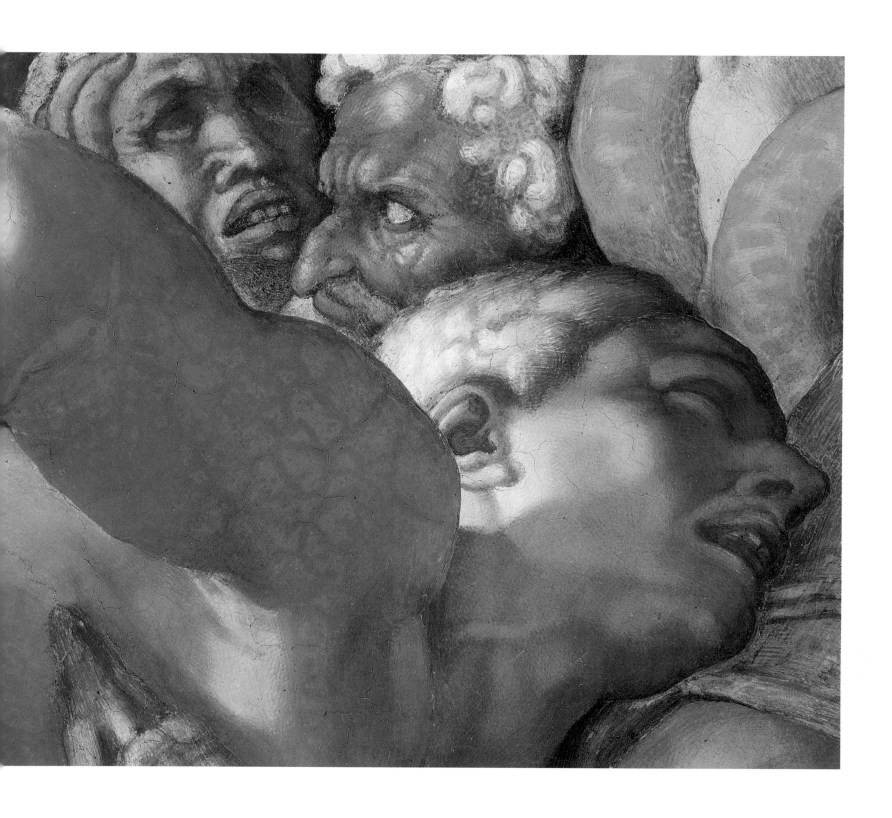

No less marvelously portrayed than the rest are those who keep their eyes
fixed with heart-felt emotion on the serpent, the sight of which has already
lessened their grief; among them is a woman who has been bitten
and reduced to terror and who now in her great and obvious
need is supported by another figure offering clear and welcome assistance.

VASARI, "Life of Michelangelo Buonarroti"

THE PUNISHMENT OF HAMAN

Haman, vizier of the king, became annoyed at
Mordecai, a Hebrew who refused to bow when
Haman passed by. So Haman persuaded King
Ahasuerus to issue an edict proclaiming the
extermination of the Hebrew people. Esther, the
young wife of the sovereign and a cousin of
Mordecai, convinced the king to revoke the
decree and to punish Haman.

In the Punishment of Haman, the vizier is
crucified. This is a significant variation on the
biblical story of the hanging, and its
introduction in the scene does not seem to be a
coincidence. Haman represents evil defeated by
the cross and the evildoer punished by divine
justice.

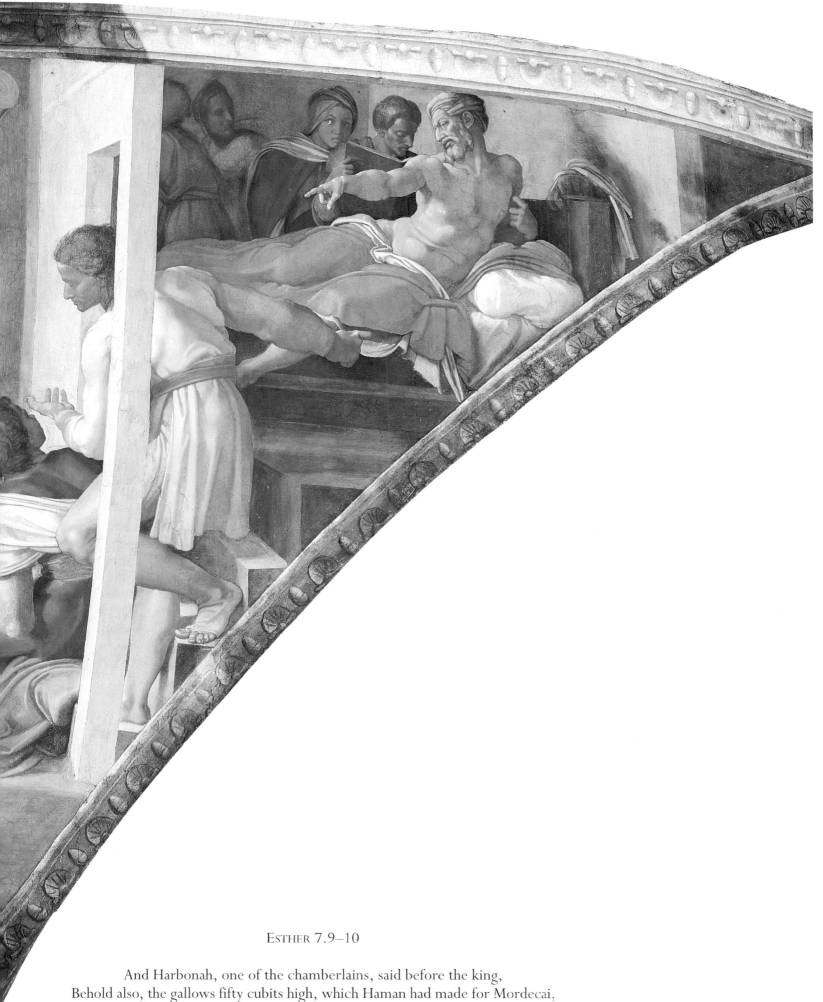

ESTHER 7.9–10

And Harbonah, one of the chamberlains, said before the king,
Behold also, the gallows fifty cubits high, which Haman had made for Mordecai,
who had spoken good for the king, standeth in the house of Haman.
Then the king said, Hang him thereon.
So they hanged Haman on the gallows that he had prepared for Mordecai.
Then was the king's wrath pacified.

Overleaf: The Punishment of Haman,
details.

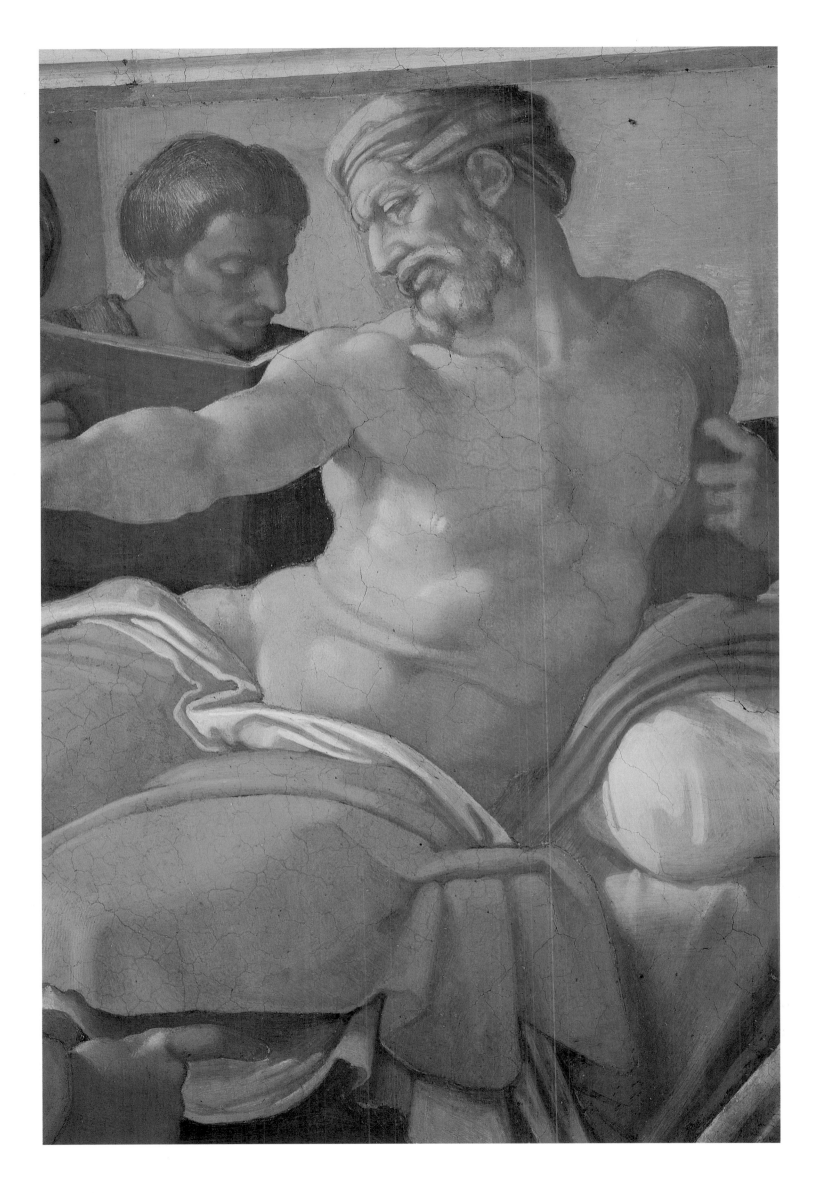

The Costumes Worn by the Ancestors of Christ

Edward Maeder

Opposite: Eleazar-Mathan *lunette, detail of Eleazar. Situated in the top left area above the entrance wall, this was perhaps the first lunette to be painted. In the shadows behind Eleazar the other members of the little family—a woman and a boy—can be seen.*

The examination and evaluation of costume in works of art is a subject of considerable controversy. Although it is possible to glean a great deal of information from representations of clothing in paintings and sculptures as well as from textiles such as embroideries and tapestries, this information must be properly understood to be of any benefit. The observer must have a thorough understanding of fibers and weaving techniques and an extensive practical knowledge of clothing construction. It is often possible to determine the kind of textile portrayed in a painting (silk, wool, or linen) and the exact cut of a garment from the visual evidence. The interpretation of this information is neither casual nor unscientific. It is based on the examination of a variety of contemporary sources, from written descriptions such as wardrobe accounts and letters to technical treatises on textile manufacture and dyeing methods.

The challenge is to remove oneself from the built-in prejudices of how clothing is observed and understood in our own time. The ways in which clothing is worn and what it means were as crucial in the early sixteenth century as they are today. This form of nonverbal communication is far more than merely well-placed draperies in pleasing colors. It is a series of carefully considered clues to enhance the form and identity of the wearer.

Sources for the creation of biblical costumes have frustrated both artists and scholars since Christian imagery began appearing in works of art. What inspired the artist? What sources were used? How were those sources interpreted? Which contemporary elements can be seen?[1] These are some of the questions I will address regarding the costumes worn by the Ancestors of Christ in Michelangelo's Sistine Ceiling frescoes.

As it is not possible to discuss every costume in an essay such as this, I will concentrate on several costumes that illustrate the theory that engravings and woodcuts were, consciously or unconsciously, used as sources; that certain elements of cross-dressing (wearing clothing of the opposite sex) were used to confuse the viewer and to place the images out of recognizable context; and that no less than nineteen of the garments were made of a type of two-colored textile that was popular, inexpensive, and easily available in the first decades of the sixteenth century in Italy. I will show that the red shadows on the pale green garment of Aminadab, son of Aram,[2] are not the result of a "Mannerist device," but are the rendering of a changeable, two-colored fabric called, in Italian, *cangiante*. I will also substantiate a theory that in spite of published information to the contrary,[3] Michelangelo was aware of the prevailing fashionable textiles and that his family was closely involved with the textile trades in Florence.[4] Four years

ago, when I had the privilege of viewing with Dr. Fabrizio Mancinelli the newly cleaned lunettes from the scaffolding, I discussed these observations, and in the past months, I have been able to find evidence to support these conjectures.

A key component in many of the figures is the disposition and treatment of the head covering. It is well known that Jews in the Middle Ages were required to wear a specific form of hat and that in some locations certain colors were also required. The coif (a small linen cap worn by Christian men and seen in early fourteenth-century paintings),[5] while easily associated with the past in the Christian community, remained a style worn by Jews, often under a cylindrical hat with a brim.[6] Color restrictions were also important. As late as 1503 the Jews in Bern, Switzerland, were still required to wear yellow,[7] and the color appears in some form in virtually every lunette in the Ceiling. An example of the coif, a fashionable garment

of male attire, is used in an altered form in the costume of the wife of Mathan. The small lappets, or flaps over the ears, are survivals of cords originally used to tie the coif in place. The exotic turbanlike hat with what appears to be a braid of hair wrapped over it is possibly based on a man's hat, which will be described later. Similar forms of the linen coif are also seen in the lunettes with Boaz and Abiud. A German woodcut from the *Nuremberg Chronicles* of 1493 illustrates this same form of "Jewish" headgear.[8] Many of the figures in this cycle have survived in Michelangelo's drawings; they are presumably of a preliminary nature. In some cases the changes seen in the finished paintings are noteworthy.

Meshullemeth, mother of Amon, described by de Tolnay as "a beautiful young woman with tender features,"[9] is wearing a fantasy headdress often found on exotic figures, usually on Jewish women. It was a form particularly favored at the end of the fifteenth century in Flanders. The sausage-like turban appears to be covered in rich, two-colored fabric held in place with additional cords or wrappings. The form is remarkably similar to several found in the *Nuremberg Chronicles.*[10] This same source includes other figures wearing hats virtually identical to that worn by David in the *Jesse-David-Solomon* lunette. He is described in the Bible as "old and stricken in years; and they covered him with clothes, but he gat no heat."[11] De Tolnay described the head covering as a "pale green hood with an acorn on top."[12] The shape and relationship to the head are virtually identical to those on another figure in the *Nuremberg Chronicles.*[13] It is likely that the "acorn" is a

Above and opposite: Various styles of headdress worn by the Jews are illustrated in wood engravings reproduced in the 1493 Nuremberg Chronicles. Several figures in the lunettes wear similar types of headdress.

version of the "pointed hat" (*pilus cornutus*) that various statutes and regulations required Jews to wear throughout the medieval period.[14] Woodcuts of hats with an acorn attachment were included in the late-fifteenth-century regulations in Frankfurt-am-Main.[15]

Two Sistine figures wear garments clearly connected to Italian engrav-

ings of the 1490s. The first is Josaphat, described in de Tolnay as wearing "gray trousers, a mantle in red and green changing colors, and a light green cap."[16] Since the cleaning of the lunettes, it is clear that the red is, in fact, orange; the green is yellow, and the green cap is a shade of lavender-gray-green. The Bible describes him as wealthy.[17] Most notable in Josaphat's attire are the long, full, loose "trousers" tied at the ankle. They are similar to a garment worn by a figure in an engraving by Christophano di Michele Martini, called "il Robetta," the *Adoration of the Magi* of ca. 1496.[18] Long, sometimes loose leg-coverings have been associated with figures from the East, in particular the Magi, since earliest times. Similar garments appear in the sixth-century depiction of the Three Magi in Ravenna in the church of S. Apollinare Nuovo.

The second figure is the woman in the *Azor-Sadoch* lunette, in which we note the curious form of her overgarment pulled off her left shoulder to expose the chemise, or linen shift. A possible prototype for this extremely affected and illogical manner of wearing the garment could be related to an aesthetic clearly illustrated in an engraving of the Mantegna school known as *Four Women Dancing*, ca. 1497.[19]

As previously mentioned, the headpiece worn by the wife of Mathan is

Top: The "pointed hat" with an acorn-shaped decoration that the Jews were supposed to wear is illustrated in the regulations of Frankfurt-am-Main dating from the end of the fifteenth century.
Below: Giovanni Bellini, Celebration of the Feast of Corpus Christi in Piazza San Marco, *detail, 1490s. Gallerie dell'Accademia, Venice. At the end of the fifteenth century, the cylinder-shaped hat was associated with Armenian Jews.*

Christophano di Michele Martini, called "il Robetta," Adoration of the Magi, *ca. 1496. Engraving.*

School of Mantegna, Four Women Dancing, *ca. 1497. Engraving.*

possibly adapted from a male hat. In late-fifteenth-century Venice this form of "top hat" or cylindrical hat with a brim was associated with Armenian Jews. A group of them can be seen in Giovanni Bellini's *Celebration of the Feast of Corpus Christi in Piazza San Marco* of the 1490s. This form of cross-dressing was an effective way of confusing the viewer by creating an unfamiliar atmosphere. Alteration of clothing forms associated with specific gender has been used with great frequency in the period under discussion but is generally unrecognized by modern academics. Without fully understanding the vicissitudes of current fashionable dress, as seen in the Italian peninsula in the early years of the sixteenth century, it is impossible for twentieth-century historians to grasp the significance of this visual information. I believe it was necessary for Michelangelo to establish distance both historically and emotionally between the august Ancestors of Christ and the "modern" Romans of the early sixteenth century.

Next let us consider Achim. There is no literary tradition for this figure.[20] The pale green and red cape with an attached hood covers what appears to be a coil of hair at the back of his head in such a way that it resembles the form of a headdress worn by the wife of Joatham. A twisted knot of hair or some other device would have been necessary to create the shape seen at the back of Achim's head. Is this another, more subtle form of cross-dressing?

Eleazar wears a "white shirt"[21] that is actually a form of chemise similar to that worn by several madonnas in sculptures by Michelangelo.[22] Particularly noteworthy is the rectangular band of decoration at the base of the neck. Again the question arises: Is this a form of dress worn by both sexes or was it customarily one worn by women and is here depicted on a man?

Perhaps the most fascinating discovery has been the realization that the changeable colors, referred to by so many who have written about the Ancestors of Christ, are not, in my opinion, a painterly device but a carefully rendered textile in existence at the time. References to *sarscenet,* an even-weave, lightweight silk originally thought to have come from the Saracens,[23] occur in wardrobe accounts in Italy and England. The origins of this silk fabric are unclear, but I would like to suggest that it was introduced into Europe in quantity by Crusaders returning from the Holy Lands. It is created by using a warp of one color and a weft of another. The play of light on the fabric creates highlights of one color and shadows of the other. When placed in sunlight, a modern silk illustrates the effect. Using this weave is a relatively easy way to achieve an iridescent, rich quality with a minimum of labor and expense. The earliest documentation to date is from an eleventh-century book of travels, where reference is made in Cairo to a kind of porcelain painted to resemble *bugalumun,* "so that different colors show depending on how the article is held."[24] *Bugalumun,* believed to be a form of changeable silk, appears throughout the document as a kind of textile used especially for banners and linings.[25]

Changeable, or "shot," silk was clearly in use from the beginning of the fourteenth century, as examples can be seen frequently in work of Giotto in Padua,[26] Barna da Siena in San Gimignano, and many other artists, including Andrea Mantegna. Hans Holbein the Elder used both plain and changeable silks in his panels for the *Kaisheiner Altar* of 1502.[27] Even at this early date the fabrics were primarily used in reference to biblical figures.

There was apparently a revival of shot silk in the last two decades of the fifteenth century.[28] Numerous references appear in the wardrobe accounts of Edward IV of England in 1480. In this instance the cost of "chaungeable sarscinet" was about twenty-five percent more than the cost of a solid color.[29] Large quantities of this material were in the royal wardrobe, but they are usually referred to as linings of bed curtains.[30] The king's own bed, which was made of red, green, and white striped velvet, had two "syde curtyns [side curtains] and a fote curtyn [foot curtain] of sarsinet chaungeable."[31] In 1483 Richard III's coronation accounts mention more than four hundred yards of sarsinet.[32]

One of the most significant examples of the use of changeable silk can be seen in Mantegna's *Virgin and Child with the Magdalen and St. John the Baptist* in the National Gallery, London. The gown of the Magdalen is obviously made of red and green changeable silk. The use of *cangiante* continued throughout the sixteenth century and is usually seen in the attire of people from the East, most notably in the elaborate dress of the Magi.

The two-colored effect was not restricted to silk, but could also be found in a fine wool or a combination of silk and wool known as *saia*.[33] Large quantities of this fabric are mentioned in the Medici accounts of the early sixteenth century known as the Selfridges Papers. Often made of

lamb's wool, it molded easily to the body and was utilized especially for stockings. Knitted stockings or hose had not yet come into use by the early years of the sixteenth century. Fitted leg coverings were made of cloth and cut on the bias, or at a forty-five-degree angle with the grain, which allowed them to stretch and to provide a relatively smooth covering. These stockings were sewn together in a seam up the back of the leg. I believe the hose worn by Eleazar, green with red shadows, are made from this material. Michelangelo's personal interest in clothing, and stockings in particular, can be seen in an entry found in his household accounts, in which he purchased wool to be made into stockings for his assistants.[34]

The woman shown in the lunette with Joatham wears a large mantle of red and yellow changeable fabric. Because of the drape of the fabric and the softness of the folds, it is almost certain that this, too, is wool and not silk. Reinforcing this view is the denseness of color, which is also often associated with wool.[35] The wool industry, particularly in Florence, was the basis of much of the economy in Tuscany as well as in other parts of

Hans Holbein the Elder, panels for the Kaisheiner Altar, detail, 1502. Alte Pinakothek, Munich.

199

Italy.[36] In his *Treatise on Painting,* Leonardo states: "Draperies should be drawn from the actual object: that is, if you wish to represent a woolen drapery, make the folds accordingly; and if it is silk or fine cloth, or coarse material such as peasants wear, or linen or veiling, diversify the folds of each kind of material, and do not make a habit, as many do, of working from clay models covered with paper or thin leather, because you will greatly deceive yourself by so doing."[37] It seems reasonable to assume that this approach to rendering draperies would also have been used by Michelangelo, whose family had been involved in the textile industry in Florence for generations. References to *cangiante* silk are somewhat rare in Italian inventories, possibly because this rather ordinary simple-weave fabric was quite common. It is also possible that there were many more references but they have been hitherto unnoticed. Recently a number of additional references have come to my attention, including one from 1498, a list of costumes worn by actors performing the Passion play on Good Friday in Rome, which mentions "una turca" (probably an exotic gown of Turkish origin)[38] that was lined with "cangiante giallo [yellow *cangiante*]."[39]

In the surviving inventory of the trousseau clothing owned by Cecilia Gallerani on the occasion of her marriage to Ludovico Bergamini on 7 July 1492, there appear only two references to *cangiante* silk.[40] In one case the colors yellow and turquoise are mentioned, and in the other the *cangiante* was used for lining the garment.[41] This is consistent with several references from the accounts of the coronation of Richard III in 1483.[42] We are fortunate that a portrait of Cecilia by Leonardo has survived, but it is generally accepted to have been painted before 1492, so it is most unlikely that she is wearing a costume that would correspond to anything in the inventory.

Certainly the most "fashionable" costume in Michelangelo's series of Ancestors is that of Mathan's wife. The bodice lacing under the arm is consistent with the current mode for dress closures in Italy. The small bag and key, typical of the early sixteenth century, are suspended on a cord from the waist. The short yellow oversleeve, which would normally have been tied, or in northern Europe pinned, appears to have been sewn into place. The identical garment is worn above, in the *Judith and Holofernes* spandrel, and the short, attached sleeve is even the same color, yellow. In my opinion this is evidence to support the theory that this garment was made and worn by a model for the initial design.

The belief that Michelangelo disliked weavers, as is evidenced by his writing, is based on his apparent reaction to tapestries. In his book *Michelangelo's Theory of Art,* R.J. Clements declares, "the art of weaving . . . was slighted by Michelangelo."[43] Clements's statement that "[Michelangelo's] dislike of the ornate and intricate tapestries reflecting the taste of Venice, one of the chief producers of them" is based on some kind of misunderstanding. Venice produced some of the most beautiful silks, particularly woven cloth-of-gold and high-quality damasks and velvets, but there were no tapestry workshops in that city in the sixteenth century. Venice was, however, a major supplier of raw materials for the renowned workshops of Flanders.[44] According to Vasari Michelangelo's brothers were, because of financial pressures, apprenticed to the Guilds of Silk and Wool in Florence. In fact the artist himself discussed the setting up of a textile shop for his favorite brother, Buonarroto.[45]

Although there have been only a few hints in this discussion concerning Michelangelo's connections to the textile industry, it should be stated that his family was seriously involved in that business since his great-grandfather, Buonarroti di Simone, joined the Arte della Lana in November 1388. Michelangelo's written descriptions of the Ancestors on the Sistine Ceiling leave no doubt that textiles were, so to speak, in his blood.[46] Given the importance of Florence's wool industry in the fourteenth and fifteenth centuries it would have been impossible to escape its influence.

Michelangelo was most certainly aware of the wealth of textiles avail-

A present-day example of shot silk.

able to him in the first years of the sixteenth century. Was it necessary to invent colored shadows or could the artist simply record the visual evidence of easily accessible textiles?[47]

Also important is the question of Cennino Cennini. There seems to be no evidence that Cennini, in his careful instructions on how "to make changing green drapery in fresco,"[48] was discussing anything other than the rendering of an existing textile. This has been an important point of discussion and it will certainly require additional research and scrutiny of documents, inventories, and other sources if it is to be resolved.

Since the changeable silks that have been discussed here originated in the land of the Saracens, and the Saracens lived in roughly the same geographical region as the Ancestors of Christ, I would like to propose that their use was a conscious decision on Michelangelo's part. I would also suggest that the link to God the Father in Perugino's *Baptism of Christ,* part of the lower fresco series in the Sistine Chapel, in which God is wearing red and green *cangiante,* is no accident.

Michelangelo used familiar and unfamiliar elements, the exotic and the commonplace, and combined them in a way that succeeded in making the Ancestors of Christ both lofty and strange, but nonetheless acceptable. It is my hope that further research will bring new evidence to light that will enable us to better understand the major impact the textile industry and its technology has had on the surviving visual evidence from the early years of the sixteenth century, particularly Michelangelo's frescoes on the Sistine Ceiling.

Pietro Perugino, Baptism of Christ, *detail of the figure of God. Sistine Chapel.*

THE LUNETTES
AND SEVERIES

THE ANCESTORS OF CHRIST

In the lunettes and severies that constitute the
links between the walls and the Ceiling,
Michelangelo represented the Ancestors of Christ
as they are listed in the beginning of the Gospel
according to St. Matthew. Their names are
written on rectangular tablets placed in the
center of the lunettes to divide the space in two.

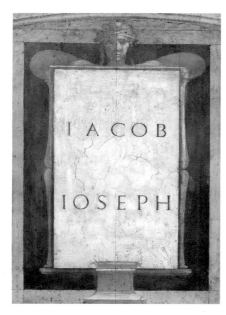

The Jacob-Joseph lunette should have been
painted last according to chronological
sequence. But, as in other areas of the Ceiling,
Michelangelo worked backward in time, from
the most recent to the most distant.
Right: Detail of the family group on the right.
The figure in the foreground must be Mary; in
the background, the bearded profile of Joseph
can be seen as well as the little Jesus. The
woman's shawl and sleeve are excellent examples
of Michelangelo's technique of using color to
create form.
Opposite: Detail with the family group in the
left half of the lunette. The male figure in the
background may be Mathan. His gaze is fixed
on his wife, who is playing with the animated
baby. The woman, who wears a rather stern
expression on her face, has a cord around her
waist to which a key and a bag are tied; these
may be an allusion to her frugal character.

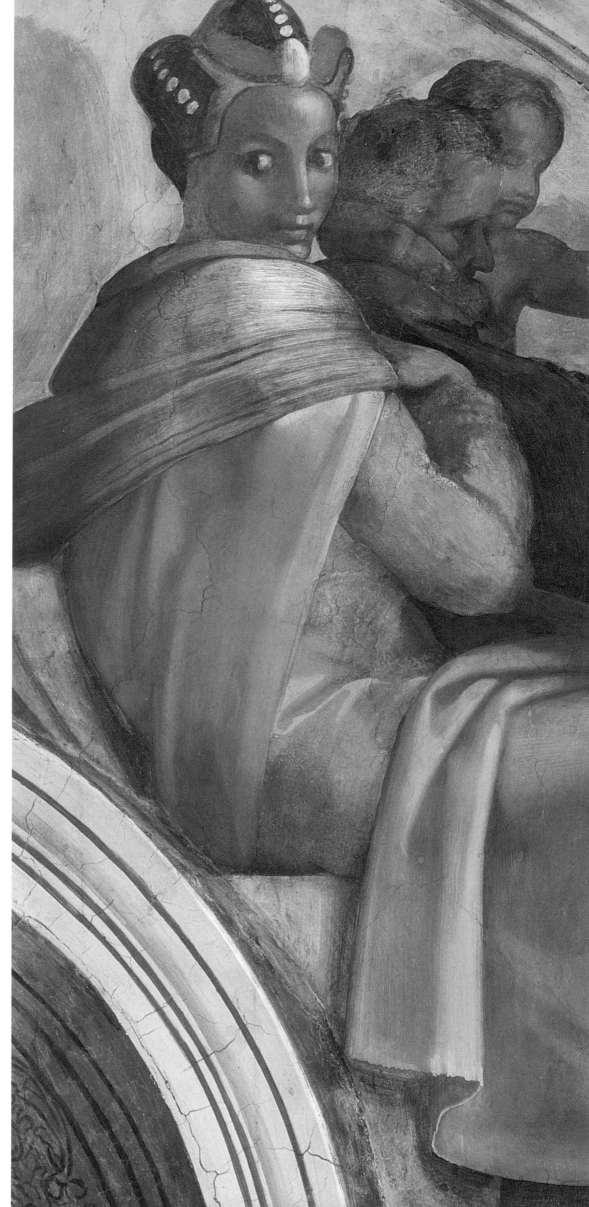

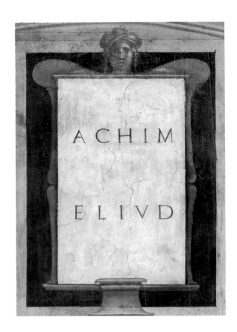

Opposite: Zorobabel-Abiud-Eliachim
lunette, detail of the male figure on the right.
The thin layer of color has been applied with
quick, skillful brushstrokes and the image
remains partly undefined and out of focus. This
summary technique characterizes the frescoes
dedicated to the Ancestors, where a naturalistic
effect is created by varying the definition of the
figures, depending on their position in the scene.
Located above the lunettes that are not
contiguous to the corner spandrels are the
severies, on which Michelangelo painted other
family groups belonging to the genealogy of
Christ. The triangular frame encloses a dark
background and a narrow space, both of which
accentuate the sad, oppressed look of the people
represented.

*Above: Severy above the Zorobabel-Abiud-
Eliachim lunette.*

207

Below: Josias-Jeconias-Salathiel *lunette. The brothers Josias and Salathiel are thought to be portrayed here with their parents. The lunette would thus contain one family group, as seems to be suggested by the fact that the two adults are looking at each other, and by the game played by the two boys, which creates a point of contact between them.*

Below: Severy above the Josias-Jeconias-Salathiel lunette. The feeling of solitude the families seem to convey, and the postures of the various individuals, which express fear, worry, and anguish, have been interpreted as indications of lives spent awaiting the Redemption.

There is a close relationship between the theme of the Ancestors and that of motherhood, which Michelangelo has represented, with much psychological insight and from many different points of view, in the lunettes and severies of the Sistine Chapel.

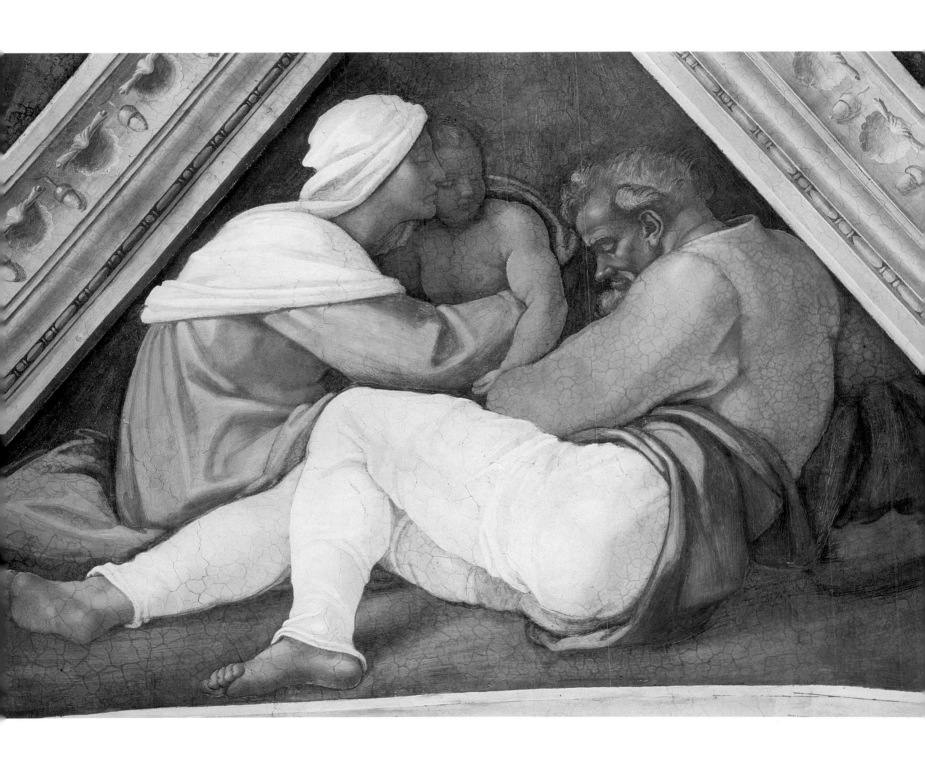

Ezechias-Manasses-Amon lunette, *detail of
the young mother rocking her child.
Meschullemet, Amon's mother, is wearing an
elaborate turban that emphasizes her Hebrew
origins.
Each of the groups in the halves of the lunettes
was painted in one day in true fresco (on wet
plaster), without the help of cartoons.
Michelangelo used only a preliminary design,
which was drawn freehand with the point of a
brush that had been dipped in a dark color.*

Severy above the Ezechias-Manasses-Amon lunette. In the severies more than in the lunettes, the mothers appear as the principal figure in each of the families portrayed. In only one case, the severy above the Josias-Jeconias-Salathiel *lunette, is the female figure not in the foreground.*

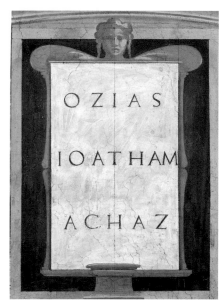

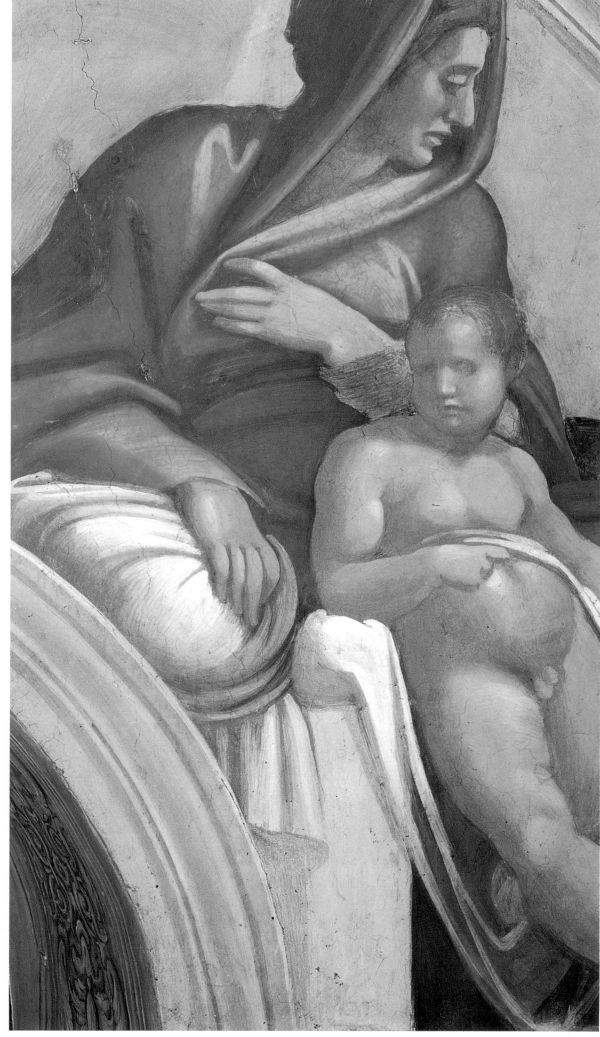

Bottom and right: Ozias-Joatham-Achaz lunette, detail of the two figures in the left half of the lunette, engaged in animated conversation; and detail of the mother figure in the right half.

"All the possible ways, complexions, movements, postures, and conditions of the human body and all the moods of the soul can be seen represented here....and so natural, alive and appropriate that it would almost be possible to say that nature herself could barely add anything."
(M. Tramezino, Roma trionfante)

Opposite: Asa-Josaphat-Joram *lunette, detail of King Josaphat. The body of this figure is rendered with large, concise blocks of color in sharp, strident tones. His facial features have been painted in detail. Josaphat's headdress and his long, wide trousers tightened at the ankles clearly indicate that he is from the East.*

Above: *Severy above the Asa-Josaphat-Joram lunette.*

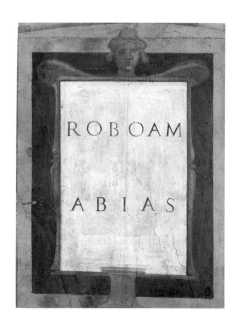

Roboam-Abias *lunette, details of the sleeping figure in the right half of the lunette, and the pregnant woman in the right half pointing to her womb. The Ancestors seem to have been represented engaged mainly in waiting and in reproducing; they live waiting and preparing for the birth of Christ.*

Opposite: Severy above the Roboam-Abias *lunette.*

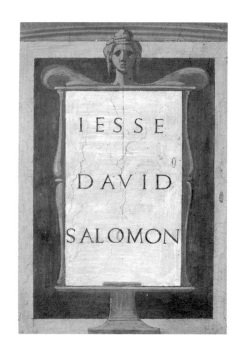

Jesse-David-Solomon *lunette, detail with David dressed in the Arab manner.*

Opposite: Severy above the Jesse-David-Solomon *lunette. The severies are surmounted by rams' skulls and pairs of bronze nudes, which are mirror images of each other. It has been suggested that the impression they convey of being imprisoned is in contrast with that of the nudes surrounding the Genesis scenes.*

Salmon-Booz-Obeth *lunette, detail of the*
figure in the right half of the lunette.
Michelangelo created a remarkable caricature of
a quarrelsome man, who seems to be reflected in
the head carved in the end of his stick, and with
whom he appears to be having a discussion.

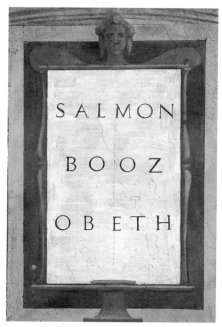

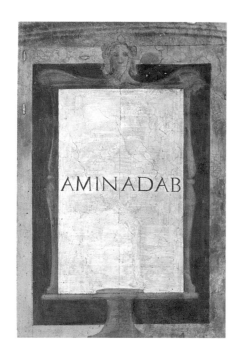

In the last two lunettes, Aminadab on the left
and Naason on the right in relation to the altar
wall, the artist represented young people. Absent
are children, who round out practically all the
family groups in the other lunettes.

The Syntax of Form and Posture from the Ceiling to the *Last Judgment*

Pierluigi De Vecchi

The impressive effect of unity and harmony in the very richly articulated system of decoration Michelangelo created for the Sistine Ceiling relies as much on the painted architectural structure as on the relationships between sizes, gestures, and rhythms established by the placement across the Ceiling of figures outside the narrative scenes. The vast surface-area to be painted, as well as the specific dimensions and the shape of the Ceiling, required the invention of a formal, metrical system that is without precedents in the figural culture of the Renaissance. The enormity of the task was most likely one of the reasons for Michelangelo's repeated attempts to refuse the commission, which Condivi takes special note of in his biography of the artist.[1] This problem must have proved a greater obstacle for Michelangelo than the difficulty of painting figures that were "large and foreshortened," a challenge which, in 1506, led Donato Bramante to doubt the artist's willingness to undertake the immense enterprise.[2]

Once the decision had been made, however, there was a surprisingly swift evolution from the concept of the Ceiling as a surface to be decorated with a rhythmic pattern of figures and geometrical compartments, to that of the vault as a simple support for a system of images that are in many ways independent of the surface itself. The program is extremely complicated on both the formal and the iconographic level. We know from drawings in the British Museum in London and The Detroit Institute of Arts that in a matter of a few months or perhaps just weeks, Michelangelo went far beyond even the most advanced contemporary solutions for ceiling decoration, such as Pintoricchio's vault at S. Maria del Popolo in Rome or the ceiling in the Stanza della Segnatura in the Vatican Palace, and developed a completely new type. He himself described his initial project, saying "the first idea for this work was for twelve apostles in the lunettes and for the rest a kind of division into compartments filled with decorations popular at that time."[3] Michelangelo's ultimate solution emphasized the rhythmic and even the illusionistic values of the painted architectural system, enlarged the fields at the center of the Ceiling that were destined for narrative scenes, and, most notably, included other figures besides the giant Apostles, soon to be transformed into Prophets and Sibyls. These figures are of various dimensions and carry different meanings within the iconographic program of the Ceiling, yet they acquire a basic significance precisely because they define the formal, metrical arrangement of the image as a whole.

Scholars have paid more attention to the transformation and the elaboration of the iconographic program than to the development of this com-

plex, metrical structure. The vast critical debate on the meaning of the Ceiling and on the different levels of interpretation has spawned research and produced theories concerning the identification of sources and possible theological advisers to the artist. If Michelangelo himself was responsible for the change in the Ceiling's program, then it is possible that formal considerations were paramount. In any case such is the correlation between meaning and the images—the latter not so much explaining the former as giving it shape and order in a peremptory way—that there can be no doubt that the perfecting of the iconographic program and the definition of the formal structure were closely interwoven and evolved in the form of a dialogue. Adjustments and adaptations were most likely made as work proceeded but always on the basis of an extremely clear and powerfully structured initial vision.

Unlike the British Museum drawing, the Detroit drawing shows very clearly the fictive arches that span the vault; these arches point out the architectonic tension in the Ceiling decoration and become the determining factor in the rhythmic scanning of the space. There are small rectangular fields at the center of the arches; they are flanked by oval compartments whose frames are supported by small figures on either side. These figures stand over the niches intended to contain the images of Apostles or Prophets. The arches with their smaller rectangular compartments alternate with larger areas clearly meant for narrative scenes, although they are still surrounded by octagonal frames that preserve the prevailing taste for ornamental, geometric compartments.

The solution Michelangelo finally adopted is a development of an idea found in the Detroit drawing. There are, however, important variations in the final design. The arches are larger and more forceful, and consequently the fields contained between them increase in size. Michelangelo abandoned the octagonal frames of the larger intermediate areas, making them rectangular, and, finally, he substituted dynamic figures of *ignudi,* or nude youths, for the static putti holding inscription panels. The inclusion of these nudes in the formal and iconographic program of the Ceiling seems to have come only during the last stage of planning the decoration. The Prophets and Sibyls are placed higher up in the final scheme, allowing them more space and greater monumentality. These figures, with the *ignudi* and various elements of the fictive architecture, confirm the strong influence that the ideas and motifs from the first project for the tomb of Julius II exercised during the decisive phase in structuring the Ceiling's overall program.

Since the writing of Vasari's and Condivi's descriptions of Michelangelo's program, both of them precise and astute but seemingly in disagreement because they stressed different aspects of the Ceiling,[4] the discussion about the presence and relevance of illusionistic elements in the fictive architectural framework of the Ceiling—beyond that of its relation to the real architecture of the Chapel—has given rise to a variety of different readings and interpretations. The root of the problem is probably a studied ambiguity of the background, brilliantly discussed by Johannes Wilde,[5] which confounds any attempt at a systematic reconstruction of the actual space designed by Michelangelo. The use of illusionistic devices, obvious in several parts of the Ceiling and especially in the openings to the sky above the figures of Zechariah and Jonah at each end of the Chapel, does not at all imply a desire to create an authentically and completely illusionistic structure. This would have been impossible given the dimensions of the painted surface, and in any case it was contradicted by the representation of the figures frontally rather than foreshortened from below. The result is an unprecedented and accurately calculated mixing of illusionistic elements with a system of compartments, intended to give the simultaneous impression of absolute structural unity and a clear articulation of the parts. The clearly defined formal and expressive qualities—gestures and movement, in the narrative scenes as well as in the Prophets, Sibyls, and *ignudi*—also permit a high degree of legibility. It has been astutely observed with regard to the recent cleaning of the frescoes that the tones and juxtapositions of color that Michelangelo chose work toward the same end, even suggesting that he assigned color a structural function.[6]

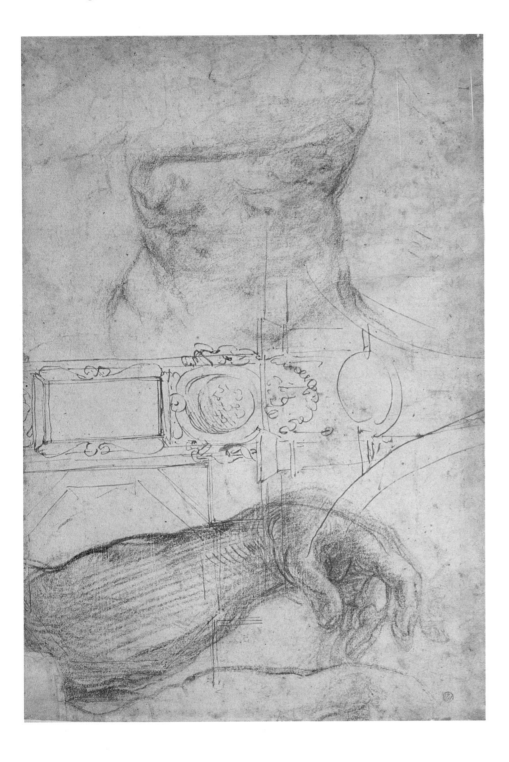

The painted architectural framework guarantees unity through symmetry and repetition; the metrical variations follow a rigorous and musical rhythm (a-b-a-b-a-b-a-b-a), beginning at the entrance wall and moving toward the altar. The figures that fall outside any narrative context underscore this pattern, emphasizing the elements of variation. Above all else, however, they give the symmetrical background-structure a powerful vitality and animation, separating and articulating the succession of images and arranging themselves according to a series of transverse axes—almost bay by bay—that complements the reading of the Genesis scenes along the longitudinal axis.

The degree to which these figures are incorporated into the architectural framework varies depending on the type of figure. The essentially symmetrical pairs of putti flanking the thrones of the Prophets and Sibyls, painted to imitate stone relief and supporting the cornice that breaks forward above them, are the most integrated. Despite their sometimes remarkably dynamic poses, the so-called bronze nudes, located at the same level as the putti and flanking the animal skulls at the peaks of the spandrels, are distinguished by the fact that the figures in each pair are mirror images of each other. The huge Prophets and Sibyls present a lively contrast to these images; they are "natural" and clearly individuated by gesture, pose, and expression.

On the level above, nearer the center of the vault, we find ten pairs of nude youths seated on plinths who turn toward the transverse axis of the smaller narrative fields and support the bronze medallions and garlands of

oak leaves. They seem to belong to an intermediate reality between the strong physical and psychological individualization of the Prophets and Sibyls and the minor figures, which are represented as sculpture and are assimilated into the architectural framework.

The first two *ignudi,* to the left of the *Drunkenness of Noah,* are rigorous mirror-images of each other, while the two pairs around the *Sacrifice of Noah* are only partially symmetrical. The lower parts of the figures on the left are mirror images, but in the torsion of the chest and head the principle of *contrapposto* prevails. Both figures, however, extend their inside arm

Above: Bronze nudes above the Jesse-David-Solomon *lunette.*

Below: Bronze nudes above the Roboam-Abias *lunette.*

toward the center to hold the medallion ribbon. The two figures on the right lean outward symmetrically, differing only in the placement of the arms they extend in toward the Ceiling. In the following pairs variety and *contrapposto* slowly prevail over mirror images. At the same time that the size and dynamic conception of the figures increase, the relationship in each pair depends on rhythmic correspondences that are ever freer and more complex and liberated from any concern for symmetry. The importance and effectiveness of the relationship between the figures can be appreciated, by way of contrast, in Adamo Scultori's otherwise faithful

illustrations of single figures taken out of their context.

The choice of pose is connected to the function and different levels of meaning—formal as much as iconographic—associated with each group of figures. The putti flanking the thrones move with gracefully choreographed dance steps that recall, with fresh insight, a repertory of motifs specific to the glazed terra-cotta reliefs that decorate choir lofts. The poses of the bronze nudes, enclosed in narrow triangular fields that seem to excite the artist's love for *difficoltà*, or complexity, in his inventions, are often forced, affected, or even acrobatic.

It is significant that the praise Vasari, in his description of the Sistine Ceiling, lavishes on Michelangelo's supreme ability to paint the human body reaches its climax in the passage on the *ignudi* and their "beautiful attitudes [which] differ in all, some are seated, others are in motion, while others again are supporting festoons of oak-leaves and acorns...."[7] The movements and poses of the *ignudi* are free not only of the requirements and conventions of narrative painting, but also of specific expressive demands or of any need to demonstrate a spiritual state through the physical, which is the case even with single figures such as the Prophets and Sibyls. The poses of the *ignudi* appear to be governed exclusively by the rhythmic relationships generated and formed by the complementary placement of pairs, the succession of figures, and, more generally, by their structural relationship to the Ceiling as a whole.

As in the case with the Prisoners planned for the Julius tomb (which are also strictly related to an architectural framework), this coordinated sequence of figures introduces the principle of variations on a predefined scheme—here the seated, nude male figure holding the ribbon of a medallion. The variations obtained by modifying the relationships between limbs—the inclination of chest and pelvis, twisting the head and/or the chest itself, the placement of limbs, or the effects of tensed or relaxed muscles—gave Michelangelo the best opportunity to demonstrate his knowledge of anatomy and his supreme mastery of the representation of the human body. Many of his contemporaries, including Vasari, recognized in the inspired beauty of his figures the apex of Michelangelo's talents as an artist. In addition these variations created the unbroken rhythm, figure to figure and bay to bay, which so powerfully animates the Ceiling, making it a unified image, and at the same time allows the viewer to scan the vault in a clearer temporal sequence. The *ignudi,* by extolling the beauty of the human body, considered the culmination of divine creation,[8] also demonstrate to the highest degree the conception of the body as perfect architecture, which through the continued variation of poses is complete, complex, dynamic, and expressive. This variety reveals the infinite possibilities for the correlation of members in a system that nonetheless preserves unaltered its absolute structural and organic coherence, becoming model and metaphor of every artistic creation.

The recent cleaning and restoration of the Sistine frescoes resulted in numerous important discoveries about Michelangelo's technique, his working procedure, and the length of time he took to paint various parts of the Ceiling. Among other things, we learned that while the *ignudi* of the first bays were systematically painted after the narrative scenes from the *Creation of Eve* forward, Michelangelo executed these nudes before the corresponding Genesis story. Such a change in working method should be evaluated in relation to the others instituted during the second phase of work on the Ceiling, that is, after the scaffolding had been taken down and rebuilt to paint the second half of the vault, and, especially important, after the artist had had the chance to see and study from the floor what he had so far completed.

The structure of the vault itself, polycentric and irregular in its dimensions, which increase toward the altar wall, forced considerable adjustments in the decorative, metrical scheme designed at the beginning of the project and in particular in the dimensions of the figures, which become ever larger. Yet, beyond getting bigger, as do the Prophets and Sibyls, the *ignudi* on the second half of the Ceiling also tend to project beyond the architectural frames of the narrative panels, invading the picture fields themselves. They assume a dynamic, plastic relief that is decidedly more monumental than that of the *ignudi* in the first bays.

It has been said many times that the interruption in the painting of the vault between the summers of 1510 and 1511 and the opportunity of seeing the frescoes from the floor contributed to Michelangelo's shift to a larger scale and a more rapid pace of execution. He also abandoned his

Michelangelo, Dusk, *Tomb of Lorenzo de'Medici. Medici Chapel, S. Lorenzo, Florence.*

concern for defining details and concentrated on the overall effect, moving from a structure based largely on the articulation and coordination of parts to their definite subordination to a much more dynamic and unitary image. With the emphasis on the visible relief given the *ignudi* in the last bays, the "beauty of the compartments" and the "diversity of poses"[9] were further imbued with a polyphonic effect which is more complex, in which the individual elements receive greater emphasis, and which, at the same time, is more consolidated and compact. Michelangelo's figures seem only to acquire their full formal value and expressive meaning when inserted into a structure that transcends them, arranging them in a metrical system of precise rhythmic relationships, and that contributes, on the other hand, to the variation and complexity of these rhythms in order "to avoid the sense of surfeit which comes from sameness."[10] The integration of architectural framework and painted or sculpted figures is a constant in the middle years of Michelangelo's artistic career, appearing first in the initial projects for the Julius tomb, then in the Sistine Ceiling and the design for the facade of S. Lorenzo, and finally in the New Sacristy and the Medici tombs.

During this period Michelangelo conceived his figures and his architectural framework simultaneously in an efficacious and inextricable plastic-expressive interaction, in syntactical systems that point at the same time to the highest degree of complexity and articulation—that is, to a powerful individualization of the parts—and to an extreme organic unity. These elements are always combined, and they lend themselves to both immediate understanding and analytical contemplation. In both cases, however, they are controlled by a rhythm that is fixed and absolute. It seems significant in this regard that when one of the two elements (the figures) is missing, as in the vestibule of the Laurentian Library, its absence is in a certain sense compensated by charging the architectural framework itself with expressive or emotional values. This game of contrasts and tensions involved the introduction of *licenza,* or license, into the canonical system of the orders. Artists, according to Vasari, "were under great obligation to Michelangelo, seeing that he [had] thus broken the barriers and chains whereby they were perpetually compelled to walk in a beaten path."[11]

The scope of the transformation of artistic language is fully evident, however, only in the dramatic contrast between the frescoes of the Sistine Ceiling and the *Last Judgment,* painted some thirty years later. In the *Last Judgment* Michelangelo deliberately refused any architectonic "support" for his image, arriving, through successive planning phases, at a conception of this fresco that was almost in opposition to the spatial configuration of the Chapel as it was defined over a period of forty years, from Sixtus IV to Leo X. Nor did he avoid changing the lighting of the Chapel or upsetting the rhythmic continuity of the walls by eliminating compartments and frames, by literally cutting away the facade on which he was preparing to paint his vision of the end of time.

In the long iconographic tradition of the *Last Judgment,* the subject was presented as a solidly structured image, arranged according to a system of calculated symmetries and correspondences, which was read vertically in two orders. There was a clear distinction between the heavenly zone, with the figure of Christ judging flanked by the Virgin, John the Baptist, and the college of judges consisting of the Apostles amid bands of angels, saints, and patriarchs; and the terrestrial zone, with the resurrection of the flesh and the separation of the Elect and the Damned. This kind of representation of the *Last Judgment* had evolved slowly and in relation to the very nature and profound meaning of the image, conceived as a metaphor of the universal order and of a fixed and immutable divine design. Michelangelo used this structure as his point of departure, but dismantled it, progressively negating the architectonic system of superimposed bands and moving toward a whirling composition based on the interconnected and opposing movements of individuals and groups of figures.

Michelangelo, Dawn, *Tomb of Lorenzo de' Medici Medici Chapel, S. Lorenzo, Florence.*

The background of the fresco represents an undetermined and undeterminable space. It completely lacks any elements that allow it to be measured, yet its profundity is suggested by the foreshortened figures, the figural groups that recede in perspective, the improvised differences in proportion, and the relationships of color and light, whose full impact is being revealed by the present restoration. Against this background a "second reality" opens abruptly from the real, coherent, and measured space of the Chapel. The syntax of the bodies alone defines the structure of the image painted on this vast wall as well as the rhythmic relationships between its

separate parts. It also determines its meaning on a figurative level and especially its very strong emotional impact on the viewer.

In the absence both of an architectural counterpoint and a solid structural articulation of an image defined by a long iconographic tradition, the study of the poses in the representation of the *Last Judgment* can no longer be based on the principle of variation nor on single figures, even if conceived in rhythmic relationships and in succession. It must depend, rather, on the interwoven movements and the dynamic coordination of figural groups. Michelangelo painted over an enormous field composite schemes

Last Judgment, *detail of the Judging Christ and, next to him, the Virgin, John the Baptist, and a multitude of the Elect.*

he had been experimenting with since his youthful *Battle of the Centaurs* relief, in the cartoon for the *Battle of Cascina,* and in some of the more complicated narrative scenes on the Ceiling, such as the *Deluge* or the corner scenes depicting the *Brazen Serpent* and the *Punishment of Haman.*

In effect, Michelangelo's particular conception of the *Last Judgment* as an event taking place directly and dramatically before the eyes of the spectator transformed an essentially atemporal and eternal image into a narrative painting, a representation of an event under way. He had to translate the formal image into a dynamic structure that depends on the eloquence of

the human body, on unequivocal gestures in certain key places, such as those of the Judging Christ, St. Peter, and Charon. The composition relies on a number of elements: the infinite variety of poses and their connections and contradictions; the contrast between movement on the surface and into depth; the impression of the instantaneous gathering and dispersion, like storm clouds across the sky, of the groups of the Blessed pressing against Christ and the Virgin, of the wingless angels who carry the instruments of the Passion aloft with difficulty, as if defying the force of a maelstrom threatening to carry them away, and of the bodies freeing themselves

Left: Last Judgment, *detail of the Damned.*
Right: Last Judgment, *detail of the ascent of the Elect.*

233

Last Judgment, *detail of Charon's boat.*

with great effort from the earth, ascending, hovering suspended in the void, struggling violently, or falling toward the fiery abyss. The nudity of these figures, which can certainly be read as the redemption of the body on the glorious day of the resurrection of the flesh, must have seemed to the artist an essential instrument of the formal organization and expressive development of the image.

One can certainly understand how Vasari could say that here Michelangelo achieved the "perfection of art," the culmination of all his previous experiments in representing the human body in motion, with the "greatest possible variety of poses and strange and dissimilar gestures," up to the full affirmation of their intrinsic expressive value: "…the number of figures, with the grandeur and dignity of the composition, are such, while the expression of every passion proper to humanity is so fully and so wonderfully expressed, that no words could do the work justice."[12]

Similarly, Condivi articulated the decisive importance of the representation of the human body in the *Last Judgment* at the beginning of his description of the fresco: "in this work Michelangelo expressed all that the art of painting can do with the human figure, leaving out no attitude or gesture whatever." In his conclusion he reaffirms, "[suffice] it to say that, apart from the sublime composition of the narrative, we see represented here all that nature can do with the human body."[13]

These two descriptions are complementary in a significant way: they praise the results of the artist's creative abilities and the successful imitation of nature itself, both at the moment of execution (Vasari) and on contemplation of the finished work (Condivi). However, there was opposition to the *Last Judgment,* and it seems inevitable that it was precisely the representation of the human body that became the focal point for the accusations of obscenity and the more specifically formal criticisms of Michelangelo's supposed demonstration of scandalous, or at least monotonous, "anatomical virtuosity." There seems to be a common root to these accusations and criticisms[14] in the resounding alarm at the "catastrophic" image Michelangelo painted in the Sistine Chapel, in the reaction to his extreme expressiveness and his genius, or what Vasari called his *terribilità,* and to the scene's unprecedented structural organization. Michelangelo seemed to some to force the rules themselves, to overturn the syntactical foundations of Renaissance figural language. The results of his radical vision were destined to find more fertile ground in and more passionate and understanding devotion by artists later in history, from Peter Paul Rubens to Théodore Géricault and Eugène Delacroix.

Last Judgment, *detail of the Damned in the lower left corner of the fresco.*

The *Last Judgment*: Notes on Its Conservation History, Technique, and Restoration

Fabrizio Mancinelli,
Gianluigi Colalucci,
and Nazzareno Gabrielli

Historical Notes

The documentation concerning the conservation history of the *Last Judgment* was and remains scarce despite the research undertaken over the last few years. Documented interventions after the sixteenth century are very few, and the restorations carried out in the Sistine Chapel under Popes Urban VIII (1623–43) and Clement XI (1700–21) seem not to have included the *Last Judgment*. This can perhaps be explained by the fact that the fresco, because of its particular nature—its location on the altar wall and because it was within easy reach—must surely have been carefully and constantly maintained. Certainly this was true under Paul III, who by *motu proprio* in 1543 created the office of *mundator,* or cleaner, charged with the responsibility of "cleaning away the dust and other kinds of dirt, as previously mentioned, from the paintings in the said chapel of Sixtus, both those on the ceiling of events fulfilled and those on the wall of events prophesied, and to make all efforts to keep them free from dirt."[1] The *mundatores* are documented as active through the pontificate of Gregory XIII (1572–85). Thereafter the documents refer to a *custos,* who most likely had an assistant, although we cannot be certain when precisely this office was established.

Aside from this ordinary maintenance, the sixteenth-century interventions on the *Last Judgment* were not restorations so much as tamperings with the fresco. These censorious interventions were undertaken under Pius IV and perhaps also under Pius V, following the decree of the Council of Trent laid down on 21 January 1564. Michelangelo, who died on 18 February 1564, less than a month after the Council's decision, never saw the consequences of its order.

The payment made to Daniele da Volterra's heirs in 1567 for the work he did on the *Last Judgment*—Daniele had died the year before, strangely, like Michelangelo, on 18 February—seems to indicate that his intervention took place in 1565, since this is the date indicated in the document. This intervention was planned during the preceding months; the first payment for the scaffolding was made on 23 August 1564 to the Florentine carpenter Master Zanobio di Mariotto. We know that this payment was for the *Last Judgment* because the next payment, on 7 September—this time for the necessary wood—records explicitly "17 scudi and 60 baiocchi paid for other wood taken away to make the scaffolding on the *Last Judgment* wall in

Opposite: Tests in progress for the cleaning of the Last Judgment.

Sixtus's Chapel."[2] After the advance he was given in August, Zanobio was paid on 12 November and again on 20 January, 7 April (when a second purchase of wood was also made), and 23 June 1565. He received the balance, including payment for dismantling the scaffolding, on 8 December 1565.

The final payment includes a clear description of what sort of scaffolding was used. The document says, in fact, that it was 42 palmi (30 ft. 11½ in. [9.42 m]) high, essentially covering half the *Last Judgment*, built in three stages one above the other, the first entirely covered with planks, with a door to climb through, this scaffold being 12 palmi (8 ft. 9½ in. [2.68 m]) deep and 60 palmi (43 ft. 11½ in. [13.4 m]) wide, essentially the width of the wall, with a parapet in front and curtains pulled in front of that, and four marble stairs.[3] This document also specifies that the scaffolding was dismantled afterward, evidently before 8 December.

It is unclear how many figures Daniele da Volterra worked on. Bottari, in his commentary on Vasari's *Life of Michelangelo,* maintained that Daniele did not finish the task assigned to him and that after his death, "St. Pius V gave the job, at Cardinal Rusticucci's request, to Girolamo da Fano." So far no documentary evidence has been discovered which confirms this. It is a fact, however, that while the repainting of St. Blaise and the partial reworking of St. Catherine were executed in fresco after Michelangelo's original plaster was removed, the other interventions were all painted with tempera. This as well as evident qualitative differences and different ultraviolet florescences suggests that different artists worked at different times to cover the nude figures of the *Last Judgment*.

The many sixteenth-century drawings and engravings, apparently derived from the original fresco and not from copies, that reproduce several figures without their loincloths long after Daniele's death make it quite clear that censorious interventions were undertaken on the *Last Judgment* at various points in time. Examples include Ambrogio Figino's drawing of Minos, dated circa 1586, Federico Zuccari's drawing of his brother Taddeo copying the *Last Judgment,* probably executed after 1590, as well as some of Cherubino Ruberti's engravings, particularly his 1591 series. Furthermore, the loincloth covering St. Peter's nudity is a repainting of an earlier drapery that is still discernible underneath. This confirms that there were several interventions and that they were undertaken at different times. They continued at least into the eighteenth century, when J. Richard noted in his *Description historique et critique de l'Italie* that he had seen in 1762 "some very mediocre artists working to cover with draperies the most beautiful nude figures on the wall and on the ceiling."

There is no documentary evidence for the work some say was undertaken under Gregory XIII to raise the level of the floor around the altar, with the consequent loss of a strip of fresco at the bottom of the *Last Judgment*. In Ambrogio Brambilla's 1582 engraving depicting the Sistine Chapel during a papal mass, however, as well as in the first state of Vaccari's 1578 print, there are four steps leading up to the altar, as there are now, while according to Paris De Grassis there were originally three. Nonetheless, as John Shearman has noted, the addition of a step, which certainly happened, does not necessarily imply that the level of the floor pavement changed. We find confirmation of Shearman's interpretation, at least for the period after the painting of the *Last Judgment,* in the fact that the plaster of Michelangelo's fresco overlaps the marble door frame to the right of the altar, which now connects the Chapel with the stairs going down to St. Peter's and which in the fifteenth century—the door frame bears the coat of arms of Alexander VI (1492–1503)—led into the sacristy. The door to the left of the altar, which today opens into the sacristy, offers further evidence. It was broken through either during or after the pontificate of Julius III (1550–55), since it was under this pope that the floor of the sacristy vestibule was raised to the level of the altar, thus creating in the space below a well for the stair leading to St. Peter's. The coat of arms we see on the architrave is Clement XI's, but it is not original to the door frame and was added to it after the preexisting arms were removed.

The creation of this door, whenever it occurred, prompted the destruction, or at least the repainting, of the base, which according to the documents Perin del Vaga had painted under Michelangelo's fresco at the end of 1542. A payment dated 15 November of that year tells us that a certain Giovanni Battista Olgiatto was paid "for the cloth he provided for the cartoon made by Master Pierino, painter, for the base running underneath the painting by Messer Michelangelo in Sixtus's chapel."[4] The present base, usually dated to the eighteenth century although in reality it is difficult to say and it seems older, offers no significant clues except that it reaches the level of the architrave of the original door, which itself seems not to have been raised. Thus it seems unlikely that Michelangelo's fresco was mutilated in the way that past comparisons with Venusti's copy of the *Last Judgment* have suggested. The present state of the fresco seems to vary little, moreover, from the situation recorded by certain engraved copies, such as those by Bonasone and Ghisi, both executed after 1545.

As far as the period after the sixteenth century is concerned, we know that between November 1662 and February 1663 restructuring work was undertaken in the area around the altar, specifically "on the marble stairs of the throne and the altar of the chapel,"[5] although it seems that the preexisting situation was not modified. The documents are so far silent on any restorations of the *Last Judgment* in the seventeenth century. Those which concern Lagi's interventions in the Chapel between 1625 and 1628 deal exclusively with the fourteen scenes from the lives of Moses and Christ on the lateral walls, the figures of the Popes above, and the backs and the chiaroscuro bases of the seats below.

Mazzuoli's intervention, undertaken from 1710 to 1712, like Lagi's and the others under Clement XI, apparently did not include the altar wall. Mazzuoli restored the biblical stories, the Popes, and the Ceiling, while Germisoni and Pietro Paolo Cristofani repainted the fictive tapestries on the lower register of the walls.

According to eighteenth-century sources, however, a restoration of the *Last Judgment* was planned. Taia furnishes a series of extremely important clues about the fresco's state of conservation. He wrote, "Certainly the saltpeter, the dust and humidity (if corrective measures are not immediately undertaken) could in a few years reduce these excellent paintings to an irreparable state, as has evidently happened from year to year, especially in the *Last Judgment,* which is cracking and producing at various places ugly stains of white niter, calcinating the color itself."[6] It is unclear what Taia was referring to when he spoke of white nitrate stains and calcinated colors, or what he meant when he said that the phenomenon occurred "from year to year." Nonetheless, since it is impossible that seeping rainwater was the cause, one might assume that he was talking of the same damage identified by Vincenzo Camuccini in 1825. The latter noted in particular the damage to the sky (the "horizon") above the group of souls rising from the dead and Charon's barge. He reported this to the Academy of St. Luke, saying specifically that "there was once a time when unintentionally they tried to destroy this masterpiece by applying a strong corrosive agent across the entire painting." That this corrosive agent was indeed applied, provoking the damage now visible, was confirmed, as we will see below, during the present restoration. When this happened is less clear. If the whitening is the same as that reported by Taia, then it is likely that this destructive intervention dates back to an undocumented restoration of the seventeenth or the very early eighteenth century. If, on the other hand, it is something else, then its source might be found in the 1762 intervention noted by Richard in his *Description historique et critique de l'Italie* and which might be linked with Stefano Pozzi.

Camuccini's observations were made after a test cleaning undertaken on

Overleaf: View of the Last Judgment *before the cleaning and a diagram of the patches on it, which were executed in both true fresco and a secco.*

◼ ◼ ◼ ◼   *Additions made in secco*   ▨▨▨▨   *Patches repainted in fresco*

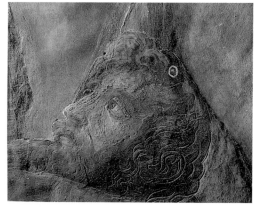

the group of angels carrying the Column of the Passion in the right lunette with a possible restoration of the entire fresco in mind. Called on to evaluate the artist's work, the Academy of St. Luke rejected this possibility, not so much because it criticized the results of the trial cleaning, which it judged positively, but because it feared that the undertaking might make more evident the damage provoked by earlier restoration and noted by Camuccini himself. After this attempt to clean the *Last Judgment,* the only one actually documented, the subject of further restoration was not raised again until the present day. Seitz's intervention in 1903 and Biagetti's in 1935–36 were undertaken only to consolidate the plaster. The accusations that Biagetti had emphasized the white "scorch marks" by too forceful a cleaning are totally unfounded since no cleaning was undertaken.

The State of Conservation

The surface area of the *Last Judgment* measures 591 square feet, or 180.21 square meters (this figure was calculated by a computer based on photogrammetrical reliefs). Its state of conservation is extremely varied due to the number of successive interventions over the centuries. This lack of a homogeneous surface is made especially clear by the tonal discontinuity across the painting. The lowest level, with the Resurrected Souls and the Damned descending from Charon's barge, has darkened considerably, and even more so in comparison with the sky above, which was greatly lightened in the past due to the corrosive agents referred to by Camuccini. The central part of the composition is also extremely dark, particularly in the peripheral band of figures, including the group of saints and the Elect surrounding Christ and the Virgin. The two lunettes above are markedly lighter and more legible. The reason the lunette with the column is easier to read is certainly due to the cleaning Camuccini undertook in this area in 1825. Similar circumstances might explain the state of conservation of the left lunette. The same is true of the much-retouched group of the Elect behind St. Peter, even though the artist stated that he had worked only on the group of angels in the right lunette.

Besides being extremely dark, the painted surface has been stained and made opaque by foreign substances, predominantly animal glues, which provide the ideal conditions for the development of microorganisms. Colonies of fungus are especially prevalent on the upper part of the wall, and their removal leaves small, round stains that are lighter in color than the surrounding area because the fungi have reached even the patina closest to the pigment.

Past restorers added small amounts of vegetable oil to the glue—or more correctly the glue water ("acqua di colla")—that was used to brighten the darkened colors. The oil served both to make the glue easier to work and to reinforce the glue's capacity to revivify the fresco's colors. In some cases it seems that oil alone was applied, again with the intention of intensifying the tones. Where the plaster was more porous the oil was absorbed, but in many instances it remained on the surface, creating irregularly shaped stains and channels along the craquelure of the plaster.

The film of foreign matter across the *Last Judgment* is very uneven. Where it is thicker, the surface appears dark and vitreous, and where it is thinner, the painting is brighter and dry. The fresco did not suffer from seeping rainwater because the wall was protected by the Sacristy rooms immediately behind it. This is most likely the reason less glue was applied to this fresco in past restorations than to the Ceiling. The consistency of the layers is therefore noticeably thinner, especially in comparison to the stratum of glue on the lunettes.

Numerous areas of retouching are evident across the fresco, all of them of low quality at best. There are also many patches of test cleanings or traces of attempts to clean the painting, all, with the exception of Camuccini's, undocumented. It is impossible, therefore, to date them, although they are presumably relatively recent. The retouchings can be divided into two general categories: those executed with full-bodied color and often covering Michelangelo's *pentimenti*, or corrections, which have created chalky, dull masses of dark brown color; and those executed with small, dark, monochromatic, semitransparent and usually cross-hatched brush-strokes that were intended to reinforce shadings and to recover the modeling of figures flattened by the veil of altered foreign matter.

The plaster itself is in very good condition. The only area where it was seriously detached from the wall was under the marble bracket. The absence of the bronze or brass clamps that were so numerous on the Ceiling confirms that there were no static difficulties in the past, with the exception of the problems in the sixteenth century affecting the architectural structure itself. The latter most likely explain the long crack that runs across the painting at a slight diagonal. It begins in the lower center part of the fresco, splits in two at several places, and finally branches out into small cracks that end around the group of angels holding the column. As on the Ceiling, these cracks were sealed with a black putty of wax and hard resin, perhaps at the time of the intervention by da Volterra and Girolamo da Fano. The uneven and varied condition of the painted surface might suggest that the original painting has very much deteriorated. Instead we can confirm that for the most part Michelangelo's fresco is preserved in excellent condition.

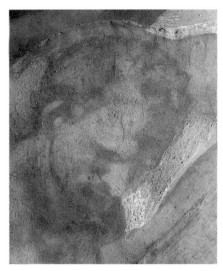

The group of angels blowing trumpets and holding up the book of the Last Judgment has suffered mechanical damage. The rings that held the metal supports for the baldachin, which until the middle of this century was normally raised above the altar for solemn occasions, can still be seen beside the angels. The poles used to raise the baldachin and the edges of the fittings themselves scratched and abraded the entire area, especially the angels on the right, and among these, particularly the one holding its trumpet on its shoulder. The black lines of the preparatory drawing are now visible in several of the damaged areas on the face of this figure.

The broad expanse of blue sky that serves as a backdrop for the protagonists of the *Last Judgment* presents an extremely complex and unique situation. Here the color is divided into zones, noticeably different in shape and tonality, by very light lines that follow the seams of the *giornate,* or days' work. Scholars have often debated the possible reasons for these whitish lines, but no convincing solution has been offered. The most recent examination of the fresco revealed the significant fact that *secco* retouchings are present along the *giornate* seams; some of them may be original and others, because their color does not match its surroundings, are clearly restorations.

The sky was painted in fresco (color applied to wet plaster) with lapis lazuli, a precious yet extremely delicate pigment, and then finished *a secco* (on dry plaster) with the same color. Only a few traces of the finishing work remain, and they now appear almost black, caused in part by the dirt overlaying it and in part by the deterioration of their glue binder. The sky, for reasons explained above, is divided into several zones. The upper band is lighter and clearly defined below by the undulating line of *giornate* seams. The center band is darker and tends toward gray. The lowest zone, just above the horizon, is extremely light. The surface, as compact as slate, is almost entirely grooved by a series of generally horizontal brushstrokes. These are dense and fine above, but they become wider and very light until they are almost white where they touch the figures crowded on the earth below.

Originally it was thought that these bands, which have virtually no

Top: Last Judgment, *detail of the Elect to the left of Christ. The irregular dark spots are the result of retouchings in oil, applied for a brightening effect.*

Above: Last Judgment, *detail of the cross-hatched strokes applied to touch up the body of one of the angels surrounding the Flagellation group. For this retouching, dark paint was applied in short brushstrokes.*

Right: Last Judgment, *detail of the touch-ups in brown applied to the shoulder of the so-called St. Andrew.*

thickness at all (in the past this phenomenon was attributed to the action of lime that was not sufficiently spent), might be due to an application of an acidulated substance, brushed on during a cleaning in the seventeenth or eighteenth century (judging from the reports of Taia and Camuccini) to lighten the veil of foreign matter deposited over Michelangelo's sky and thus to reinforce the modeling of the figures. Moreover, since wine had been used to clean Raphael's Stanze and the Sistine Ceiling, it was also suggested that the agent responsible for the damage to the *Last Judgment* was an acidic wine, that is, one that was turning to vinegar.

Later investigations carried out in collaboration with Giovanni Torraca proved this hypothesis to be groundless. It was found that a weak acid like vinegar, which can be found in nature also in this form, cannot discolor lapis lazuli. Further research and observations seem to suggest that these bands are the remains, or better, the mark, of lost *secco* finishing work. Originally they must have been intended to strengthen certain areas of the sky and, especially at the bottom, to hide the seams between *giornate*. This finishing work must have had a certain thickness; it may have been lost in part during the seventeenth- and eighteenth-century cleanings and in part for mechanical reasons linked to the periodic dustings that continued until the middle of this century.

To the list of damages suffered by the blues we should add those suffered by the pigments applied *a secco* and those that were painted in fresco but

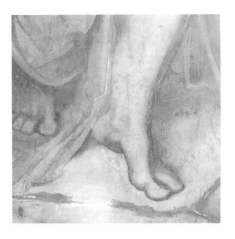

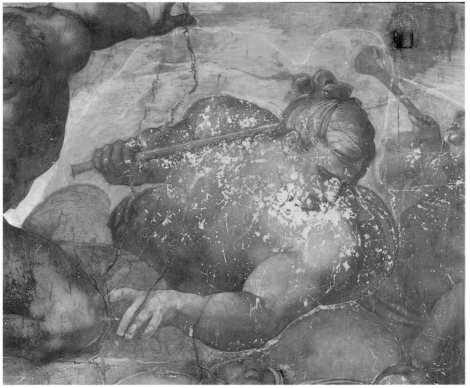

did not carbonize well and were therefore weak and not cohesive. In both cases past cleanings precipitated the loss of considerable quantities of color. The slight flaking of pigment in the areas repainted by Daniele da Volterra was caused, on the other hand, not by old restorations but by the contraction of the glue layer due to variations in the climatic conditions in the Chapel. The different technique Daniele used to apply his color was also a contributing factor.

Above: Last Judgment, *one of the demons below Charon's boat viewed in raking light. It is possible to make out the lines of indirect incision by which the cartoon was transferred to the wall and, in the lower right-hand corner, the* pentimenti *in the foot of one of the Damned.*
Right: Last Judgment, *detail showing the seams between* giornate *directly below* Jonah *before the cleaning.*

Michelangelo's Technique and the Relative Documents

The information we have about the painting of the Ceiling comes almost exclusively from indirect sources, most often Michelangelo's own correspondence. Payments for the *Last Judgment,* on the other hand, are numerous and provide extremely accurate information about Michelangelo's salary as well as about the pigments and scaffolding used.[7] The payments for the scaffolding and the preparatory operations extended over more than a year, from 16 April 1535 to the end of April 1536. The length and difficulty of this period was due in large part, according to Vasari, to disagreements between Michelangelo and Sebastiano del Piombo. Vasari says that Sebastiano persuaded the pope "to have it done in oils, while Michelagnolo did not wish to do it except in fresco. As Michelagnolo did not declare himself one way or the other, the wall was prepared in Sebastiano's fashion, several months passed and nothing was done, but on being approached, Michelagnolo declared that he would only do it in fresco, and that oil-painting was a woman's art and only fit for lazy and well-to-do people like Fra Sebastiano. Accordingly he removed the incrustation made by the friar's direction, and prepared everything for work in fresco."[8]

Vasari's account is confirmed by the documents. The demolition of the "first plaster of the facade" took place on 25 January 1536, fully nine months after work began. The payment to the brickmaker Giovanni Fachino for the bricks to be used for the curtain wall in front of the altar wall was made on 13 February of the same year. The payments for pigments began on 18 May 1536 and attest to a series of acquisitions that continue later, during the period when the Pauline Chapel was painted. These orders for the disbursement of funds are rather general; they record the amount paid but not the specific color purchased. An exception is made for the blues, which are almost always the extremely expensive lapis lazuli, or ultramarine, purchased the first time in Venice and then in Ferrara, the native city of the commissar of papal works, Jacopo Meleghino, who handled all such payments. On 21 November 1537 ten pounds of azurite, called "azuro todescho" (German blue) in the documents, were ordered from Ferrara—the only exception, it seems, to orders for ultramarine.

The brick curtain-wall Michelangelo had built offered him a support very different from the tufa of the Ceiling. It was laid at the beginning of 1536, and it projected almost 9 in. (24 cm) in front of the preexisting wall. This is more or less the figure Vasari reported: "Michelangelo now caused an addition to be made to the wall of the Chapel, a sort of escarpment, carefully built of well-burnt and nicely chosen bricks, and projecting half a braccio at the summit, in such sort that no dust or other soil could lodge on the work."[9] It seems unlikely, however, that this was the reason the wall curved slightly outward. The optical effect it created is the more likely reason, given the attention the artist paid to the foreshortening of his figures and their complex placement in space, not to mention the characteristics of the *pentimenti*.

As on the Ceiling, a layer of finer plaster, the *intonaco,* was laid over the rougher *arriccio,* but here no final and even thinner coat of plaster, or

intonachino, was laid. The latter is sometimes replaced by a white or whitish preparatory ground. The area of the sky was prepared with a thin glaze of red ocher so light that it seems almost pink. The *arriccio* is about ¼ in. (7 mm) thick, and the *intonaco* about ⅛ in. (4 mm); the plaster on the upper parts of the lunettes is thinner since there is no under-layer of *arriccio.*

The plaster is made up primarily of pozzolana and lime in the proportion of three to one. (This information can be traced back to Federici; the higher value refers to the inert material.) On rare occasions the days' work intended for figures were prepared with marble dust, evidently to give them a smoother and more compact surface. For the most part all the *intonaci* are very finished and compact—or *stretti* (literally, "pressed"), to use restorers' jargon. This phenomenon is very easy to see in raking light.

According to Biagetti the fresco was painted in 450 *giornate.* This figure will have to be revised since there are many *giornate* in the lunettes, where the number of days' work has already been checked, which were not recorded on Biagetti's diagram.

The technique used to paint the *Last Judgment*—once Sebastiano's suggestion that oil be used was rejected, at least initially—was, as on the Ceiling, true, or *buon*, fresco. Yet the two paintings were conceived and executed in very different ways: the brushstrokes, the range of colors, the use of *secco* during the execution of the work, and the preparation of the *intonaco* itself, already discussed above. The *Last Judgment* has none of the limpid, transparent colors of the Ceiling, and the liquid brushstrokes and glazes of color on the Ceiling are abandoned in the *Last Judgment* for richly colored impastos painted with heavy brushstrokes that are always quick and rough. The technique of preparing the shaded areas of the figures with terre verte,

or *verdaccio,* was rarely used on the Ceiling and does not appear at all in the *Last Judgment*. The use of localized brown tones to prepare whole images for painting (the figure is then modeled with highlights and halftones) continues from the Ceiling and is used perhaps even more frequently in the later painting.

The number and scope of the corrections, additions, and *secco* finishing touches are noteworthy. The latter were often executed after several days, although never by scraping off the plaster, as was the case on the Ceiling. The *pentimenti* include moving and increasing or decreasing the size of some parts of a figure, sometimes substantially. In some cases they are intended to modify or even add areas of highlight. Unlike the *pentimenti* on the Ceiling, which adjusted the proportions of single details, correcting their dimensions, those on the *Last Judgment* were made predominantly for dynamic and perspectival reasons and alter the figures' arrangement and sense of movement. The *pentimenti* on the angel holding the column and on the Elect Soul between Christ and St. Peter are typical. In both cases the figure's head has been turned toward the left shoulder and depicted in full profile, significantly changing the original relationship between head and shoulders and therefore the entire composition of the figure.

Following the normal technique, the elements—trumpets, for example—that cross several *giornate* were painted *a secco*. The same is true for pigments that could not withstand the causticity of the hydrated lime; this seems to be the case for the yellow area behind Christ. Numerous finishing touches lost in past restorations were, presumably, also executed *a secco*. They would have made less obvious the shifts in tone visible today in the broader expanses like the sky and in places where adjacent *giornate* were

painted sometimes even months apart. Such finishing touches might also have masked the *giornate* seams that are now so evident. If this were the case, then they have been lost, in part because of past restorations and in part because of the combined action of flaking, due to the contracting layer of glue, and abrasion caused by frequent dustings.

The reddish-brown outlines of figures added in the background, frequently painted over several *giornate*, were also executed *a secco*. These were apparently not present in the cartoon, in which, given its dimensions, Michelangelo included only the principal figures. Yet they have an essential function in that they consolidate the structure of the composition by com

pleting it and, more important, by giving it a greater sense of depth. They were executed only after the principal figures, and they were painted with a rapid, sketchlike technique that creates the impression of a progressive blurring of the image. This technique is characteristic of Michelangelo's style since the Sistine Ceiling. Typical examples are the sketchy figures in the background of the right lunette who hold the ladder, the pole, and the sponge.

Michelangelo's palette on the *Last Judgment* was somewhat different from that of the Ceiling. Mars brown and yellow, lead orange and ivory black, which were used only in the early phases of work on the Ceiling, were not used on the altar wall. For the blues, Michelangelo no longer used blue smalt, or *smaltino*; he substituted lapis lazuli and small quantities of azurite. On the other hand we find red lake and perhaps (if the laboratory analyses confirm it) *giallolino* and orpiment on the altar wall—colors that either cannot be used or are only rarely employed (in the case of *giallolino*) in fresco.

The pigments identified up to this point, together with the technique with which they were used, document Michelangelo's increased pictorial sensibility, brought about, no doubt, by his contact with Venetian painting and his close relationship with Sebastiano del Piombo. The addition to his palette of lake, azurite, and possibly *giallolino* and orpiment is particularly important in this sense, as is the use of azurite for a specific purpose and not as a substitute for the more costly lapis lazuli (on the Virgin's mantle and the lower part of the sky). Significant, too, is the choice of lapis lazuli for the intense blue of the sky that is so important for the overall effect of the fresco. The choice of the extremely expensive ultramarine must also have been influenced by the fact that the expenses of the *Last Judgment,* unlike those of the Ceiling, were all covered by the pope. From an economic point of view, moreover, Michelangelo had no more worries; he was part of the papal household and his salary was covered, as we know from two briefs and from the payments that continued until his death.

As has been noted, a cartoon was made for all the principal figures; it was surely preceded by small compositional drawings and perhaps, as on the Ceiling, by studies drawn directly on the *arriccio,* although no evidence for them has yet come to light. On the upper part of the *Last Judgment* the cartoons were transferred to the plaster by pouncing, or *spolvero,* and the paper used seems to have been quite thick, since in some cases the edge of the small perforations left a circular mark on the plaster. On the lower part of the fresco, executed at the end of the project, the method of transfer changed to indirect incision, a technique Michelangelo had used in the later narrative scenes on the Sistine Ceiling.

Beyond any actual economic considerations which may in a secondary way have influenced some of his choices, the artist who emerges from the tests and cleaning so far completed is tied technically, as was obvious, to

Last Judgment, *details of the right lunette after the cleaning.*

the canons of *buon fresco.* Yet he is also more a painter than the artist who executed the Sistine Ceiling, one capable of using color and light in ways that seem not only to follow but also to anticipate Venetian techniques.

Last Judgment, *detail of the Elect below the left lunette, photographed while the cleaning was in progress. The area that had not yet been cleaned can be seen clearly in the foreground.*

The Cleaning

The preparatory phase of the restoration of the *Last Judgment,* intended to determine the fresco's condition and Michelangelo's technique as well as to develop the best method for the cleaning, took more than a year. It included both laboratory research and *in situ* tests.

The method of cleaning being used was developed with two essential requirements in mind. The first was its capacity to adapt itself to the different technical and conservation situations encountered across the surface of the fresco without changing the degree of cleaning, which must remain constant for the entire painting. The second was its capacity gradually to reach a predetermined level, thus allowing for the possibility, given the unevenness of the fresco's state of conservation, of leaving behind some part of the veil of foreign matter in order best to balance the result of the cleaning.

In the procedure designed according to these requirements, the fresco is

Two photographs taken during the cleaning of the Last Judgment *frescoes. On the left, the application of the solvent; on the right, a stage in the cleaning process.*

first washed with distilled water alone and then treated with a solution of water and ammonium carbonate (at twenty-five percent), with an intermediate phase where the diluting agent is potassium nitrate. Twenty-four hours later the ammonium carbonate solution is applied again, this time through four layers of Japanese paper. This treatment lasts between nine and twelve minutes, after which the paper is removed and the area is washed with a small, sterilized sponge soaked with the same ammonium carbonate solution. The fresco is then washed several times with distilled water. This method has produced excellent results on the figures, but a slightly different technique has been used to clean the sky. The ammonium carbonate was applied for a shorter time, and, since the pigment cannot be cleaned even with a very soft brush, the removal of foreign matter was effected with a blotter—a sponge soaked in water is laid against the painted surface so that when it is pressed and released it lifts the dirt from the color without creating any friction. Since the effectiveness of this method, developed after a long series of tests, depends largely on the restorer's manual skill, the cleaning of the sky was entrusted to a single individual.

The areas painted *a secco* can be cleaned in the same way as the sky.

When these areas are covered by retouchings, however, the retouchings must be removed first, using specific solvents and very small brushes. All the water used in the cleaning process and for the final washing is first sterilized in the research laboratory. Among the retouchings are the loincloths discussed above. A definitive decision concerning them will be made at the end of the restoration, and in the meantime we hope to clarify the question of their chronology. The repainted figures of Sts. Blaise and Catherine will obviously remain, since they were executed in fresco and cannot be removed. Furthermore, according to a standard now universally accepted by restorers, anything that constitutes a historical document rather than irrelevant information is preserved, as in the case of the fig leaves in the Brancacci Chapel in Florence.

No protective substance will be applied to the painted surface at the end of the restoration so as not to superimpose foreign and perishable material on the original pictorial fabric. Instead, a system designed to filter the air and regulate the microclimate of the Chapel has been installed. The climate control is regulated by a sophisticated monitoring system linked to sensors placed on all the walls as well as the Ceiling of the Sistine Chapel.[10] At the time of this writing, the restoration is scheduled to be completed by the spring of 1994.

THE PALETTE OF THE *LAST JUDGMENT*

Whites:	Lime white (hydrated calcium carbonate)
Yellows:	Yellow ochers of various tones (earth silicates more or less rich with hydrated ferrous oxide) *Giallolino** (lead oxide and tin oxide)
Browns:	Umber (ferrous oxide and manganese dioxide) Burnt siena (earth silicates and hydrated ferrous oxide)
Blues:	Lapis lazuli (aluminum and sodium silicates containing sulphur) Azurite (basic copper carbonate), in small quantities
Reds:	Red ocher (anhydrous ferrous oxide) Red lake
Greens:	Terre verte (ferrous silicates) Malachite** (basic copper carbonate)
Blacks:	Vine black (black obtained from burning grapevines)

* This pigment was found in only one place. Further tests must be run to confirm its presence.

** Malachite is present only in St. Catherine's dress, which, however, is part of Daniele da Volterra's repainting in true fresco.

Last Judgment, *detail of the right lunette after it was cleaned. The small figures with the ladder of the Crucifixion were added in secco.*

255

New Documents on the Construction of the Sistine Chapel

Piernicola Pagliara

Top: Sistine Chapel, brick wall with the papal coat of arms of the Della Rovere family, near the northwest corner of the Sala Regia. (On the left is the jamb of the large window designed by Antonio da Sangallo the Younger.) The placement of so many coats of arms near the corners, at the height of the windows and in the battlement, makes the chapel look like a completely "Sistine" structure. Above: Sistine Chapel, south facade, the papal coat of arms of the Della Rovere family, at the height of the windows. The edge of the wall to the right of the coat of arms is smooth, and the seam of mortar above it is thicker than the others and continues on to the left portion. These two features are evidence that the coat of arms was placed in the wall during construction of the chapel, rather than by breaking into a preexisting wall. Hence, the brick wall was built during the time of Pope Sixtus IV.

We have always known from Aurelio Lippo Brandolini and other sources that Sixtus IV's chapel in the Vatican Palace replaced the Capella Magna (Large Chapel), and that it was built on the same site, using, at the very least, the older chapel's foundations.[1] John Shearman then underlined the imperceptible irregularities in the chapel's plan, which narrows toward the altar wall; they can be explained by supposing the building was reconstructed on the medieval foundations.[2] One might also suppose that the pavement of the older chapel was more or less at the same level as that of the Sistine Chapel since, in 1391, the canonization of St. Brigid took place in both the Capella Magna and the Capella Parva (Small Chapel) on the other side of the Aula Regia. The height of the latter had remained unchanged since the thirteenth century.[3] Neither the internal nor the external appearance of the Sistine Chapel, however, gives the impression that much of the older building was preserved. The external brick facade is completely homogeneous, with the exception of the restored battering on the north wall. Furthermore, it is very similar to other brick walls built in Rome in the last decades of the fifteenth century. They are characterized by thick mortar beds and bricks, from 1¼ to 1½ in. (3 to 4 cm) high, often laid on end rather than lengthwise (usually one with its short side facing outwards for every two laid lengthwise).[4] In addition, one finds the Della Rovere coat of arms at all levels and on all sides of the chapel; many of them were inserted into the wall during its construction.[5] No comment is required concerning the wholly "Sistine" character of all parts of the building that were not subsequently altered.[6]

It is difficult, even after careful examination, to imagine that this brick casing encloses a monument of which a substantial part predates the reign of Sixtus IV. Yet proof that this is indeed the case was found at the end of 1989, when part of the modern, restored plaster was removed from the interior of the south wall of the chapel, that is, the one closest to St. Peter's. The area exposed was on the first pilaster strip from the corner toward the Sala Regia, at the level of the fictive tapestries, and it revealed an opening in the masonry that was later walled up.[7] This opening was flanked by brick jambs, measured about a yard (or meter) across and was splayed toward the exterior of the chapel.[8] The jamb on the left seems to stop 3¹⁵⁄₁₆ in. (10 cm) below the fifteenth-century bench, that is, just a little above the present level of the chapel floor, and it rises 2⅔ yards (2.5 m) above the floor and then it seems to end.[9] The corresponding jamb on the right was more profoundly altered when the tufa masonry, which could well date to the time of Sixtus IV, used to close the opening was consolidat

ed with the preexisting wall.[10] The configuration and dimensions of this opening indicate that it was most likely a door.[11]

There is no doubt that this door was closed before the fictive tapestries were executed because the opening is still covered by painted *intonaco* (the upper layer of plaster), some of which is surely original.[12] It seems unlikely, furthermore, that this opening was cut through and then closed after Sixtus's reign since the staircase descending to St. Peter's, renovated by Donato Bramante for Julius II, was located on the other side of the wall from about 1506 or 1508.[13] Furthermore, there was certainly a stair in the same place at least by Alexander VI's death in 1503, when, for the conclave called to name his successor, the entrance from the Aula Regia to a staircase opposite the Scala del Maresciallo was walled up. This stair descended from the Aula Regia to the Paradiso and, as we will see below, almost certainly existed before Sixtus IV's reign.[14] Thus at least the south wall of the chapel, to a height above the level of the floor pavement, predates Sixtus's chapel.

A twice-published document and the building itself offer clues that at least part of the old chapel was preserved. Among his collection of epigrams on Sixtus' works, between the one on the Sistine Chapel (*De phano quod sixtus in palatio condidit*) and the one on the library, Brandolini dedicated one to the "Paradiso," *De loco qui Paradisus dicitur a Sixto edificato* (and which in fact was only renovated by the Della Rovere pope).[15] This Paradiso has nothing to do with the atrium of Old St. Peter's, also referred to as the Paradiso, nor with Nicholas V's projects.[16] Baldassare Peruzzi's plan (Uffizi

Top: Brick wall on the south side of the Borgia Tower (1492-94).
Center: Sistine Chapel, detail of the south-facade brick wall.
Bottom: Brick wall in San Aurea at Ostia (1483). In these and other brick walls in Rome dating to the last two decades of the fifteenth century, as in those of the Sistine Chapel, the bricks are often laid on end rather than lengthwise; later they were arranged this way less frequently. On the other hand, it became customary rather early on to use thinner mortar seams.

Top left: Sistine Chapel, view from the north. The uniform brick facing dating from the fifteenth century partly covers earlier walls.
Above left: Sistine Chapel, view from the south.

572) showing the rooms to the south of the Sistine Chapel and adjacent to the "stairs which descend from the palace to St. Peter's"—later replaced by the Scala Regia—allows us to identify the Paradiso mentioned by Brandolini with the rooms below the chapel.[17] These rooms were adapted to house Paul VI's Museum of Modern Religious Art in 1973. On the Uffizi drawing, the corridor leading from the upper landing of the staircase to these rooms is labeled "andito ale Camere del paradiso" (corridor to the Paradise rooms), and just below, by the south wall of the Sistine Chapel, one reads, "scarpa dela cappella di papa sixto" (escarpment of Pope Sixtus's chapel). The term "Paradiso" is again used to refer to this group of rooms later in the century in a plan attributed to Mascherino.[18] According to Brandolini, Sixtus improved the lighting in these rooms, which had been so dark they deserved the name Inferno, and thus transformed them into a paradise:

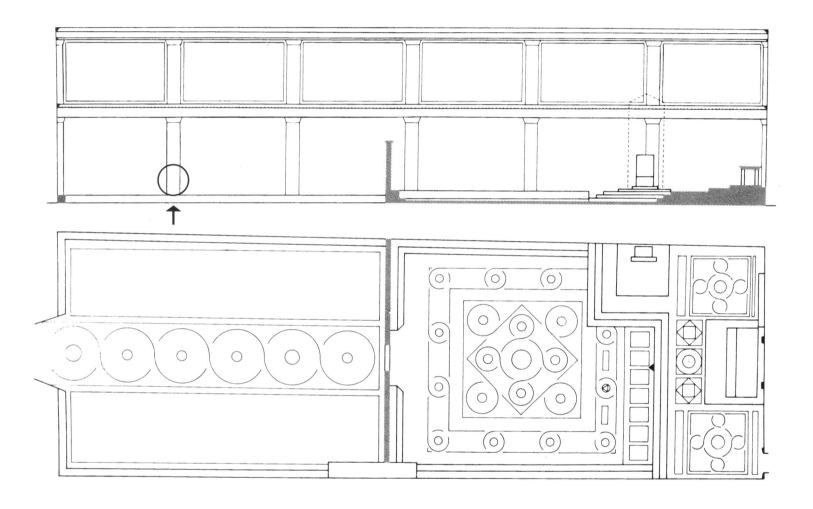

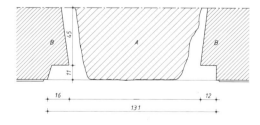

A = Tufa masonry
B = Brick ends

It had been night here, even in the middle of the day;
it was a gloomy spot, neither a dwelling nor a place fit for men;
it seemed a dark dungeon and unworthy even to be a dungeon,
appropriate only as a cave intended for use by sheep, not men.
Hell was its nickname since one seemed to be living close to the
underworld there; in fact, it was hardly a dwelling place at all.
But Sixtus drove the darkness away and brought back the light of the
sky, and to this place, that had been unaccustomed to it,
he gave back the light of day.[19]

Top: Sistine Chapel, elevation of the left wall and floor plan. The arrow points to the position of the opening cut into the wall under the fictive tapestries.

Above: Diagram of the opening made in the wall.

The groin vaults installed in these rooms, with Della Rovere arms carved on the keystone of each one, offer further evidence of Sixtus's intervention here.[20] The outer, northern wall, on the other hand, must antedate Sixtus's renovations because the windows on that side are unequally spaced and do not correspond to the interior division of the rooms.[21]

The rooms of the Paradiso must originally have had wooden ceilings, which supported the floor of the Capella Magna. This seems likely given the surviving accounts of the lively conclave of 1378, the first held in Rome and in the Vatican after the Babylonian Captivity. On the second day a crowd of local people broke into the conclave to demand a Roman pope, chanting unceasingly for twenty-four hours, "we want a Roman."[22] The night before, the horde had invaded the Vatican Palace and the rooms below those designated for the conclave. There the people pounded on the wooden ceilings, keeping the cardinals awake, "and from below they were pounding vigorously against the roof of the room, so that *their Excellencies,* the cardinals, were hardly able to get any rest...and they kept it up all night."[23] Among the rooms where the conclave took place, this document can only refer to those beneath the Sala Ducale, partially vaulted but after 1378, and the Capella Magna, since the Sala Regia was supported by groin vaults dating to the

thirteenth century and which are still visible today.[24] Indeed, an emergency escape door was cut into the floor of the chapel, a measure possible only with a wooden floor. One document recounts that this hole "was in the floor of the large chapel, more or less in the center of the chapel... he said that he came out into a residence that was below the above-mentioned roof and that, from there, they had access to a door leading to a vineyard."[25] Five cardinals attempted to escape to the vineyard mentioned in the document, corresponding today to the Belvedere, by means of this emergency exit; they were quickly rounded up and brought back to the palace.[26] This document must refer to the large chapel since, while the cardinals fled undisturbed, the people had already invaded the other, small chapel, where the ballots had been opened and where they found the newly elected pope. This evidence must, however, be used cautiously since none of the numerous other sources, each of which contributes some colorful details to our knowledge of the incident, mentions the chapel. In fact, one of the cardinals declared, "through a small hole that had been made in the roof I climbed down into the residence of the chamberlain."[27] Another witness added, "I climbed down into that room by way of a ladder that was perched very dangerously on top of a cupboard that was none too stable; the reason that the ladder had been placed there was that it was much too short."[28]

Brandolini offers us another useful clue when he writes that the rooms beneath the chapel were as dark as Hades. This poet was almost blind from birth, and, furthermore, his description could not have come from personal experience since he came to Rome in 1480, after the rebuilding of the chapel had begun. None of this, however, rules out the possibility that Brandolini's report is true.[29] At that time light must have entered these rooms unobstructed from the north, since it is only Pius V's wing, built in the sixteenth century, that makes them dark today. In the mid-sixteenth

Left: View of the opening made in the wall. Fictive tapestries were painted on the plaster covering the hole. Part of this plaster is original; the hole was therefore closed up before the chapel was decorated.
Top: Detail of the right jamb of the opening in the wall.
Above: Detail of the jamb, the splay, and the volcanic tufa that filled the hole. The tufa is of a type in use in Rome during the second half of the fifteenth century and the first half of the next century; it could therefore have been part of the work performed at the orders of Sixtus IV.

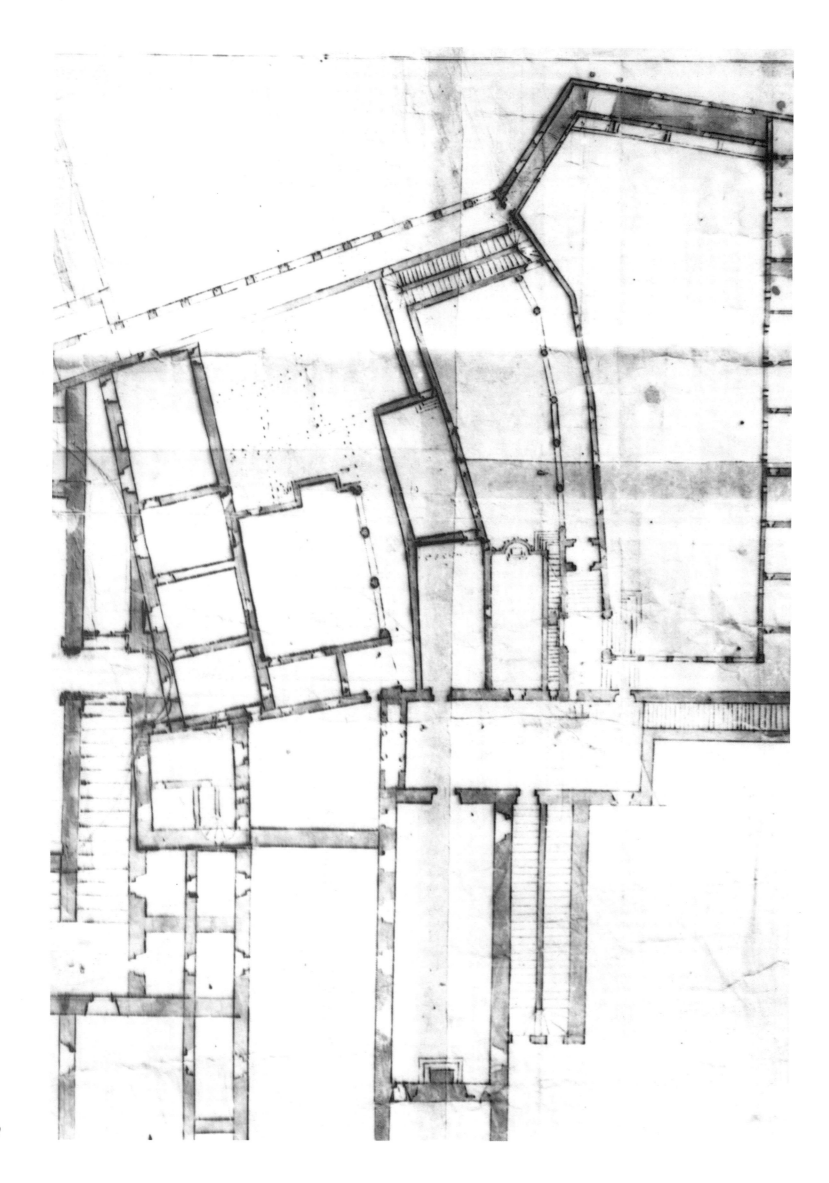

century, the view toward the Belvedere was still open and clear, the addition of the Borgia Tower notwithstanding, as Giovan Battista Naldini's drawing *View from the Sistine Chapel* demonstrates.[30] On the other hand, the windows on the south side, now adjacent to the upper part of the Scala Regia, must already have been walled up in 1480. They are no longer visible, but they were up until the last century, when Steinmann, in his survey, showed them both in plan and section. They are significantly splayed at the top in order to admit light despite some sort of a barrier blocking their lower section.[31] This obstacle must be a staircase, perhaps uncovered, which even before Bramante's stair led from the Sala Regia along the south side of the chapel to the rooms below, connecting the chapel with the rooms which from Sixtus's time were certainly assigned to the chapel's ministers. The events of the 1378 conclave prove that there was no internal connection between the chapel and the floor below. Furthermore, even then this stair must have continued to the portico of St. Peter's and was not remodeled until Bramante's project.[32]

The evidence examined thus far indicates that the outer shell of the Capella Magna to the level of the floor of the chapel itself must have been retained almost in its entirety, while the interior space was rearranged and vaulted. Further investigations, permitted by a continuation of the restoration of the painted tapestries, will allow us to check how far the preserved medieval walls extend horizontally above the chapel's floor. It is likely that the west wall, like those on the north and south (and obviously the one toward the Sala Regia), also corresponds, in part, to the original medieval structure.[33] The fact that the two lower orders have frescoed pilasters and that marble was used on the first only for the cornice but on the second for the entire entablature, leads us to believe that the medieval walls were preserved at least to the level of the first cornice.[34]

The suggestion that Sixtus's project preserves a large part of the earlier medieval building seems to be at odds with the various written sources that imply the pope completely rebuilt the chapel. Yet only the encomiastic texts, which tend to exaggerate in order to praise, allude to a building con-

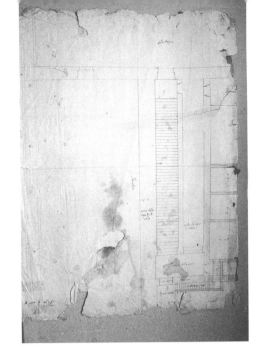

Opposite: Bramante's workshop, plan for the transformation of the Vatican Palace (Uffizi 287 A, Florence). Partial reproduction with the Sistine Chapel, the Capella Parva (Small Chapel), the staircase later called the Scala Regia, and the Aula Regia.

Above: Ottavio Mascarino, plan of the structures to the south of the Sistine Chapel, with the rooms of Paradiso indicated. Accademia di San Luca, Rome.

Below: Baldassarre Peruzzi, plan of the structures to the south of the Sistine Chapel, on the level of the Paradiso rooms (Uffizi 572 A, Florence). At the top right is the staircase that leads up to the Aula Regia and down to St. Peter's. The reference to the Paradiso rooms makes it possible to identify them as the rooms under the Sistine Chapel described by Brandolini.

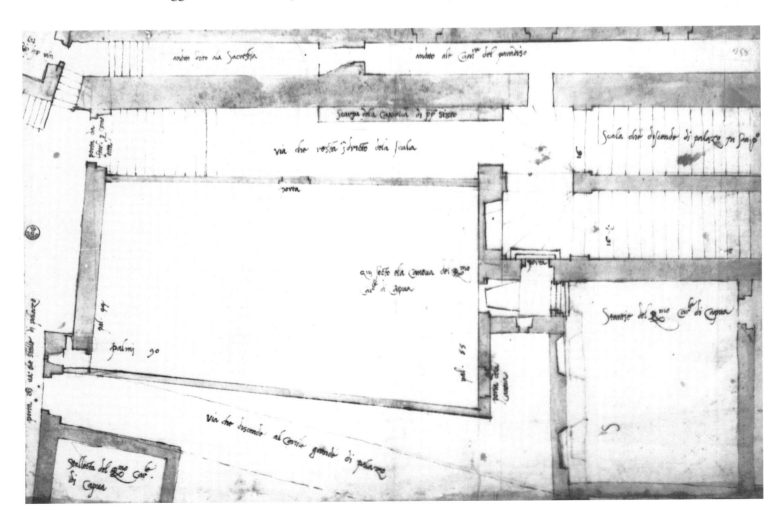

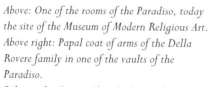

Above: One of the rooms of the Paradiso, today the site of the Museum of Modern Religious Art.
Above right: Papal coat of arms of the Della Rovere family in one of the vaults of the Paradiso.

Below right: Sistine Chapel, detail of the left wall with the cornices on the first, second, and third levels.

structed anew from its foundations. This is especially true of Andrew of Trebizond (who used the terms "funditus diruisti" [completely demolished] for the old chapel) and to a lesser extent of Brandolini.[35] The chroniclers Jacopo Gherardi and Sigismondo de Conti use the generic term "instauravit"

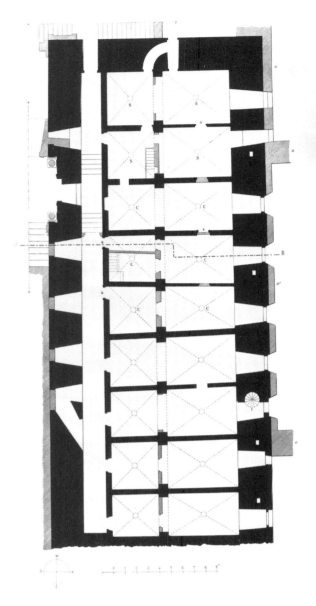

(restored)—significant because Sigismondo writes "fundavit" (founded) for the church of S. Maria del Popolo, which Sixtus completely reconstructed—and they mention explicitly only the work for which Sixtus was really responsible, including the mosaic floor pavement, the frescoes, and the vaulting.[36] The pope's restoration was, furthermore, only slightly less demanding than a complete reconstruction. The peripheral walls were preserved, but the vaults above and below the chapel were added, and the apartment below was renovated. The entire medieval structure, which Brandolini called unstable and which Pietro del Massaio's plan shows to be summarily but effectively buttressed, was consolidated, reinforced with a battered basement, and refaced with a layer of brick.[37] This procedure was common in Rome; I know of seventeenth-century examples.[38] The battering, which extends upward to the entablature of the first order, had to absorb the thrust of the new vaults of both the Paradiso and the chapel. The

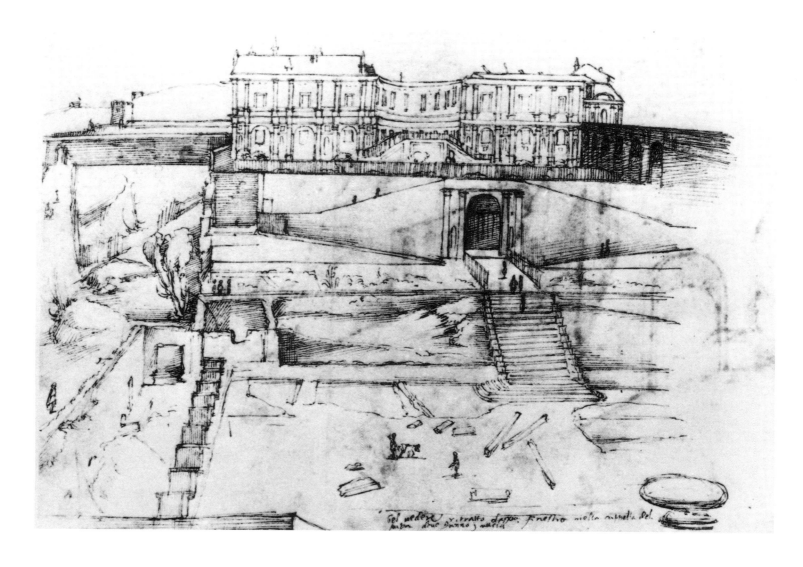

The courtyard of the Belvedere, as seen in View from the Sistine Chapel, *attributed to Giovan Battista Naldini, ca. 1560 (Fogg Art Museum, Cambridge, Massachusetts). In the mid-sixteenth century, the view from the choir toward the Belvedere was unobstructed. It was later blocked by Pius V's wing, which greatly reduced the light coming into the chapel and, especially, into the Paradiso below.*

crenellations above the cornice served the same defensive purpose in times of unrest as they would in military buildings.

Our understanding of Sixtus's reasons for modifying the Capella Magna is enriched by both the chronicle of the conclave of 1378 and Brandolini's epigram. They can be added to demands, noted by Shearman, created by the changing ceremonial needs that evolved during the time the papacy was in residence in Avignon.[39] As Brandolini noted, the consolidation of an unsafe structure was one of Sixtus's goals, but he also needed to increase security in an area of the Vatican complex essential to papal conclaves, which the dramatic events of less than one hundred years before had demonstrated to be so lacking. Security may also be the reason that conclaves were not held in the Vatican Palace in the years immediately after the papacy returned for good to Rome. It was only some twenty years later, under Calixtus III, that the Vatican was used once again for conclaves. The vaults above and below the chapel were difficult to break through and made the chapel soundproof, so that nothing of the proceedings could be overheard, thus avoiding any leaking of information. Conclave rules, and particularly an injunction in force in Avignon requiring that all windows less than about nine yards above the floor be walled up, seem also to have dictated the position of the chapel's windows, placed approximately ten yards (10.07 meters) above the floor.[40] It was not, then, necessary to wall up the windows every time a pope died—with the exception of those made more easily accessible by the vault of Bramante's stair and the roof of the sacristy.[41] Brandolini clarifies the fact that the Paradiso was put at the disposal of the chapel's ministers. Clerics, chaplains, and perhaps initially the sacristan, as well as a varying number of singers and the masters of ceremony, had their communal lodgings and their archive here, near the place where they carried out their daily responsibilities.[42] The poet noted that

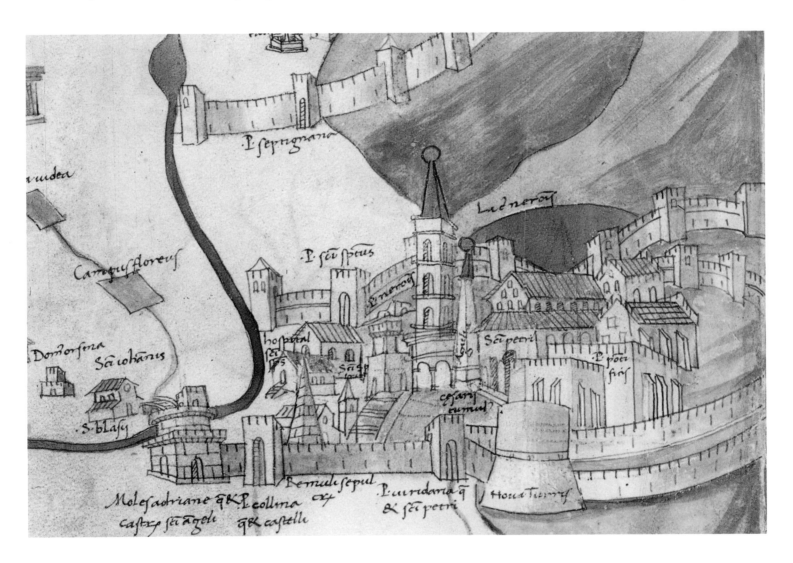

Sixtus, after having taken care of a temple for the gods, did not forget the lives of the men who were in charge of the religious ceremonies.

Looking at Sixtus's building in this new light, we are forced to rethink our understanding of the architect, the chronology of the construction, and the biblical proportions of the chapel. The architect had to be, above all, an expert builder and consolidator, and Giovanni de Dolci fits this profile. (The man responsible for the innovative interior architecture must have had a different training.[43]) The consolidation of the masonry could have been done well before February 1477, when the Capella Magna was used for the last time, since only the construction of vaults above and below the chapel and its interior decoration required that it be closed.[44] Finally, if the altar wall indeed coincides with its medieval predecessor, then the proportions of the Sistine Chapel, at least in terms of its ground plan, are due to the old Capella Magna rather than to Sixtus's design.[45]

Pietro del Massaio, map of Rome in Ptolemy's Cosmography, *detail with the Vatican Palace. In the building with buttresses to the right of the church and above the "palace of the pope," one can recognize the old Capella Magna (Large Chapel).*

265

NOTES

MICHAEL HIRST, "OBSERVATIONS ON DRAWINGS FOR THE SISTINE CEILING"

1. "E dichono avere arsii tutti que' chartoni, ma non chredo di tutti. Doghomi, ma la volontà vostra s'à a eseguire...." P. Barocchi and R. Ristori, *Il carteggio di Michelangelo*, Florence, 1965, vol. 1, p. 318.

2. Compare, for example, the Uffizi study for the head of Zechariah, Uffizi 18718 recto (Tolnay Corpus 153 recto), which measures 17⅛ x 10⅞ in. (435 x 277 mm).

3. The case of Pontormo shows clearly enough that we are not concerned with a practice on the way out in the first half of the century.

4. The drawings are Wilde 7 recto, Tolany Corpus 154 recto, and Wilde 14 recto, Tolnay Corpus 165 recto.

5. Tolnay Corpus 168 recto.

6. For the drawing, Wilde 10 recto, Tolnay Corpus 154 recto, see the comments in Michael Hirst, *Michelangelo and His Drawings*, New Haven and London, 1988, p. 71.

7. Tolnay Corpus 139 recto and 143 verso.

8. Ibid., 144 recto and 136 recto.

9. Ibid., 163 recto and 164 recto.

10. For the important identification of a fragment of cartoon for Haman on the verso of the Haarlem sheet, see Carmen Bambach, "A Note on Michelangelo's Cartoon for the Sistine Ceiling Haaman," *Art Bulletin*, vol. 65, 1983, pp. 681ff.

11. Tolnay Corpus 155 verso.

12. Ibid., 160 recto.

13. See Carmen Bambach Cappel, "Michelangelo's Cartoon for the *Crucifixion of St. Peter* Reconsidered," *Master Drawings*, vol. 25, 1987, pp. 131ff.

14. Hirst, *Michelangelo and His Drawings*, p. 76.

GIANLUIGI COLALUCCI, "THE TECHNIQUE OF THE SISTINE CEILING FRESCOES"

I would like to dedicate my nine years of work on Michelangelo's frescoes in the Sistine Chapel to the memory of Cesare Brandi.

1. Giorgio Vasari, *Lives of Seventy of the Most Eminent Painters, Sculptors, and Architects*, New York, Charles Scribner's Sons, 1896, vol. 4, pp. 86-87.

2. Ibid., pp. 87, 89-90.

FABRIZIO MANCINELLI, "THE PROBLEM OF MICHELANGELO'S ASSISTANTS"

1. Vasari 1896, vol. 4, pp. 84-85.

2. On the subject of Michelangelo's involvement in the Condivi biography, see P. D'Ancona, "Ascanio Condivi e Giorgio Vasari biografi di Michelangelo," in Ascanio Condivi, *Michelangelo: La Vita*, ed. P. D'Ancona, Milan, 1928, pp. 7-20; Johannes Wilde, "Michelangelo, Vasari, and Condivi," in *Michelangelo: Six Lectures*, ed. J. Shearman and M. Hirst, Oxford, 1978, pp. 1-16.

3. Ascanio Condivi, *The Life of Michelangelo*, trans. Alice Sedgewick Wohl, ed. Helmut Wohl, Baton Rouge, Louisiana, 1976, p. 58.

4. Giorgio Vasari, *Le vite de' più eccellenti pittori, scultori, e architettori nelle redazioni del 1550 e 1568*, ed. R. Bettarini and P. Barocchi, Florence, 1987, vol. 6, pp. 5-7.

5. L. Bardeschi Ciulich and P. Barocchi, *I ricordi di Michelangelo*, Florence, 1970, p. 1.

6. Charles H. Wilson, *Life and Works of Michelangelo Buonarroti*, London, 1876, pp. 125-26.

7. Karl Frey, *Sammlung ausgewählter Briefe an Michelangelo Buonarroti*, Berlin, 1899, vol. 6, pp. 10-11; Ernst Steinmann, *Die Sixtinische Kapelle*, Munich, 1905, vol. 2, pp. 705-06.

8. P. Barocchi and R. Ristori, *Il carteggio di Michelangelo*, Florence, 1965, vol. 1, p. 376.

9. For the text of Granacci's letter, see ibid., vol. 1, pp. 64-65, 376-77.

10. The quarrels with Jacopo di Sandro are documented in a letter from Ludovico Buonarroti to Michelangelo dated 7 October 1508 (".... per l'ultima tuo resto avisato chome Iachopo di Sandro t'à

ingannato. Io me ne maraviglio, perché à viso di buono; ma gia più volte ti dissi che tutti questi piagnioni erano chattivi uomini....Io mi chredevo che chotesto Iachopo fussi un apostolo. Non si può fidare di persona....") and from Michelangelo to his father on 27 January 1509 ("Di qua s'é partito a questi dì quello Iachopo dipintore che io fè venire qua; e perché e' s'é doluto de' casi mia, stimo che è si dorrà ancora costà. Fate orechi de merchatanti e basta; perché lui e' mille torti e are' mi grandemente a doler di lui. Fate vista di non vedere."). The entire texts of both letters are published in Barocchi and Ristori, pp. 85-86 (October), 88-89 (January).

11. I have made this suggestion previously. See Fabrizio Mancinelli, "Il cantiere di Michelangelo per la volta della Cappella Sistina," in *La pittura in Italia: Il Cinquecento*, Milan, 1985, p. 539. It is interesting to note that Jacopo di Sandro is the only one of Michelangelo's assistants virtually ignored by Vasari, who notes only his collaboration with Domenico and Davide Ghirlandaio and Andrea del Sarto in their biographies (see Vasari 1987, vol. 3, p. 496; vol. 4, p. 362; vol. 5, p. 437). It seems as if his quarrels with Michelangelo at the time of the painting of the Sistine Ceiling earned him a sort of *damnatio memoriae*. The other *garzoni*, with the exception of Agnolo di Donnino, each warranted his own biography; whether it was long or short depended on his artistic merit as well as on Vasari's goodwill. Vasari even collected a number of facts about Agnolo di Donnino, whose ability was probably not superior to Jacopo's, which he includes in his life of Cosimo Rosselli, who was, according to the biographer, a close friend of Agnolo's.

12. For Jacopo di Lazzaro's biography, see Giorgio Vasari, *Lives of the Most Eminent Painters, Sculptors, and Architects*, London, Henry G. Bohn, 1865, vol. 2, pp. 344-47. See also Vasari, ed. Gaetano Milanesi, Florence, 1878–85, vol. 3, pp. 679-80. A. Venturi suggested long ago that Jacopo assisted Pintoricchio in the Borgia Apartments; see *Storia dell'arte italiana* VII, 2, pp. 616, 639. For more information about Jacopo see G. Richert, "Iacopo Torni," in Thieme-Becker, *Künstlerlexikon*, Leipzig, 1939, vol. 33, pp. 292-93.

13. Giorgio Vasari, *The Lives of the Painters, Sculptors, and Architects*, New York, E. P. Dutton & Co., 1927, vol. 2, p. 143.

14. For Granacci's life, see Vasari 1865, vol. 3, pp. 452-57; Vasari 1878-85, vol. 5, pp. 339-45. For other information about Granacci and his relationship with Michelangelo, see Charles de Tolnay, *Michelangelo: The Youth of Michelangelo*, Princeton, New Jersey, 1947, pp. 12-13, and C. von Holst, *Francesco Granacci*, Munich, 1974.

15. For this artist, see Vasari 1865, vol. 4, pp. 296-304; and S. Meloni Trkulja, "Giuliano Bugiardini," in *Dizionario biografico degli italiani*, Rome, 1972, vol. 15, pp. 15-18.

16. Vasari 1865, vol. 4, p. 297.

17. For Agnolo di Donnino, see Vasari 1865, vol. 2, pp. 177-78; and on his life see A. Forlani, "Agnolo di Domenico di Donnino," in *Dizionario biografico degli italiani*, Rome, 1960, vol. 1, p. 449.

18. Barocchi and Ristori, vol. 1, p. 64.

19. For Bastiano da Sangallo's life, see Vasari 1865, vol. 4, pp. 470-93.

20. Ibid., vol. 4, p. 472.

21. Barocchi and Ristori, vol. 1, p. 110.

22. On Giovanni Trignoli and Bernardino Zacchetti, see Steinmann, vol. 2, pp. 162-63; A. Mercati, "Due pittori reggiani amici di Michelangelo," *Atti e memorie della R. Deputazione di Storia Patria per le Provincie Modenesi*, vol. 12, 1919, pp. 47-49, and "Notizie supplementari su G. Valle e il pittore Giovanni da Reggio," ibid., vol. 14, 1992(?), pp. 142-43; W. Wallace, "Michelangelo's Assistants in the Sistine Chapel," *Gazette des Beaux-Arts*, 1987, pp. 207-08.

23. Bardeschi Ciulich and Barocchi, p. 23; Barocchi and Ristori, vol. 2, p. 74; Wallace, p. 208.

24. Wallace, pp. 203-4.

25. For the payment to Rosselli see Bardeschi Ciulich and Barocchi, p. 3. We may infer that Rosselli was perhaps involved in the construction from the record of the last payment. On 27 July Piero received thirty gold ducats "per resto di ponte e de l'ariciato e di quelo one fato insino in questo di." The formula "per resto di....e de....e di" indicates that the sum constituted the balance of payments for the scaffolding, the plastering, and for whatever had been finished earlier. According to Charles de Tolnay and P. Barocchi, Piero was the "povero uomo legnaiuolo" whom Vasari credited with building Michelangelo's scaffolding and the artist to whom he gave the ropes from Bramante's scaffolding so that he could provide a dowry for his daughters. See Charles de Tolnay, *Michelangelo: The Sistine Ceiling*, Princeton, New Jersey, 1949, p. 187; and Giorgio Vasari, *La vita di Michelangelo nelle redazioni del 1550 e del 1568*, ed. P. Barocchi, Milan and Naples, 1962, vol. 2, pp. 411-12, n. 310). For other documentary notices of Rosselli, see Wallace, p. 205 n. 21, 313.

26. For Piero Basso, see Wallace, pp. 204-5, 212 n.16. Unlike de Tolnay and Barocchi (see note 25 above), Wallace identifies Piero Basso as Vasari's poor carpenter. According to Wallace, Rosselli cannot be the man Vasari mentions because he was an architect, and indeed Michelangelo himself refers to him as such in a letter written to his brother in August 1518 (see Barocchi and Ristori, vol. 2, p. 71). The formula "per resto di ponte" thus refers to a simple finishing of the structure. For my interpretation of the meaning of this formula, see note 25 above.

27. Barocchi and Ristori, vol. 1, p. 75.

28. Ibid., vol. 1, p. 73. In the letter Michi refers to an offer of assistance from a certain "Raffellino dipintore," who worked for Pier Matteo d'Amelia and who was available to come to Rome for the salary he had received from Pier Matteo, that is ten gold ducats a month. It does not seem, however, that Michelangelo accepted this offer. Referring to himself, Michi wrote, "E se per me non v'è niente, datene avixo, che sono sempre per fare tutte quelle chose che a voi sia utile e honore."

29. Ibid., vol. 1, p. 77. The confirmation that Michi was available was relayed to Michelangelo by his brother Buonarroto, who wrote, "Io ò cierciho di questo Giovanni Michi e stamani l'ò trovato e ò gli dato la lettera, la quale à avuto tanto chiara quanto sia possibile. E dicie che a ogni modo tu l'aspetti, che vuole venire ma che a una facienduza di due o tre di e dipoi si partirà e che sarà chostà 2 o 3 dì dopo il fante."

30. I would like to correct what I have said in the past concerning the possibility that Michi may have been a sculptor. See Fabrizio Mancinelli, "Michelangelo all'opera," in *La Cappella Sistina: I primi restauri, la scoperta del colore*, Novara, 1986, p. 253. In truth there is nothing that indicates one way or another what his profession was. In theory, if Pietro Urbano assisted Michelangelo as he was painting in the Sistine Chapel, as Wallace maintains, he might have been assigned the task of making the clay models Vasari says were used to study foreshortening. See Wallace, p. 208. For Michi, see also Steinmann, vol. 2, pp. 162-63, and de Tolnay 1949, p. 190, who defined him as a "confidential man of affairs," as did Karl Frey, in "Studien zu Michelangelo, I," *Jahrbuch der Preussischen Kunstsammlungen*, vol. 15, 1895, pp. 95-99.

31. Barocchi and Ristori, vol. 1, pp. 66-67.

32. Bardeschi Ciulich and Barocchi, p. 3. Other than the first payment made on 11 May, Michelangelo also made payments immediately after the contract was signed—on 17 and 27 July—and after Granacci had left.

33. This news comes from a letter Michelangelo sent Buonarroto in Florence asking his brother to give Granacci a letter evidently attached to his. See Barocchi and Ristori, vol. 1, p. 74.

34. Granacci's presence in Florence in August is documented by a letter Barocchi dates to Saturday, 19

or 26 August; see Barocchi and Ristori, vol. 1, p. 80. In it Michelangelo asked his father, Lodovico, to tell Buonarroto "che mi facci chomperare o da Francesco Granacci o da qualche altro dipintore un'oncia di lacha, o tanta quanta è può avere pe' decti danari, che sia la più bella che si trova in Firenze; e se e' non ve n'e' che sia una cosa bella, lasci stare." It is unclear if this lacquer was intended for the Sistine Ceiling, although no trace of it has been found. The text of a letter sent to Buonarroto on 2 September refers, perhaps, to different pigments; see Barocchi and Ristori, vol. 1, p. 82. Michelangelo informed his brother that "l'aportatore di questa sarà il Ghiozo choriere, il quale à un sacchetto di libre dua e mezo in tutto, entrovi cholori li quali m'à portato qui Lodovicho e il Granacio [evidently in Florence] perche te lo mandi." The amounts are so small that they must have been samples of pigments. Michelangelo writes about pigments, or, more precisely, blues, in two other letters, one written in May to Fra Jacopo di Francesco (see note 31) and the other to Buonarroto on 29 July, in which Michelangelo tells his brother, "io ò mandato intorno a mezo agosto danari costà per chomperare azurro"; see Barocchi and Ristori, vol. 1, p. 75.

35. De Tolnay 1947, pp. 114-15.

36. It is not specified in the April 1508 notice (Bardeschi Ciulich and Barocchi, p. 1) if the twenty ducats was a flat rate or a monthly payment. The second seems more likely, however, since otherwise the duration of employment would have to have been very short. The "Raffellino dipintore" of Michi's 22 July letter (see note 28 above) was paid ten ducats a month by Pier Matteo d'Amelia. The sum Michelangelo proposed is thus twice that salary, but it was probably not excessive for the kind of work expected, especially since it was for the pope and given that the painters had to come from Florence.

37. Because the Sistine vault is polycentric—a so-called Roman vault—and therefore very irregular, analytical projections based on actual measurements of the vault could not be made before the scaffolding had been built. See Fabrizio Mancinelli, "La progettazione della volta della Cappella Sistina," in *Studies in the History of Art* (acts of the 1988 symposium Michelangelo Drawings), forthcoming.

38. See, for example, B. Biagetti, "La volta della Cappella Sistina: Primo saggio di indagine sulla cronologia e la tecnica delle pitture di Michelangelo," in *Rendiconti della Pontificia Accademia Romana di Archeologia,* vol. 12, 1936, p. 220, and Wallace, p. 206.

39. Barocchi and Ristori, vol. 1, p. 125. The letter is addressed to his father: "gli è costà un garzone spagnuolo che à nome Alonso, che è pictore, el quale comprendo che sia amalato; e perché un suo o parente o amicho spagnuolo, che è qua, vorrebbe sapere come gli sta.... vi prego, o voi o Buonarroto intendessi un pocho dal Granaccio, che lo conoscie, chome gli sta."

40. Wallace, p. 210.

41. Vasari 1927, vol. 2, p. 144.

42. For Michelangelo's relationship with Julius II, see Vasari 1896, vol. 4, p. 78.

43. Wilson, pp. 155ff.

44. Steinmann, vol. 2, pp. 160-67; Biagetti, pp. 200-20; de Tolnay 1949, pp. 113-15, 190.

45. Wallace, pp. 203-16.

46. None of Michelangelo's cartoons for the Ceiling have survived, but there are clearly visible traces of the two methods for transferring these drawings to the wet plaster: pouncing and indirect incision. The drawings for the first half of the vault were extremely accurate and were therefore almost always transferred by pouncing.

47. For the sequence of execution of the first phase of the painting of the Ceiling, see Gianluigi Colalucci's essay in this volume.

48. For an analysis of Ghirlandaio's working method, see Artur Rosenauer, "Domenico Ghirlandaio e bottega: Organizzazione del lavoro per il ciclo di affreschi a S. Maria Novella," in *Tecnica e stile: Esempi di pittura murale del Rinascimento italiano,* Florence, 1986, pp. 25-30; Christina Danti, "Osservazioni sugli affreschi del Ghirlandaio a S. Maria Novella a Firenze," in *Le pitture murali: Tecniche, problemi, conservazione,* ed. C. Danti, M. Matteini, and A. Moles, Florence, 1990, pp. 39-52; G. Ruffa, "Osservazioni sugli affreschi di Domenico Ghirlandaio nella Chiesa di Santa Maria Novella," in *Le pitture murali: Tecniche, problemi, conservazione,* pp. 53-58; and G. Marchini, "The Frescoes of the Choir of Santa Maria Novella," *The Burlington Magazine,* 1953, p. 320. The remarks made here come both from the literature and observations I made during a visit on the scaffolding erected for the restoration of the Tornabuoni Chapel. I would like to thank my hosts there, Guido Botticelli, Fabrizio Bandini, and Christina Danti, for their kindnesses and helpful assistance.

49. Fabrizio Mancinelli and Arnold Nesselrath are conducting a study of the technique Perugino used on the ceiling to be published with the report on the cleaning of the room named after Raphael's *Fire in the Borgo.*

50. On the order of execution in the *Deluge,* see Biagetti, pp. 209-12, and Fabrizio Mancinelli, "Il cantiere di Michelangelo per la volta della Cappella Sistina," in *La pittura in Italia: Il Cinquecento,* Milan, 1988, vol. 2, pp. 540, 551.

51. On this question, see the entry on the *Deluge* in Fabrizio Mancinelli, Gianluigi Colalucci, Nazzareno Gabrielli, "Rapporto sul restauro della volta di Michelangelo," forthcoming.

52. Vasari 1896, vol. 4, pp. 85-86.

53. Evidence that assistants were used primarily on the first third of the Ceiling presents a curious analogy with what Vasari says about the technical problems that plagued the early stages of work on the Sistine Ceiling, and especially the appearance of white mold on the painted plaster. Condivi says this first occurred with the painting of the *Deluge*—the first scene executed on the Ceiling—but Vasari states that it became apparent "when he had completed about one-third of the painting," and adds, as if to justify the chronological incongruity, "according to what he told me." Vasari has perhaps confused the timing of the outbreak of the mold and the departure of the assistants, for which he gives us no precise chronology.

54. The *tondi* on the first half of the Ceiling seem to be less damaged by previous cleanings than those on the second, that is, the last four, which are poorly painted. In many instances the composition seems to have been retraced without any understanding of the original subject. There are no traces of gilding or modeling in the roundel above the *Persian Sibyl;* instead we find only a rapid and linear sketch made with a brush which, only approximate and almost illegible, perhaps covers traces of the original and now lost sixteenth-century work. Perhaps, on the other hand, it is the product of the imagination of an anonymous eighteenth-century restorer. It is unclear if the declining quality of the compositions is the result of past restorations alone, or if it can be attributed in part also to the original. On both halves of the Ceiling, the black outlines and the gilding were heavily restored, probably in the eighteenth century.

55. I have already suggested these possibilities. See Mancinelli 1988, pp. 535-52, and "Tecnica di Michelangelo e organizzazione del lavoro," in *Michelangelo e la Sistina: La tecnica, il restauro, il mito,* Rome, 1990, pp. 56-57. According to de Tolnay, the use of assistants continued until the end of the project: "It must be supposed that until the end of the work he was assisted by *garzoni,* but it is true that, after the *Temptation* was done, the execution was almost completely in the hands of Michelangelo while the *garzoni* executed only the architectural framework and the secondary-decorative parts, as, for example, the bronze-coloured medallions, the frames of the spandrels, and in part the marble-coloured Genii, the putti below the tablets and the bronze-coloured nudes." De Tolnay 1949, p. 115. Barocchi, however, prefers an earlier date for the departure of the assistants. See Barocchi and Ristori, vol. 1, pp. 375-76.

56. Two different hands seem to be responsible for the fictive marble reliefs on the thrones on the second half of the Ceiling, one on the left and one on the right. It is possible, however, that one of these hands is Michelangelo's. One can also detect a drop in the quality and a change in technique in the bronze nudes, especially those at the end of the Chapel. Yet these figures show no traces of transferred cartoons, and it is difficult to imagine that an assistant would have executed them without the master's drawings. The roundels are too difficult to judge given their condition (see note 54 above).

57. In a letter Barocchi dates to July-August 1510, Michelangelo wrote to his brother, "Io mi sto qua all'usato, e arò finita la mia pictura per tucta quest'altra sectimana, cioé la parte che io chominciai." Barocchi and Ristori, p. 106. On 5 September he wrote to his father, "io resto avere cinquecento ducati di pacto fatto guadagniati, e altrectanta me ne dovea dare el papa per mectere mano nell'altra parte dell'opera, e llui s'è partito di qua e non m'à lasciato ordine nessuno, i' modo che mi trovo sanza danari né sso quello m'abbia a fare." Ibid., p. 108. The end of the first campaign on the Ceiling can be dated, therefore, to the period between the July-August and the September letters.

58. This date comes from a letter Michelangelo sent his father on Saturday, 4 October: "Padre charissimo, io andai martedì a parlare al Papa; il perché v'avserò più per agio. Basta che mercoledì mactina io vi ritornai ellui mi fece pagare quatrocento duchati d'oro di Chamera.... Pregate Idio che io abi onore qua e che io chontenti el Papa." Ibid., p. 121.

59. Michael Hirst, " 'Il modo delle attitudini': Il taccuino di Oxford per la volta della Sistina," in *La Cappella Sistina: I primi restauri,* p. 213.

60. Barocchi and Ristori, vol. 1, p. 137.

61. Ibid., vol. 1, p. 101.

John Shearman, "The Functions of Michelangelo's Color"

1. It must be said that not all of us had quite failed to discern the true nature of the vault's color (see note 3). And we seem to have forgotten how Goethe reflected in August 1787 on shifting opinions in Rome on Michelangelo: "The great heat, which grew steadily worse and set limits to any excessive activity, made one look for cool places to work in, and one of the most pleasant was the Sistine Chapel. At that time the artists had just rediscovered Michelangelo. In addition to all the other qualities they admired, they said that he surpassed all others in his sense of colour, and it became the fashion to dispute whether he or Raphael was the greater genius." J. W. Goethe, *Italian Journey,* trans. W. H. Auden and Elizabeth Mayer, Penguin Classics, London, 1970, p. 380. More striking still, perhaps, is the reaction of Le Corbusier (using the pseudonym De Fayet), in "La Sixtine de Michel'Ange," *L'Esprit Nouveau,* vol. 14, 1922 (?), p. 1609: "La Sixtine est une oeuvre pictural de haute et définitive formation. Tout ce qu'on doit exiger de la peinture y est. Tout ce qu'on en peut atteindre s'y trouve. On entre: plafond. Etonnement: la couleur la plus somptueuse et la plus fraîche. La gamme la plus digne à grande base de gris et de blanc, avec des ocres, jaunes, rouges, les terres vertes et l'outremer. Quel progrès de la 'peinture-couleur' invoquer depuis ceci?" There is a remarkably sensitive appreciation of Michelangelo's color in Giovanni Testori's introduction to the *Rime,* ed. E. Barelli, 3rd ed., Milan, 1987, p. 7. (I have not been able to check whether the text is the same in the first edition, 1975.) A characteristically intelligent and mutinous comment on the function of Michelangelo's color in relation to distance was made by Benjamin Robert Hayden; in 1826 Thomas Lawrence had commissioned William Bewick to paint replicas of the *Prophets* and *Sibyls* for the Royal Academy Schools, and a scaffolding was erected for this purpose in the Chapel. "What absurdity,"

remarked Hayden, "to pull things from dark recesses, sixty feet high—things which were obliged to be painted lighter, drawn fuller, and coloured harder than nature warrants, to look like life at a distance, and to bring them down to the level of the drawing room, and adore them as the purest examples of form, colour, expression and character." *Life and Letters of William Bewick, Artist*, ed. T. Landseer, 1871, vol. 2, p. 114. We owe this text to my wife, Deirdre.

2. E. Platner and C. Bunsen, *Beschreibung der Stadt Rom*, II, i, Stuttgart-Tübingen, 1834, p. 245.

3. To avoid intolerable recycling of argument, I must refer to my broader historical treatment of the phenomenon in "Isochromatic Color Compositions in the Italian Renaissance," *Color and Technique in Renaissance Painting: Italy and the North*, ed. Marcia B. Hall, Locust Valley, 1987, pp. 151ff. I should add that the hypothesis raised there about the Sistine Ceiling was first spelled out, with a confidence I would now temper, in my Ph.D. thesis, "Developments in the Use of Colour in Tuscan Painting of the Early Sixteenth Century," London University, 1957, pp. 145ff.

4. I use a notation system in which a slash [/] indicates a color change and a hyphen a color value.

5. In the Oratorio frescoes rocks are pale-blue/pink-violet and pink/green in the *Preaching of the Baptist* and pale-pink/pale-violet in the *Flight into Egypt*.

6. At an earlier point in his career, the effect was contrived but confused, as in the robe of God the Father in the *Beast with the Horns of a Lamb* (B. 74) from the Apocalypse series.

7. One recalls the young artist's studies in the fishmarket, when preparing the scaly monsters in his painted copy of Schongauer's *Temptation of Saint Anthony*, as he described them to Condivi: "Michelangelo worked with such diligence that he would not apply color to any part without first consulting nature. Thus he would go off to the fish market, where he observed the shape and coloring of the fins of the fish, the color of the eyes and every other part, and he would render them in his painting...." One may assume that it was equally easy for him to become familiar with exotic fabrics. Ascanio Condivi, *The Life of Michelangelo*, trans. Alice Sedgewick Wohl, ed. Helmut Wohl, Baton Rouge, Louisiana, 1976, pp. 9-10.

MATTHIAS WINNER, "JONAH'S BODY LANGUAGE"

1. "Many of the figures exhibit the most remarkable foreshortenings, and every one of the details is most admirable. Who could behold the powerful figure of [Jonah], which is the last in the chapel, and where by the force of art, the vaulting, which in fact does here spring forward, is compelled, by the bending attitude of that figure, to assume the appearance of being driven backwards and standing upright?" Vasari 1896, vol. 4, p. 104.

2. Charles de Tolnay, *Michelangelo: The Sistine Ceiling*, Princeton, 1945, vol. 2, pp. 199ff., pls. 230-32, 238; Charles de Tolnay, *Corpus dei disegni di Michelangelo*, Novara, 1975-80, vol. 1, pls. 119, 120 recto and verso.

3. De Tolnay 1945, vol. 2, pl. 231; de Tolnay 1975-80, pl. 120.

4. See de Tolnay 1975-80, pls. 166-173, 168 verso; Michael Hirst, " 'Il modo delle attitudini': Il taccuino di Oxford per la volta della Sistina," in *La Cappella Sistina: I primi restauri, la scoperta del colore*, Novara, 1986, pp. 208-17. See also Michael Hirst, *Michelangelo and His Drawings*, New Haven and London, 1988, p. 37.

5. De Tolnay 1975-80, f. 170 verso.

6. Ibid., pl. 170 recto.

7. Hirst 1988, p. 213.

8. Vasari 1896, vol. 4, pp. 205-6.

9. "But most remarkable of all is the prophet *Jonah*, situated at the head of the vault, because, contrary to the curve of the vault and by means of the play of light and shadow, the torso which is foreshortened backward is in the part nearest the eye, and the legs which project forward are in the part which is farthest. A stupendous work, and one which proclaims the magnitude of this man's knowledge, in his handling of lines, in foreshortening, and in perspective," Ascanio Condivi, *The Life of Michelangelo*, trans. Alice Sedgewick Wohl, ed. Helmut Wohl, Baton Rouge, Louisiana, 1976, p. 48.

10. *La Cappella Sistina*, p. 40 (illustration).

11. Vasari 1896, vol. 4, p. 138.

12. Condivi 1976, p. 83. See also Vasari 1896, vol. 4, p. 138.

13. This problem was recently discussed by Arnold Nesselrath in *Michelangelo e la Sistina: La tecnica, il restauro, il mito*, exh. cat., Vatican Museums, Rome, 1990, n.21, with illustrations of the Ottley engravings.

14. In *Michelangelo e la Sistina*, n.30, Nesselrath attributes the drawing (now in the museum of the Rugby School of Art) to Giulio Clovio. He dates it to before 1534, when Michelangelo had the brick curtain wall built to support the projected *Last Judgment*, destroying the two lunettes with the Ancestors of Christ on the existing wall. Yet the head of the Prophet in this drawing does not correspond with the one that was frescoed. In the drawing he has curls and his mouth is closed. The same head for Jonah appears in a print by Adamo Scultori (1530–1585), first published in 1585 (see *Michelangelo e la Sistina*, n.99). Can we suppose a common source for both copies of the Jonah?

15. Condivi 1976, p. 83.

EDWARD MAEDER, "THE COSTUMES WORN BY THE ANCESTORS OF CHRIST"

1. Leonardo, in his *Treatise on Painting*, cautions the artist: "As far as possible avoid the costumes of your own day, unless they belong to the religious group.... Costumes of our own period should not be depicted unless it is on tombstones in churches, so that we may be spared being laughed at by our successors for the mad fashions of men and leave behind only things that may be admired for their dignity and beauty." Codex Urbinas Latinus 1270, trans. Philip McMahon, Princeton, New Jersey, 1956, chapter 574, p. 208.

2. In this most striking figure, Charles de Tolnay, who regularly described the color combinations used in the garments, is strangely silent. It is possible that these colors were not visible prior to the cleaning. Charles de Tolnay, *The Sistine Chapel*, Princeton, New Jersey, 1949, p. 90.

3. R.J. Clements, *Michelangelo's Theory of Art*, New York, 1961, p. 328.

4. Giorgio Vasari, *Lives of the Most Eminent Painters, Sculptors, and Architects*, New York, 1979, vol. 3, p. 1833: "In time Ludovico's [Michelangelo's father's] family increased, and being in poor circumstances, with slender revenues, he set about apprenticing his sons to the Guilds of Silk and Wool."

5. L. Schneider, *Giotto in Perspective*, Englewood Cliffs, New Jersey, 1974, fig. 20, the *Mourning of the Clares*, San Francisco, Assisi (Alinari 49725). The elders on the left wear coifs (small linen caps) under their normal headgear.

6. Albrecht Dürer's woodcut the *Martyrdom of St. John the Evangelist*, 1498, includes a group of Jews, one of whom is wearing such a hat on top of a linen coif. Los Angeles County Museum of Art, Prints and Drawings Department, 69.4.

7. *Anselm Berner Chronic*, 1826, p. 249. It is noted here that the color yellow, previously reserved for Jews, has now nearly become a Swiss national color: "So hat de gel farbe, so vor Judas heiss angefangen, und die gmeinst worden, der eine swytzer-gel gnemt."

8. *Nuremberg Chronicles*, p. XV recto. This figure is Nimrod (the Hunter), son of Cush and grandson of Noah (Genesis 10.8–9). It should be noted that Kroeberger, the printer of the *Chronicles*, had a distributor in Venice (Jacopo Philippi Foresti) as early as 1483. This information comes from *The Nuremberg Chronicles*, San Francisco, 1930, p. XIV.

9. De Tolnay 1949, p. 88.

10. *Nuremberg Chronicles*, p. XX verso. This figure is Bethuel (Latin: Bathuelis), mother of Rebecca, wife of Abraham (Genesis 25.20).

11. I Kings 1.1–2.

12. De Tolnay 1949, p. 90.

13. *Nuremberg Chronicles*, p. XVI recto. Grandson of Noah, Meshech (Latin: Mosoch), son of Japeth (Genesis 10.2).

14. A. Rubens, *A History of Jewish Costume*, pp. 106, 107. The Fourth General Council of the Lateran (1215), which ruled that Jews should in future be distinguished by their clothing, was more important than any of the preceding Church Councils and remained for generations the authority on all disputed points of canon law. It was summoned by Innocent III, the pope who supported King John of England against the barons over the Magna Carta.

15. Ibid., p. 100.

16. De Tolnay 1949, p. 89.

17. II Chronicles 17.1 and 21.1.

18. J.A. Levenson, K. Oberhuber, J.L. Sheehan, *Early Italian Engravings from the National Gallery of Art*, Washington, D.C., 1973, pp. 296-97.

19. Ibid., pp. 228, 229. This engraving has been attributed to Zoan Andrea.

20. De Tolnay 1949, p. 86.

21. Ibid.

22. De Tolnay, *The Youth of Michelangelo*, Princeton, New Jersey, 1947, for example, pl. 44. This sculpture, believed to have been begun in 1501, was sent to Flanders in 1506. It is mentioned in a letter written from Rome on 31 January 1506. (Note: "Alexander Monschron & Co., who ordered the sculpture, was engaged in buying and selling English cloth and had establishments in Rome and Florence," p. 157.)

23. S.W. Beck, *The Draper's Dictionary: A Manual of Textile Fabrics, Their History and Application*, p. 286: "A stuff of silk that has apparently changed little from the time of its introduction into this country [England] in the 13th century until now. It derives its name from having been made by the Saracens, probably in Spain. Du Cange (Charles Du Fresne, 1610-1688, *Glossarium ad scriptores mediae...*, 1688) renders it *pannus saracenici operis* and Skinner (Stephan, 1623-1667, *Etymologicon linguae anglicanae...*, London, 1671) *sercum saracenicum*. It was not extensively used until the fifteenth century, when, owing probably to some improvement in the manufacture, it was eagerly bought, and displaced the older kindred fabric, cendal."

24. W.M. Thackston Jr., ed., *Naser-e Kosraw's Book of Travels*, Cambridge, Massachusetts, 1986, p. 54. I am grateful to Dr. Irene Bierman, Department of Fine Arts, UCLA, for bringing this reference to my attention.

25. Ibid.

26. *Giotto in Perspective*, p. 8. "Another basic requirement for good painting according to the quattrocento humanists was the direct observation of nature." I believe the *cangiante* fabrics were directly observed and rendered from life.

27. Hans Holbein the Elder (1460-1524), *Presentation of the Infant Christ in the Temple*, Alte Pinakothek, Munich, inv. nr. 723. The (changeable silk) textile worn by the figure on the right is certainly of Italian origin.

28. See note 21.

29. N.H. Nicholas, *Privy Purse Expenses of Elizabeth of York: Wardrobe Accounts of Edward the Fourth*, London, 1830, p. 116. In 1480 the accounts listed "grene sarsinett at iij s ijd. the yerd" (three shillings-two pence/yard) and "sarsinettes chaungeables.... price of every yerd iiij s." (four shillings).

30. Ibid., p. 135. At the time of Edward's coronation the inventory boasted more than one hundred fifty yards of "sarsinettes chaungeable and other diverse colours [sarsinettes]" as well as "curtyns of sarcinet iij (3.)."

31. Ibid., p. 143.

32. A.F. Sutton and P.W. Hammond, *The Coronation of Richard III, the Extant Documents*, New York, 1983, p. 145.

33. *Saia* was a fine serge of silk and wool, favored for stockings. G.R.B. Richards, *Florentine Merchants in the Age of the Medici,* Cambridge, Massachusetts, 1932, p. 314.
34. L. Bardeschi Ciulich and P. Barocchi, *I ricordi di Michelangelo,* Florence, 1970, pp. 92-93. I am grateful to Dr. William Wallace for bringing this information to my attention.
35. In order to obtain *cangiante* in wool it was necessary to spin the wool tightly and to weave it in twill pattern or a variation of twill.
36. Richards, p. 314.
37. Leonardo da Vinci, *Treatise on Painting:* Codex Urbinas Latinus 1270, trans. and ed. Philip McMahon, Princeton, New Jersey, vol. I, chapter 573, p. 207.
38. Jacqueline Herald, *Renaissance Dress in Italy 1400-1500,* London, 1981, p. 230.
39. Marco Vattasso, *Per la storia del dramma sacro in Italia,* Rome, 1903, p. 99. I am grateful to Franca Camiz for bringing this reference to my attention.
40. "A short cape of crimson damask lined in changeable silk taffeta with black knots in circles." In M. Bellezza Rosina, *Tessuti serici italiani, 1450-1530,* p. 68.
41. Ibid.
42. Sutton, Hammond, p. 145.
43. See note 3.
44. G.T. Van Ysselsteyn, *Tapestry: The Most Expensive Industry of the XVth and XVIth Centuries,* Brussels, 1969, p. 34.
45. "Encourage Lodovico and Giovansimone on my behalf, and write and tell me how Giovansimone is getting on, and apply yourself to learning your trade and working at the shop, so that you may know what you are about when you need to: which will be before long. On the tenth day of November" (1507). E.H. Ramsden, *The Letters of Michelangelo,* vol. 1, p. 40. The letter is addressed "to Buonarroto di Lodovico di Buonarrota Simoni in Florence, deliver to the shop of Lorenzo Strozzi, Arte di Lana, in Porta Rosa." British Museum, London.
46. P. Barocchi et al., *Il carteggio indiretto di Michelangelo,* Florence, 1988, vol. I, p. XI.
47. During the discussion that took place at the congress on the restoration of the Sistine Ceiling (March 1990), it was noted by the late Professor André Chastel that if *cangiante* was only an artistic device, why were there not *cangiante* rocks or *cangiante* trees or *cangiante* people? Why was this device, with one or two notable exceptions, restricted to costumes and draperies if it did not originate in textiles produced at the time?
48. Christina J. Herringham, *The Book of the Art of Cennino Cennini,* London, 1899, p. 71.

Pierluigi De Vecchi, "The Syntax of Form and Posture from the Ceiling to the *Last Judgment*"

1. Condivi 1976, p. 39.
2. See the letter from the carpenter, Piero Rosselli, in Rome to Michelangelo in Florence on 10 May 1506 in P. Barocchi and R. Ristori, *Il carteggio di Michelangelo,* Florence, 1956, vol. 1, p. 16.
3. Ibid., vol.3, p. 8.
4. "In these compartments Michelagnolo has used no perspective foreshortenings, nor has he determined any fixed point of sight; but rather accommodated the division to the figures, than the figures to the division...." Vasari 1896, p. 92. "Starting from the brackets which support the horns of the lunettes, up to about a third of the arch of the vault, a flat wall is simulated...." Condivi 1976, p. 39.
5. Johannes Wilde, *Michelangelo: Six Lectures,* Oxford, 1978, pp. 51-56.
6. See John Shearman's essay in this volume.
7. Vasari 1896, p. 94.
8. See especially John O'Malley, "Il mistero della volta. Gli affreschi di Michelangelo alla luce del pensiero teologico del Rinascimento," in *La Cappella Sistina: I primi restauri, la scoperta del colore,* Novara, 1986, pp. 92-148.
9. These are expressions used by Condivi to describe the Sistine Ceiling frescoes. "In all things, in the beauty of the compartments, in the diversity of poses, in the contradiction of the contours of the vault, Michelangelo displayed consummate art." Condivi 1976, p. 48.
10. Ibid., p. 42.
11. Vasari 1896, vol. 4, p. 115.
12. Ibid., p. 144.
13. Condivi 1976, pp. 83, 87.
14. On the reaction of Michelangelo's contemporaries to the *Last Judgment,* see especially Pierluigi De Vecchi, "Il Giudizio Universale: Fonti iconografiche, reazioni, interpretazioni," in *La Cappella Sistina: I primi restauri,* pp. 189-98.

Fabrizio Mancinelli, Gianluigi Colalucci, and Nazzareno Gabrielli, "The *Last Judgment:* Notes on Its Conservation History, Technique, and Restoration"

1. "Tam picturas testudinis et parietis praedictarum in dicta capella Sixti iam confectarum .... a pulveribus et aliis immunditiis praefatis mundare et a mundatis tenere omni cum diligentia."
2. "S(c)uti 17 b. 60 se le dano per altri legnami tolti p(er) farne il ponte nella Cappella di Sisto alla facciata del Giudicio."
3. "Alto p(almi) 42 fatto a tre palchi l'uno sopra l'altro el primo e turrato in t.o di tavole, con una porta di potere salire qual ponte sia largo p. 12 lg.o p. 60 con suo parapetto devanti et tirato le tende divanti con 4 scale del m.ro."
4. "Per la tela che ha data per lo cartone che fa m[aestr]o Pierino pittore della spalliera che va sotto la pittura di m[esser] Michelangelo in la cappella di Sisto."
5. "Alla scalinata di marmo per il soglio e l'altare della Cappella...."
6. "Certo che il nitro, il polvere e l'umidita (se non si usa pronto rimedio) in pochi anni potrebbero ridurre queste egregie pitture in stato da non potersi piu riparare, come si vede notabilmente esser accaduto in esse da un anno all'altro, e nella facciata del *Giudizio* massimamente, che sputa e rompe a luogo a luogo in brutte macchie di nitro bianco, incalcinandone il colore stesso."
7. An in-depth study of the documents preserved in the State Archives in Rome and the Archivio Segreto at the Vatican is under way under the direction of Anna Maria De Strobel.
8. Vasari 1927, vol. 3, p. 119.
9. Vasari 1896, vol. 4, p. 138.
10. This system was designed by the technical services department of the Governatorato with technology and financing provided by Adelchi Carrier. The project was directed by Stefano Marino and supervised by Massimo Stoppa.

Piernicola Pagliara, "New Documents on the Construction of the Sistine Chapel"

1. Aurelio Lippo Brandolini wrote about the Sistine Chapel, "Here where a splendid temple rises to the sky/...it had deteriorated with age and disuse and it was a holy place only in name/...here he commanded that a soaring edifice be erected...." ("Hic ubi sydereum consurgit ad aethera templum/...squalebat senio atque situ vix nomine phanum/...hic celsam iussit se tollere molem...."). Biblioteca Apostolica Vaticana, Vat. Lat. 5008, f.59r.; and Urb. Lat. 739, f.78v., published by Eugene Muntz, *Les Arts à la cour des papes,* Paris, 1882, vol. 3, p. 135, and Ernst Steinmann, *Die Sixtinische Kapelle,* Munich, 1905, vol. 1, p. 123. Andrew Trebizond addressed the pope, "You have completely demolished the chapel...after the walls had become unstable and the wood roof had fallen into disrepair...and you have erected a new one." ("Tu sacellum...parietibus labentibus, tecto tabullato et desidenti...funditus diruisti, novum...absolvisti."). See J. Monfasani, "A Description of the Sistine Chapel Under Pope Sixtus IV," *Artibus et Historiae,* vol. 7, 1983, pp. 9-18, with special reference to p. 11.
2. John Shearman, "La costruzione della cappella e la prima decorazione al tempo di Sisto IV," in *La Cappella Sistina,* Novara, 1986, p. 26, and "La storia della Cappella Sistina," in *Michelangelo e la Sistina,* exh. cat., Vatican Museums, Rome, 1990, p. 21. Based on Brandolini's epigram, Steinmann had already suggested that the new chapel was built on the foundations of the older one.
3. "And so we crossed the entire chapel to the other chapel and we came back in procession to the large chapel." ("Et sic ivimus per totam capellam usque ad aliam capellam et reversi fuimus processionaliter ad magnam capellam."). J. P. Migne, ed., *Patrologiae Lutetiae Parisiorum 1857-86,* 161 vols., col. 1359-60, cited by Steinmann 1905, vol. 1, p. 120; and M. Dykmans, *Le Cérémonial Papal,* Bibliothèque de l'Institut Historique Belge de Rome, XXIV-XXVII, Rome, 1977-85, vol. 3, p. 238. According to F. Ehrle and H. Egger, the groin-vaulted room below the Aula Regia was built by Innocent III, *Studi e documenti per la storia del palazzo apostolico vaticano,* Vatican City, 1935, p. 52 and pl. 1, and according to D. Redig de Campos, by Nicholas III, *I palazzi vaticani,* Bologna, 1967, p. 29.
4. On the north side the wall has been restored with modern, smooth bricks to the level of the windows of the Apartment of the Masters of Ceremonies. Toward St. Peter's and in the exposed areas on the short sides of the chapel, the walls are uniformly built with whole bricks 10¼/10⅝ x 5⅛/5½ x $1\frac{3}{16}$/$1\frac{9}{16}$ in. (26/27 x 13/14 x 3/4 cm) and gray pozzolana mortar in beds $\frac{9}{15}$/1 in. (1.5/2.5 cm) thick. Thus a unit of five brick courses is between 10⅜ and $11\frac{13}{16}$ in. (26.5 and 30 cm) high. One finds walls that are similar with regard to the size of the bricks and the number of them laid on end but which have thinner mortar beds, at Sant'Aurea (1483, bricks: $10\frac{7}{16}$/$10\frac{11}{16}$ x 5⅛ x 1¾ in. [26.5/27 x 13 x 4.5 cm]; mortar beds: ¼-⅜ in. [0.7/1.0 cm]; and units: 9/9⅞ in. [23/25 cm]), the Borgia Tower (1492-94), and the side wall of San Pietro in Montorio (circa 1483, bricks: 10⅝ x 5⅛ x 1⅜/$1\frac{11}{16}$ in. [27 x 13 x 3.5/4.2 cm]; mortar beds: ⅜/$\frac{9}{16}$ in. [1/1.5 cm]; unit: 9⅞ in. [25 cm]). Before the second half of the fifteenth century, brick walls in Rome, even in the Vatican palace, were built with reused bricks (the Tower of Innocent III, on the inner curtain of "tufelli"; the outer sheath is brick). See Redig de Campos, p. 24. New bricks were used for the walls of Nicholas V's palace; see Ehrle-Stevenson, *Gli affreschi del Pinturicchio nell'Appartamento Borgia,* Rome, 1897, pp. 29-33. The brick sheaths over the walls in this building did not yet have any value of their own since they were covered with stucco and *sgraffitto* decoration imitating *opus quadratum;* see Ehrle-Stevenson, p. 31. In the first decades of the sixteenth century, mortar beds tended to become thinner, in imitation of ancient Roman buildings (Piernicola Pagliara, "Note su murature e intonaci a Roma tra Quattrocento e Cinquecento," *Ricerche di storia dell'arte,* vol. 2, 1980, pp. 35-44), while walls like those of the Sistine Chapel were either intended to be stuccoed or used as a reinforcing sheath (for example, the battered basement of the Villa Medici); see Pagliara, "Matériaux, structures, et techniques mis en oeuvre dans la construction de la Villa Médicis," in *Villa Medici,* vol. 3, forthcoming. The brick facade of the chapel displays, therefore, all the characteristics of a work dating to the 1470s and eighties while the Della Rovere arms date it specifically to the reign of Sixtus IV.
5. The papal arms of the Della Rovere family are found over the entire Sistine Chapel. Today there are seven in the crenellation (one on the north, three on the west, and three on the south), five at the level of the chapel windows (two on the north and three on the south), and three on the battered walls (two on the north, one of which is on the wall of the Sala Regia, and one on the south).
6. The powerful buttresses pierced by arches on the north and south sides of the chapel, one of which partially covers the Della Rovere arms, were added later. One might suppose, although it has not been proven, that they can be dated to ca. 1570, when

Vignola and Pirro Ligorio corrected the building's structural faults; see Redig de Campos, p. 167; Shearman 1986, p. 33. For the other important modifications to the chapel, see Shearman 1986, pp. 30-33, and Redig de Campos, p. 167.

7. This discovery was made during the restorations, directed by Fabrizio Mancinelli, by the restorer Bruno Baratti and Master Mason Fezzardi, thanks to the latter's attention to and curiosity about the way masonry incorporates the history of a building. By removing a small patch of modern plaster, Mr. Fezzardi revealed what became the definitive proof of the hypothesis that a considerable part of the medieval chapel was preserved.

8. The left jamb, which was uncovered to a height of about 84⅗ in. (215 cm), was built of yellowish bricks 1¹⁄₁₆ in. (3 cm) high, with the exception of one reddish brick 2 in. (5 cm) high. Small fragments of very finely grained plaster were found on the right splay.

9. No remains of plinths or other supporting structures were found in the area from which the plaster was removed.

10. Masonry of summarily squared stone blocks was used in the 1470s and eighties in Rome (for example, the interior walls of the upper loggia of San Marco; see Christoph L. Frommel, "Francesco del Borgo: Architekt als Pius' II und Pauls II," *Römisches Jahrbuch für Kunstgeschichte,* vol. 21, 1984, p. 90 and fig. 31) and in Lazio (Palazzo della Rovere in Grottaferrata). See Piernicola Pagliara, "Giuliano della Rovere e Grottaferrata," *Quaderni dell'Istituto di Storia dell' Architettura,* n.s. 13, 1991, figs. 1, 5; and "Raffaello e la rinascita delle tecniche antiche," in *Les Chantiers de la Renaissance,* Paris, 1991, p. 54, figs. 1, 6, 7.

11. Shearman (1990, p. 21) thought that it could be either a door or a window. The jambs, which on the interior must have supported a stone or marble cornice, and the splays, which open only outward, are more suited to a door.

12. According to the restorers, the plaster and the fresco decoration that cover the central part of the opening are original. This does not allow us to exclude the possibility that Frommel raised during discussions at the symposium. He suggested that the opening was made at the same time the Sistine Chapel was built and closed immediately afterwards because of an error in construction. This hypothesis is problematic, however, because the bricks of the jambs are not the same as those used for the chapel's facade. The likely existence of a staircase which must by Sixtus's time have run along the south wall of the chapel, located in the same place as the stair Bramante renovated in 1506 and corresponding today to the Scala Regia, also makes the idea that a door would have been opened on that side of the building unlikely.

13. Burchardus, *Diarum sive rerum urbanarum commentarii (1483-1506),* ed. Thuasne, Paris, 1883-85, vol. 3, p. 429. Flights of rectilinear ramps which allowed the pope to be carried on a litter from the third hall to St. Peter's must have existed at least from the time of Innocent VIII; see Ehrle-Stevenson, p. 13, and Burchardus 1883-85, 15 April 1487 and 29 June 1489. The staircase must be the same one that Bramante transformed in 1506 when, on 21 May, Julius II was carried to St. Peter's "through the entrance to the palace, where a guard or sentry was generally stationed, where they tore down the staircase which the popes used to descend in order to build a new one in such a way as to allow them to ride from the Aula Regia to the St. Peter's" ("per portam palatii, ubi solet guardia seu custodia teneri, eo quod scalam per quam soliti fuerant pontifices descendere, demolierant pro nova facienda, tali scilicet modo quod equis ire possint ex aula regali usque S. Petrum"); see Burchardus, p. 429. The demolished staircase, normally used by the popes to descend to St. Peter's, must, at least in part, have been located where Bramante reconstructed it; see Frommel 1976, p. 73.

14. The estimate for the work done for the conclave (15 September 1503) notes that the following were

walled up: "the window high up in the first large room [the Aula Regia] and one on the side above the door of the old staircase [the stairs to the Cortile del Maresciallo] and that door and the one opposite it that leads down to the Paradiso...." ("il fenestre in capite aule prime et una ad latus supra hostium antiqui ascensus et ipsum hostium et illud in apposito quod descendit ad paradisum...."). It also specifies that the "door of the large room in front of the Paradiso [was walled up] with new, whole bricks" ("porta aule ante paradisum cum mattonibus integris"). See Burchardus, ed. Celani, p. 372. A "door that leads to the Paradiso" ("porta que ducit ad Paradisum") in the Sala Regia is also noted by Paris de Grassis in March 1505. Biblioteca Apostolica Vaticana, Chigi L.I.17, f.338.

15. Biblioteca Apostolica Vaticana, Vat. Lat. 5008, f.59v and Urb. Lat. 739, f. 78v., published by Muntz, 1889, vol. 3, p. 135, and G. De Luca, "Un umanista fiorentino e la Roma rinnovata da Sisto IV," *La Rinascita,* vol. 1, 1938, pp. 85-86.

16. On the Paradiso and Nicholas V's projects for the Vatican Palace, see Manetti and Carroll W. Westfall's commentary in *In This Most Perfect Paradise,* 1974, pp. 263-83.

17. Florence, Uffizi, A572. This drawing is reproduced in H. Wurm, *Baldassare Peruzzi Architekturzeichnungen,* Tübingen, 1984, pl. 511, and is cited in Frommel 1969, p. 38, n. 47. The principal subject is the apartment of the Bishop of Capua, Nikolaus von Schenberg, who died in 1537 (Frommel 1969, p. 38, n. 47), located to the south of the large staircase.

18. Rome, Accademia di San Luca, Fondo Mascherino, 2489. See Frommel 1969, pp. 14, 16, 38, and fig. 10, and P. Marconi, A. Cipriani, and E. Valeriani, *I disegni di architettura dell'Archivio storico dell'Accademia di S. Luca,* Rome, 1974, vol. 2, p. 22, fig. 2489. This plan, dated about 1585, shows the "sala Regia," the "scala che va a sala Regia," the "scala che va a S. Pietro," and all the rooms to the west of the Pauline Chapel as well as the Paradiso.

19. Nocturne hic fuerat media quoque luce tenebre
Nec domus hec hominum: carcer opacus erat
indignus quoque carcer erat tantum antra fuere
Inque usus ovium condita non hominum
Inferno cognomen erat: cui vivere in illa
contigit instigia vix erat ille domo
expulit at tenebras sixtus coelumque reduxit
insolitumque loco reddidit ispe diem.

20. Steinmann, vol. 1, pp. 154, 155, and Redig de Campos, p. 66.

21. See Steinmann, vol. 1, plate VI. While the Palazzo Medici in Florence already had windows placed regularly on the facade, in Rome in the Palazzo Venezia and in other buildings erected in the following decades, a regular disposition within each single room was preferred; see Frommel 1984, figs. 7, 9. The windows of the Paradiso follow neither the first nor the second principle.

22. Archivio Segreto Vaticano, Arm. 54, vol. 19, ff. 97-101. Gayet, *Le Grand Schisme d'occident,* Paris, Florence, Berlin, 1889, vol. 2, pp. 124ff.

23. "Et percutiebant de subtus fortiter solarium conclavis, sic quod D. Cardinales modicum potuerunt quiescere...et per totam noctem duraverunt." Archivio Segreto Vaticano, Arm. 54, vol. 19, f. 97-101, from the testimony of the Cardinal of Sant'Angelo.

24. For the room beneath the Sala Regia, see note 4, and for the rooms below the Sala Ducale, see Redig de Campos, pp. 29, 41, 121.

25. "Erat in solo capelle majoris, circa medium cappelle...dixit quod exibat ad unum domum que erat subtus dictum solarium que habebant unam portam que exibat versus vineam."

26. Archivio Segreto Vaticano, Arm. 54, vol. 19, f. 59r., and Gayet, vol. 1, p. 370, from the testimony of Menendus di Cordova. On the cardinals brought back to the conclave, see Gayet, vol. 1, p. 20.

27. "Per unum parvum foramen quod fuerat factum in solario descendi inferius in hospitio camerarii." Gayet, vol. 1, p. 377.

28. "Ego descendi in illam cameram per quandam scalam que multum periculose stabat super unum dressatorium, quod male erat firmum et scala fuerat posita ibi quia nimis erat brevis." Ibid.

29. On Aurelio Brandolini and his blindness, see A. Rotondo in *Dizionario biografico italiano,* vol. 14, Rome, 1972, pp. 26-28.

30. James S. Ackerman, *The Cortile Belvedere,* Vatican City, 1954, cat. no. 30, fig. 25. Naldini's drawing is in the Fogg Art Museum, Cambridge, Massachusetts, n. 1934.214.

31. Steinmann, vol. 1, pl. 6. Bramante's stair and the Scala Regia which replaced it, both of them vaulted, rendered this device ineffective. It must, therefore, antedate them.

32. See notes 14 and 15.

33. Early in 1991, on the occasion of the restoration in progress, it was established that the lowest level of the chapel's altar wall, beneath the brick curtain wall built in preparation for Michelangelo's *Last Judgment,* is made of pieces of tufa. See L. Dorez, *La Cour du Pape Paul III d'après les registres de la Trésorerie secrète,* Paris, 1932, vol. 2, p. 26: 20 February 1536, "crostatura di mattoni per la facciata della Cappella di Sisto che ha dipinge Michelangelo" ("a sheath of bricks for the facade of the Sistine Chapel which Michelangelo painted"). The upper levels are built of brick all the way through and date, therefore, to the pontificate of Sixtus IV.

34. This does not imply that the walls of the Cappella Magna, whose height must have been proportional to the length and width of the chapel, were just this high but only that they were preserved to that level.

35. See note 2.

36. Jacopo Gherardi da Volterra, *Il diario romano,* in *Rerum Italicarum Scriptores,* ed. E. Carusi, vol. XXIII, 3, Turin, 1904-11, p. 40, 11 March 1481: "The pope went out into the large room adjacent to the smaller rooms. It is being used as a chapel until the bigger construction that is being built today with enormous efforts and great expense will be restored." ("Exivit pontifex in propinquam cubiculis aulam quae pro sacello habetur quandoque quousque aliud maius erit instauratum quod egregio opere et magno sumptu reedificatur quotidie.") Sigismondo dei Conti, *Le storie dei suoi tempi,* vol. 1, p. 205: "The hall or chapel above, where the Pope performs the holy sacraments with the Cardinals, was...[verb missing], once the ceiling, the mosaic floor, and the marble seats had been restored, beautiful pictures...." ("Aulam insuper, sive aediculam, in qua Pontifex cum Cardinalibus sacra facit, testudine, pavimento tessellato, marmoreisque sedilibus renovatis, egregia pictura....") Cited by Steinmann, vol. 1, p. 136.

37. Ptolemy, *Cosmographia,* and Steinmann, vol.1, fig. 58.

38. See the example of the Villa Medici cited in note 5.

39. Shearman 1990, pp. 19, 20.

40. Dykmans, p. 4, Ceremoniale di Pierre Ameil on the conclave after the death of Urban VI: "The chamberlain must make sure that these doors are walled up as well as all the windows that are located less than four rods [about nine yards] away from the ground or the roof." ("Caveat camerarius quod parte murentur et omnes fenestre que sunt basse prope terram vel solarium ad minus ad quatuor cannas.")

41. Biblioteca Apostolica Vaticana, Vat.Lat. 12417, the Diary of Paris De Grassis, f.5v, on the conclave in the Sistine Chapel after the death of Julius II, "All the windows located high up had been carefully closed off with canvas and hemp so as to keep the wind from coming in. The two windows that are located above the sacristy, i.e., above the altar, were walled up and also the one in the entrance area of the chapel to the left was partly walled up." ("Fenestrae omnes altae fuerant diligenter cum tela et stuppa incollatae ut ventus nullo modo intraret. Duae autem fenestrae que sunt super sacristiam, idest supra altare fuerunt muratae, et etiam illa in ingressu capellae ad sinistram fuit semimurata."). See also Shearman 1972, p. 9 n.58.

42. On the organization of the clergy that served the Sistine Chapel, see G. Moroni, *Le cappelle pontificie,* Venice, 1841; Steinmann, vol. 1, pp. 149-665; B. Guillemain, *Le Cour pontifical d'Avignon 1309-76,* reprinted 1962; Shearman 1986, pp. 33ff.; B. Schimmelpfennig, "Die Organisation der Päpstlichen Kapelle in Avignon," *Quellen und Forschungen aus italienischen Archiven und Bibliotheken,* vol. 50, 1971, pp.

80-111, and *Die Zeremonien bücher der römischen Kirche in Mittelalter,* Bibliothek des deutschen Historischen Instituts in Rom, vol. 40, Tübingen, 1973; A. Roth, "Primus in Petri aede sixtus perpetuae harmoniae cantores introduxit: alcune osservazioni sul patronato musicale di Sisto IV," in *Un pontificato ed una città. Sisto IV (1471-84),* ed. M. Miglio, F. Niutta, D. Quaglioni, and C. Ranieri, Vatican City, 1986, pp. 217-41.

43. On this attribution, see E. Muntz, "Giovannino de'Dolzi, l'architetto della Cappella Sistina," *Il Buonarroti,* ser. 2, 13, 1879, p. 348; Steinmann, vol. 1, pp. 130-33; Redig de Campos, pp. 69-70.
44. 2 February 1477: Shearman 1986, p. 27, and Shearman 1990, p. 24.
45. E. Battisti, "Il significato simbolico della Cappella Sistina," *Commentari,* vol. 8, 1957, pp. 96-104.

PHOTOGRAPH CREDITS

INDEX